County Compan...

Devon
Judy Chard

Cadogan Books, London
Century Publishing, London

Contents

Writing: Judy Chard
Editorial Assistant: Leone Turner
Illustrations by Pauline Pears
Series design by Information Design
Workshop
Cartography: Line and Line

ISBN 0 946313 857

First published 1984 by Cadogan
Books Ltd, 15 Pont Street, London
SW1X 9EH in association with Century
Publishing Co. Ltd, Portland House,
12-13 Greek Street, London W1 V5LE

Typeset in Great Britain by Grange
Filmsetting Ltd, Birmingham and
Budget Typeset, Penge, London
Printed in Great Britain by Purnell &
Sons (Book Production) Ltd, Paulton,
Bristol

How to use this guide   **4**

Devon

Complete Guide   **6**

Places to visit, towns and villages
in alphabetical order

Detailed Maps   **136**

Map 1   136
Map 2   137
Map 3   138
Map 4   139

Town Directory   **140**

Barnstaple   140
Bovey Tracey   140
Brixham   140
Combe Martin   140
Dartmouth   140
Exeter   141
Great Torrington   142
Ilfracombe   142
Kingsbridge   142
Lynton & Lynmouth   142
Newton Abbot   142
Okehampton   142
Paignton   143
Plymouth   143
Seaton   144
Sidmouth   144

South Molton   144
Teignmouth   144
Tiverton   144
Totnes   144

Street Plans

Exeter   141
Plymouth   143

Leisure A-Z   145

Air Sports   145
Angling   145
Aquariums   156
Archaeological   157
Art Galleries   158
Bird Reserves   159
Boat Trips   159
Caravan & Camping Sites   160
Castles   166
Church Buildings   167
Country Parks   168
Crafts   170
Cricket   173
Events   174
Farms   176
Gardens   177
Golf Clubs   180
Historic Homes   183
Horseracing   186
Industrial Archaeology   186
Lighthouses   188
Local Industry   188
Mills   189
Museums   190
National Parks   196
Nature Reserves   199
Other Historic Buildings   201
Picnic Sites   202
Railways   203
Riding   205
Sports Centres   208
Swimming Pools   209
Tourist Information Offices   211
Unusual Outings   213
Walking   214
Water Skiing   217
Windsurfing   218
Women's Institute   219
Woodlands   219
Zoos   221

Acknowledgements   224

How to use this guide

Complete Guide

The first section of the book describes all the major towns and villages of interest in Devon. They are included, along with outstanding attractions, in alphabetical order. After each name there is a map reference locating the place on one of the detailed maps. Places of interest to be found in the various towns and villages are described in this section but all details of their opening times, charges, facilities and other information can be found in the Leisure Directory. All places of interest in bold have a listing in the Leisure Directory under the relevant section. For example:

Bickleigh Castle (Historic Homes)
This indicates that the details for Bickleigh Castle can be found in the Historic Homes section of the Leisure Directory. **Finch Foundry Museum** indicates that the details for this museum can be found under the Museums section of the Leisure Directory.

Maps

Four detailed maps of sections of Devon on which are located all major places of interest and other important features such as caravan parks can be found on pages 136-139.

Town Directory

The major towns are listed here with the facilities and places of interest to be found in and nearby those towns. All details about the places to visit can be found in the Leisure Directory. For example:
Museum: Maritime Museum
This indicates that details for the Maritime Museum (under Exeter in the Town Directory) can be found in the Museums section of the Leisure Directory. Street plans of some major towns can also be found in this section with places of interest located.

Leisure A-Z

This section lists activities and places to visit, giving all important details. A full list of the topics included can be found on the Contents list at the front of this book. All entries are in alphabetical order. Where relevant, a map reference is given immediately after the name of the place of interest, locating it on one of the detailed maps. A page reference is given if the place is described in the Complete Guide.

The telephone number of the place is given, followed by the location and all other details.

Symbols

- 🚐 caravan park
- 🎣 angling
- ⛳ golf course
- 🛈 tourist information centre
- 🅿 Parking
- 🍴 licensed restaurant
- ☕ snacks
- ♿ access for disabled visitors
- 🏪 shop
- 🪑 picnic site
- 🏊 swimming pool
- 🍷 bar
- ⛵ sailing
- ∪ riding
- ⛺ campsite
- PO post office
- ▼ place of interest

Complete Guide

Appledore   Map 1 Ab

This is still a delightfully unspoilt village with old seamen's
cottages and narrow winding streets dating back to 1335. It
stands on the peninsula which includes Northam and
Westward Ho! on the estuaries of the rivers Taw and
Torridge. Ships have been built here from Elizabethan
times when they fought in the Armada. The modern
shipyard was built in 1969 and is one of the largest covered
yards in Europe. The Quay itself is a good starting point
for a walk, if you can resist exploring the side streets which
include a roof top look-out in Bude Street and the Georgian
Market Street. Beyond the Customs House and Lifeboat
Station is Hinks Yard, where replicas of such boats as the
Golden Hind have been made by craftsmen using original
woodworking tools. There is also the **North Devon
Maritime Museum.**

Northam sadly has been spoilt, an outstanding example
of what 'development' can do and is doing to so many parts
of Devon. Stephen and William Burrough of Burough
lived nearby, the notable sixteenth-century navigators.
Charles Kingsley made Burough the centre of his epic
novel *Westward Ho!* which is full of scenes from this corner
of Devon. The church at Northam is most impressive from
the outside; its tower is a landmark for shipping crossing
the dangerous bar at the estuary mouth.

To the north of Appledore lies **Braunton Burrows**
(Nature Reserves) made famous by Henry Williamson, for
this too is *Tarka The Otter* country. There is a great
expanse of sand dunes supporting rare plants and birds,
part of which is a National Nature Reserve. Beyond are
Saunton Golf Course and Saunton Sands with a
magnificent three mile sandy beach.

Westward Ho! is a village built to commemorate the
famous historical novel by Charles Kingsley. The
foundation stone was laid in 1863 by the Duchess of
Portland; Trinity Church was built in 1870, and by 1872
there were some scattered villas and a single line of shops.
A golf course was laid out and the United Services College

opened for the sons of officers in 1874. Rudyard Kipling was one of its first pupils and based *Stalky & Co.* on his experiences there. Sadly, many of the recent buildings are entirely alien to Devon. There is a two mile long Pebble Ridge, and a superb sandy beach affording first class surfing.

Instow is a small seaside resort opposite Appledore on the beautiful estuary where the rivers Taw and Torridge meet. It has its own quay dating back to 1620, now the H.Q. of the North Devon Yacht Club. The old village lies on the hillside and the church of St John the Baptist is a fourteenth-century building as far as nave and chapel are concerned, while the font and wall of the nave are Norman. There is a mural to a student, John Downe, son of the rector who died in 1640 after only two years at Oxford. Another mural commemorates Sibthorpe, the famous professor of botany at Oxford who died in 1797.

Just one and a half miles south of Instow is **Tapeley Park House & Garden** (Gardens), a William and Mary mansion set in a beautiful Italian garden with many rare plants. There is also a walled kitchen garden and lily pond set in woodland.

Arlington Map 1 Bb

Miss Rosalie Chichester, aunt of the famous Sir Francis, left **Arlington Court** (Historic Homes) to the National Trust in 1947. It contains a delightful museum reflecting her Victorian tastes. There are snuff boxes, musical instruments, sea shells and a watercolour painting by William Blake. The house is preserved almost as it must have been when she was a young girl, in fact walking into her bedroom, so vivid is her presence, it feels as if she herself might be encountered at any moment. On the central staircase is a display of dresses of the period from 1830 to 1910. One ancestor, Amias Chichester, had 19 sons and four daughters and Charles Kingsley refers to 'this

A

noble sight of 19 sons' in *Westward Ho!* For animal lovers, the huge park has a nature trail, Jacob sheep and Shetland ponies. In the stables are horse-drawn carriages.

Ashburton   Map 3 Bb

As one of Devon's Stannary towns, reaching its maximum population in 1831, Ashburton was later by-passed by railway and road. It is typical of many of this county's market towns and the increasing population is largely due to the popularity of the Dart Valley with retired people. Many of the houses date back to the seventeenth century, including The House of Cards in North Street where playing card motifs are picked out on the tile-hung front. There is a small but very interesting museum, **Ashburton Museum**, specialising in American Indian antiquities as well as local history. The Golden Lion pub is an old coaching inn, and the Exeter Inn was built as a private house. Between them stands the London Inn. Tea rooms provide delicious Devon cream teas. Nearby, at New Bridge, is a National Park Information Centre. The river Ashburn, on which the town stands, provided the water for many fulling and other types of mill. Ashburton 'pop' made the town famous in 1780. It was said to 'have a sharp, good taste, better than small beer and more like champagne.' When the cork was drawn there was a sharp report like a pop bottle, hence the name. It is said that once three old cronies got through a dozen bottles in six hours. Sadly the recipe died with its brewer in 1785. The Grammar School founded in 1314 produced such men as William Gifford, who became the first editor of the *Quarterly Review*, John Ireland who became Dean of Westminster, and possibly John Ford, the dramatist, born at nearby Bagtor, Ilsington. Ashburton's senior citizen is Portreeve, a Saxon officer older than the mayor and appointed annually since A.D. 821, however the claim cannot be verified. There is no doubt there was a village on the banks of the river Ashburton before the Norman Conquest. During Summer

Carnival week there is ale-tasting and a bread weighing ceremony. South of the town is the 80 acre **River Dart Country Park.**

Just north of Ashburton is a picture postcard village, Buckland-in-the Moor, with three thatched cottages lying in a wooded hollow near a boulder-strewn stream. The church has a modern clock with the words 'My Dear Mother' round the face instead of numerals. Drive south from the church to nearby Buckland Beacon whose two flat rocks by the summit have the Ten Commandments carved upon them, and sacred texts executed by local craftsmen.

Aveton Gifford   see Kingsbridge

Axminster   Map 2 Bc

The A35 runs through this small but busy market town with its Georgian buildings. Three markets are held on Thursdays when the pubs are open all day. The carpet industry was established here in 1755 by Thomas Whitty with his five daughters as loom operators, and his sister as overseer. He worked in close conjunction with the famous Adam Brothers. Many of these fine carpets are still in existence, one of which can be seen at **Saltram House** (Historic Homes) near Plymouth, and another at **Powderham Castle**. The factory, **Axminster Carpets** (Local Industry) is open to the public. The town itself is ancient, standing on the intersection of two old roads, the Icknield Way and the Fosse Way. Small traces of the Cistercian Newnham Abbey remain, founded in 1246. Great Trill, first mentioned in 1173, was one of the properties of the Drakes of Ashe. The house has been modernised to some extent and Hoskins says: 'It is practically certain that the great Duke of Marlborough was born in this house on 24 May 1650 and not at Ashe House in Musbury as is so often asserted.' Smallridge was one of the earliest homes of the Raleighs who lived here for ten or eleven generations. The parish church of St Mary is a cruciform structure with a central tower re-built in the thirteenth century above the old crossing. There is a Norman doorway, a pulpit and reading desk dated 1633. There is a carnival during the second week in September.

Axmouth   Map 4 Ba

At any time of year a week could easily be spent exploring round and about this town with its emerald marshes edging the river Axe. The estuary was once much wider, but became silted up so the mouth was almost barred by a pebble ridge, forcing the river out through a narrow outlet on the east side. Over the years many attempts have been made to re-make the harbour. A pier was built at the beginning of the 1800s, behind which ships of 100 tons could unload, and up to the time when the railway came in 1868, vessels traded regularly between Axmouth and London. Much of the pier was swept away in the gales of January 1869. At one time the Norman St Michael's church held a big congregation, sadly the attendance has now diminished. Perhaps due to its change in fortune the place has great charm, giving the feeling of a lost village with its 800-year-old Inn, the Harbour, and beautiful walks, one of the most famous being through **Downlands Cliffs and Landslip Nature Reserve**. The cliffs have always been subject to slippage and in 1839 when millions of tons came away, the villagers thought the end of the world had occurred. This has left dramatic chasms with rocks rich in fossils. Two coastguards who saw the event said, 'the sea became violently agitated, the beach heaved like the deck of a boat and then suddenly the cliff fell into the sea with a tremendous roar, forming an island three quarters of a mile long and 60 feet high.' There is nothing of this to be seen now as the sea soon dispersed the loose material. To the south of the village is a golf course. Stedcombe House to the north is a fine William and Mary mansion overlooking the river Axe, now uninhabited and belonging to the Loveridge family who live at Bindon Manor.

Bampton   Map 2 Ab

This lovely market town lies on the river Batherm with
mostly Georgian houses built of stone from the local
quarries. Once it had a castle which was much fought over
in Stephen's reign. The church of St Michael and All
Angels, originally Norman, was rebuilt in the fifteenth and
sixteenth centuries and restored in the late nineteenth
century. On the west wall look for a tablet dated 1776:

> 'Bless my little iiiii,
> Here he lies
> In a sad pickle
> Kill'd by an icicle.'

There are two yew trees in the churchyard said to be 500
years old. The town is a centre for hunting and hacking,
with trout fishing in the river Exe. The major annual event
is the fair of Exmoor ponies in October.

On the A396 to the southwest are the lodge and gates to
Suckeridge House, whose cottage has a thatched colonnade.
There are extensive lime quarries, to the south, of
considerable interest to the geologist. Bampton Castle is at
the east end of Castle Street, consisting only of a mound
with some traces of outworks; it was probably a fortified
house rather than a true castle. In the 1860s few people had
ventured down the valley to Exeter. They were a self-
supporting, close knit community, then came the Exe
Valley Flier, a saddle tank engine of the Great Western,
about which Page wrote: 'Personally I do not love the
locomotive, useful he is but ornamental he is not. Noisy,
obtrusive, where he gets his iron foot romance dies. He has
spoilt the Exe valley.' Near the fifteenth-century Exeter Inn
on the road which ran from Bampton to Rackenford is the
'ha'penny' bridge, so named after the toll that was
collected. Alongside can be seen the remains of the
medieval bridge which carried packhorses from Bampton
with lime. There is a trout hatchery two miles away along
the B3223 towards Exebridge. Whilst here, do not miss
Brushford's church of St Mary with a font dating from the

B

mid-twelfth century, and a chapel designed by Sir Edwin
Lutyens in memory of Aubrey Herbert. It commemorates
an officer of the Irish Guard, with his sword above him,
son of the 4th Earl of Carnarvon and said to be the
character, Greenmantle, in John Buchan's thriller. The oak
tree in the churchyard is thought to be over a thousand
years old. There is a wonderful feeling of remoteness.

Barnstaple   Map 1 Bb

The town still has a Georgian feel to it and claims to be the
oldest Borough in Britain, traditionally granted a charter in
A.D. 930. Until the river Taw started to silt up it was an
important port. Samuel Pepys visited here, as did
Shakespeare with his players as a kind of Elizabethan rep.
There is a three-day fair starting on the third Wednesday in
September and a pannier market on Fridays where food
used to be brought in panniers on packhorses. At the end of
the pannier market is the Queen's Hall and at the western
end the Georgian Guildhall. In the High Street opposite is
the Three Tuns Tavern, built in 1450 with its fine oak
panelling and beamed ceilings. On the opposite side of the
river is the **North Devon Leisure Centre** (Sports
Centres) with swimming pool, games rooms and other
sports facilities.

The *Oxford Dictionary of Place Names* defines
Barnstaple, with its thirteenth-century arched bridge across
the river Taw, as a post to which a warship was moored, or
'Bearda's Post'. It was of considerable economic importance
throughout medieval times and, in the early fourteenth
century, the third town in Devon. The fourteenth-century
church of St Peter's has a crooked spire and beyond in
Paternoster Row is fourteenth-century **St Anne's Chapel**
(Museums), once a grammar school, and now a museum of
local history and antiques. John Gay who wrote *The
Beggar's Opera,* was taught here. By the river is Queen
Anne's Walk, an elaborately decorated colonnade with an
ornate statue of the Queen. Here also is the Tome Stone
where bargains were struck between merchants, in the days

when word of mouth was considered binding. From here too, sailed the ships which joined Drake against the Armada in almshouses, the seventeenth-century Horwood's almshouses and school are grouped together in a lovely quiet green churchyard. In 1834 the Salem Almshouses were built, the last of their kind constructed in the town. In Litchdon Street are the pottery showrooms built by Charles Brannam, a late Victorian, much influenced by William Morris. Hugh Strong writing in the 1880s said: 'the beautifully proportioned vases have justly earned artistic compliment ... what perfection he has personally attained in this art.' They were decorated with flowers, fruit and animals. Barnstaple was also the centre for the manufacture of medieval tiles, many of which can still be seen in the churches.

In Boutport Street stand the Royal Fortescue Hotel and the Westminster Bank, which was at one time the home of rich merchants and has an elaborate plaster ceiling. Many of the seventeenth-century ceilings, which were the work of a Barnstaple school of plasterers, have been removed or destroyed.

Pilton was once a more important town than Barnstaple, but is now a suburb. The church of St Mary has beautiful woodwork and monuments, notably a rare and beautiful rood screen dated 1420. It was much 'done up' by the Chichesters of Raleigh and there is a good Renaissance monument in Beer stone dated 1569 to Sir John Chichester, twice Sheriff of Devon.

Codden Beacon, to the southwest off the A377 and a minor road to the east, is a high viewpoint and the site of a memorial to Caroline, wife of Jeremy Thorpe.

Becky Falls See Manaton

Beer Map 4 Ba

This is one of the most notorious smuggling areas of Devon. The 'master' smuggler, Jack Rattenbury, who was born in 1778, made so much money he retired and wrote

B

his memoirs in 1837. A stream runs down the middle of this traditional fishing village, overlooked by high chalk cliffs honeycombed with caves, and above the village at **Beer Modelrama** (Unusual Outings) runs the Beer Heights Light Railway where there is also a museum of model railways. Beer was once famous for its lace made specially for Queen Victoria's wedding dress. One mile north is Bovey House, now a hotel. In about 1300 it came into the possession of the Walronds of Bradfield, until 1786 when it passed to the Rolles family. Later the house remained empty and the lane leading to it was said to be haunted, but it was in fact used as a store and meeting place for smugglers. The Old Quarry, entirely underground and worked from Roman times, is one of the most exciting places in Devon for those interested in history. From here the stone originated for Roman villas, public buildings, cathedrals, parish churches, country houses and cottages, even such prestigious buildings as Exeter Cathedral and St Stephen's at Westminster.

Berry Pomeroy Map 4 Ab

Berry Pomeroy Castle must be one of the most romantic ruins in Devon, approached by a ghost-haunted drive edged with rhododendrons. The medieval castle was built on the site of an older manor house by the first member of the Norman de la Pomerai family, later the Pomeroys.

The most unusual feature is that when Edward Seymour, Duke of Somerset, acquired it, he built a mansion inside in 1548. The plan was ambitious with many huge windows, and enough remains to imagine the whole with huge fireplaces, and kitchens, but the plan was never completed. Standing on a ravine above the Gatcombe Brook, the castle retains its outer shell; the fourteenth-century gatehouse leads into a courtyard, but the reason for the ruin and non completion has never been explained. An air of mystery and evil really does hang over it, enhanced by stories of the ghost of Lady Margaret Pomeroy, murdered by her jealous sister, and of knights who preferred to

14

commit suicide by riding into the ravine rather than surrender their castle after the rebellion in 1549. It is also said that mysterious ley lines cross above it.

Bickleigh Map 2 Ac

Standing beside the river Exe among wooded hills, this is one of the best known beauty spots in Devon. It has a bridge of five arches said to be the inspiration for Simon and Garfunkel's song 'Bridge Over Troubled Waters'. The bridge was badly damaged by floods in 1809 and is said to be haunted by a headless horseman. Part of the village stands on a hill with an early Victorian rectory, where Bampfylde Moore Carew was born in 1869, who became the King of Beggars. His grave is in the churchyard.

   Bickleigh Castle is down river on the west bank. It has a beautiful Norman gatehouse with exquisite wrought iron gates, but the castle was largely destroyed in the Civil War. The north wing was rebuilt as a cob and thatch farmhouse after the Restoration. There is a tiny Norman chapel on the other side of the road, reputed to be the oldest building in Devon. Nearby **Bickleigh Mill Craft Centre and Farm** includes a restored water mill and wheel where craftsmen can be seen at work. There are farm activities, animals, a fish farm, peacocks, an agricultural crafts museum constituting a fascinating complex. At nearby Cadbury is an Iron Age earthwork commanding some of the most magnificent views in Devon. Dartmoor and Exmoor are nearly always visible, and on a good day the hills of Somerset and Cornwall.

Bideford Map 1 Ab

Many people think this is the most attractive town in North Devon, lying on the hillside on the west bank of the river Torridge. The bridge with its 24 arches is a main feature of the town; the earliest was of timber and, as was so often the case, the first stone one was built round it in 1460. The town was given to the Grenvilles by William Rufus, and

B

owes a great deal to that family. The colonisation of
Virginia and Carolina by Sir Richard of the *Revenge* led to
the establishment of considerable trade with America,
which lasted for about 200 years, and Bideford Quay was
built in 1663 by the Corporation. It was however the
tobacco trade which made the largest Bideford fortunes,
but as a result of incessant wars in the eighteenth century
and the collapse of the woollen industry, by the early
nineteenth century only a coasting trade remained. Today
it is an active and cheerful town with a good market and
shops, recommended as a place to retire to in one's old
age. Much of the town is Victorian, but Bridgeland Street
is particularly interesting, laid out by Nathaniel Gascoyne
in about 1690 and lined with merchants' houses. St Mary's
church, rebuilt in the nineteenth century, contains a fine
late Norman font and the tomb of Sir Richard Grenville.

Across the river is East-the-Water, a suburb of the town,
and at the Royal Hotel it is said Charles Kingsley wrote
much of *Westward Ho!*, there is also an exquisite plaster
ceiling with a riot of flowers and foliage. The marble statue
erected to Kingsley stands on the quay. In September
there is a Regatta and salmon fishing in the river Torridge.
At the north end of the Quay, in Victoria Park, there are
ancient guns from the Armada. **Burton Art Gallery**
contains painting, pottery and local items of interest.

Bigbury   Map 3 Bc

Bigbury stands on the west bank of the river Avon. In the
church is a large slate wall tablet with crude figures to John
and Jane Pearse, bearing a verse:

'Thus Pearse being pierced by death do peace obtaine,
Oh happy pierce since peace is Pearses gaine.'

There are also the old walls of the farmyard of Bigbury
Court, an ancient manor with a circular dovecot in the
middle of the courtyard.

Out in the mouth of the river is Burgh Island which can
be reached on foot at low tide. Archibald Nettlefold of

Guest, Keen and Nettlefold, once owned the island and converted it into a luxury paradise for his friends. It was approached most of the time by sea tractor, a huge monster which still carries people across the causeway, looking much like an amphibious greenhouse, and probably unique in the British Isles. Reminiscent of the age of *The Great Gatsby* and *Brideshead Revisited*, the hotel has been turned into time-share flats, retaining much of the atmosphere where Noel Coward and Agatha Christie once stayed. The crime writer was said to have written some of her books here. The Duke of Windsor and Mrs Simpson were also visitors, and later the Beatles. The sixties pop group, Dave Clarke Five, made a film on the island.

Standing on the crest is the ruin of the Huer's Hut where the lookout raised the cry when shoals of fish were seen. Below is the Pilchard Inn dating back to 1336 where Tom Crocker the smuggler met his end and whose ghost still visits on four days of the year.

Bovey Tracey Map 4 Ab

Nightingales can still be heard singing on nearby Chudleigh Knighton Heath, all that is left of the great heath that once covered the Bovey Basin. The area is of great interest to geologists, as the bed of an ancient lake contains lignite which has been mined since the early sixteenth century. There are potteries and brickworks as well as an industrial estate at Heathfield. The town is built on a steep hill on the edge of Dartmoor, marking a natural starting point or gateway for a tour of that region. There is an old watermill in the town and the bridge was built in 1643. Nearby **Parke** (Country Parks) is a classical mansion dating from 1820, now the H.Q. of the National Parks' Service and a reserve designed to protect vanishing species of various animals. **Yarner Wood National Nature Reserve**, to the west of the town, has well laid out woodland walks and one and a half miles away on the Haytor Road is the David Leach Pottery, son of the world famous Bernard Leach.

B

The church, St Thomas of Canterbury, has fifteenth-century furnishings; it is said to have been founded by William de Tracy in expiation of the murder of St Thomas of Canterbury in which he played a part. Recently, human bones said to be 500-years-old have been found under the floor of the church by a carpenter doing repair work. A gateway standing just off the main street is known as Cromwell's Arch, although it was probably there before his time. Lord Wentworth's troops were attacked here in 1646 by Cromwell who captured 100 horses and seven flags, while the officers were reputedly playing cards.

On the road to Challabrook Farm, is a mutilated cross that is said to have marked the grave of a Royalist officer who fell in this skirmish on Bovey Heath. Nearby is Hawkmoor, once a Domesday Manor, now a hospital.

Bradninch See Cullompton

Brampford Speke see Exeter

Branscombe Map 4 Ba

It is difficult to describe Branscombe as it consists of hamlets and houses planted haphazardly and practically reaching the unspoilt beach belonging to the National Trust. Great Seaside Farm is a good example of an Elizabethan farmhouse, and there are other interesting houses dotted about, including the homes of franklins, also of Tudor and Stuart gentry. Church Living is a medieval house, said to have another one hidden away beneath it. St Winifred's church is very atmospheric and shows a process of continuous development from the eleventh to the sixteenth century. Not far away is Barnells, the house built by Captain Ewell, Nelson's captain of the marines on the *Victory* at Trafalgar.

There are outstanding cliff top walks taking in part of the **South Devon Coast Path** (Walking). Joan Wadham, the mother of Nicholas Wadham who founded

Wadham College, Oxford, is buried in the churchyard. She married twice and had 20 children, although only 17 are shown on her memorial. The two public houses are recommended by Egon Ronay. There is an old fashioned blacksmith's forge and a bakery with wood-fired ovens. Here, 81-year-old Gerald Collier begins work at 4 a.m. and lights the oven to bake the beautiful crusty bread for which he is famous, following the traditional methods of his father which have been practised for over 100 years. Five or six faggots, collected by local farmers after trimming their hedges, are pushed into the old stone oven and lit. This is the last surviving example of wood-fired bakery, and Gerald is a bachelor so there are no children to carry on the business.

Brixham   Map 4 Ab

The old harbour of Brixham once stretched inland, but the central part of Lower Brixham has been built over this, the original Saxon settlement being at Higher Brixham. The

Replica of the Golden Hind, Brixham

whole life of the village for several centuries revolved around fishing, net making, ship building and all the allied trades. Until 1870, when Plymouth took over, it was the foremost fishing port in Devon. The Brixham fishing fleet returning under full sail in the evenings, was one of the great sights in the west of England. In 1910 there were 213 trawlers of various types fishing from the port and Brixham men held a justifiable pride in their town. The war came and the young men were called away, then when they returned, the town had virtually died and only 86 old, worn vessels were left. Fish prices fell and by 1935 only 26 boats remained. The famous Brixham fishing fleet was now practically extinct, but the town has since acquired a reputation as a holiday centre.

On the Quay is a statue erected in 1889 to commemorate the landing of William of Orange on 5 November 1688. The harbour is now a hive of activity, fish can be bought at the Fish Market. There is a full size replica of Sir Francis Drake's **Golden Hind** (Unusual Outings) afloat in the harbour, and the Marine Aquarium and Trawling Exhibition on the Quay. The **Brixham Museum** includes the National Coastguard Museum, and now has extra premises at Rea Barn Hill, complete with lecture room, laboratory and extra storage space. It has completed 25 years with exhibits associated with smuggling, and a female skeleton from a Bronze Age burial place known affectionately as 'Kate'. Brixham Pottery is open during shop hours and well worth a visit. Flora Thompson who wrote *Lark Rise to Candleford* came to Brixham with her husband when he retired from Dartmouth. They lived at a house called 'Lauriston' on New Road. She actually wrote *Candleford Green* here, and *Still Glides the Stream*, but died at Lauriston a few weeks after its completion in May 1947.

To the north of Brixham is **Berry Head** (Country Parks), an area of outstanding beauty. In 1970 the flat land here was bought from the Trustees of the family of the Rev. H.F. Lyte who wrote the hymn 'Abide with Me' whilst living here. It is the site of an Iron Age settlement and coastal fort, covering a large area with a moat and defensive

B

outer wall built in 1802 at the time of the Napoleonic invasion scare. Napoleon himself was kept in a ship, *The Bellerophon*, moored off Berry Head in 1814, the closest in fact he ever got to England. Here too is one of the smallest lighthouses in the country, only ten feet tall, and 191 feet above sea level. Cliff climbing is prohibited between 15 May and 15 July due to a breeding colony of birds including the auk, guillemot, razorbill and fulmar.

Broadclyst   Map 4 Aa

The parish of Broadclyst is very large, covering nearly 15 square miles and including valleys and wooded hills such as Killerton. Many houses like Churchill and **Killerton House** (Historic Homes) date from shortly after Domesday in the eleventh century, when the parish was full of ancient freeholders, the most interesting being the Churchills. A mile away from Killerton is Columbjohn which was bought by Sir John Acland in Elizabeth I's reign. It was garrisoned for the King during the Civil War, and in March 1646 formed the H.Q. of Fairfax, whose army was then stationed at Silverton. Cromwell also stayed here. The old house was pulled down when the Aclands moved to Killerton, but the arched Elizabethan gateway can still be seen among the trees. Killerton Gardens, now owned by the National Trust, are often called the Devonian Kew. The gardens stretch up the slope of Dolbury Hill 'Dola's burh', the remains of an earthwork. In the gardens is Bear Hut, a tiny thatched building of split tree trunks lined inside with wicker and pine cones. It was built for a bear brought back from Canada by one of the family. There is also a good example of an old ice house where food was kept, resembling an early deep freeze.

The gardens are a perfect example of a controlled wilderness and in April thousands of naturalised daffodils and narcissi bloom, followed by great azure drifts of bluebells. Then come the magnolias until late June. There are cork oaks, a handkerchief and a snowdrop tree. The chapel designed by C.R. Cockerell in 1841 was delayed whilst being built because a swallow had made her nest in the rose window and everything had to stop till she hatched her eggs. Two carved nests on either side commemorate this happy event.

Broadhembury   Map 4 Ba

Said to be the best example of a thatched village in the West Country, Broadhembury has no yellow lines, no television aerials or telegraph poles. Colour washed cottages line the broad street, covered with roses, clematis and fuschia. In 1768 the Rev. Augustus Toplady, the vicar here, wrote the famous hymn 'Rock of Ages' whilst living in Somerset.

Enormous chestnut trees lead up to the fourteenth-century church of St Andrew's, built of flint from the surrounding hills, chalky limestone from Beer, and some

Broadhembury

volcanic rock from Thorverton. There is a fifteenth-century Priest's House, whilst the Drewe Arms is the same age as the church and may originally have been the Church House. The Grange, with its gardens bounded by magnificent hedges, was bought from Dunkeswell Abbey in 1603 by Edward Drewe, an Elizabethan lawyer who already owned Sharpham. Inside the house there are beautiful plaster ceilings, a grand carved wood staircase and the well-known magnificent oak drawing room. It is a conservation area and the cottages which belong to the Drewe family can only be leased and not bought. Walter, the present member of the family, lives on the edge of the village with a beautiful garden full of magnificent azaleas and rhododendrons, many of which he has grown from seed. This lovely peaceful spot is highly recommended as a place to visit whether you are a local or visitor. It is like stepping back into the tranquillity of the past. There is an excellent book on this little known area *In the Shadow of the Blackdowns* by J.A. Sparks.

Two miles southeast is **Hembury Fort** (Archaeological Sites), a Stone Age camp 1,085 feet long and 330 feet wide, occupied for 4,000 years until Roman times and from which there are magnificent views across Dartmoor.

Buckfastleigh   Map 3 Bb

Buckfastleigh is a small market town close to the river Dart, and by-passed by the A38. Here is the main depot of the **Dart Valley Railway**, resuscitated by a group of enthusiasts after the railway between Ashburton and Totnes was closed in 1962. There is also the passenger carrying Riverside Miniature Railway. The heart of the town's prosperity was wool, but the big mill is now closed. High on a hill above the town, approached by 195 steps, is the thirteenth-century church of the Holy Trinity. In the churchyard look for the enormous seventeenth-century tomb of wicked squire, Sir Richard Cabell of Brooke Manor, who hunted a pack of black hounds, many of which became wild and vicious and inspired Conan Doyle's

B

Hound of the Baskervilles, named after a coachman who drove the author up to the moor. Under the church the ground is honeycombed with caves where the fossilised bones of hippopotami, rhinoceros, elephant and bison, 4,000 in number, have been discovered and left in situ. They constitute the richest collection of interglacial bones and teeth found in the British Isles and can be seen at Higher Kiln Quarry, together with colonies of bats who live permanently in one of the caves. There is a centre and museum open to the public; the town also has a museum of early farm machinery, and the John Loosemore Centre for Organ and Early Music contains an organ building workshop, teaching studio and recital hall.

Buckfast Abbey (Church Buildings) was founded in about 1030 and endowed by King Canute. It then suffered literally many ups and downs and in 1806 a local woollen manufacturer lowered the standing walls and built a house and mill; the house now forms part of the reconstructed Abbey. A community of French Benedictine monks acquired the site in 1882 and set out to rebuild the Abbey, carrying out the work themselves, with never more than six working at a time. On 25 August 1932 St Mary's Abbey church was consecrated by the Archbishop of Westminster, Cardinal Bourne; the tower was completed in 1938. Dom Charles Norris, who was in the army with General Montgomery during the war, came here as a young man and began to work with stained glass. His contribution to the Abbey is the huge east window with the figure of Christ, and in the modern chapel added to the main Abbey church, the entire wall from floor to ceiling, apart from cross supports, is made of glorious coloured glass. One must mention the famous bees whose honey is on sale to visitors, as is the tonic wine.

Sadly the unique House of Shells has closed, as has the delightful racecourse on the other side of the A38.

Buckland Abbey   see Yelverton

Budleigh Salterton Map 4 Aa

This is a town of comfortable villas set in large well kept gardens, much favoured by retired people. The name comes from the salt pans once at the mouth of the River Otter. Sir John Millais lived at the Octagon and painted his famous picture 'The Boyhood of Raleigh' on the beach against a wall, which still exists.

Fairlynch Arts Centre Museum, housed in a pretty marine cottage, has a reference library, lace making demonstrations and recreates a smuggler's cellar as well as other displays of local history.

Two miles to the north lies **Bicton Park** (Gardens) whose 50 acre grounds contains magnificent Italian gardens, designed by Andre le Notre, American gardens and a **Woodland Railway**. The great house built in 1713 is now an agricultural college. Sir Walter Raleigh was born at Hayes Barton which exudes a lovely air of faded gentility. For the sport's enthusiast the headquarters of the East Devon Golf Club, the Lawn Tennis and Croquet Club are located here.

Bicton Gardens, East Budleigh

25

C

Buckland-in-the-Moor see Ashburton

Chagford Map 3 Ba

This small market town on the edge of Dartmoor has no
yellow lines and unrestricted parking which is a
recommendation in itself. It is a wonderful centre for
exploring the surrounding Moor. The river Teign runs
through the town, more beautiful in this area perhaps than
anywhere else, and lower down when spring comes, there
are displays of wild daffodils, primroses, wild anemones,
bluebells and violets all along the valley.

Before 1244 there was a bridge at Chagford, meaning
gorse-ford and derived from 'chag' meaning gorse or
broom. In 1305 it was made one of the original Stannary
Towns, although it had been acting in that capacity for
years before. After tin came the wool trade, and even when
that dwindled Chagford remained an important town, full
of interesting buildings, perhaps the most famous being the
early sixteenth-century Three Crowns Inn, where poor
Sidney Godolphin, poet and dedicated King's man, was
shot and died in the porch. His ghost is often seen.

St Michael's church is a fine example of a fifteenth-
century granite building containing a memorial to Sir John
Whiddon or Whyddon, Justice of the Queen's Bench, who
died in 1575. He created a house and park at the entrance
to Teign Gorge which is a romantically beautiful place of
rocks, ravens and deer. Also in the church is a memorial to
Mary Whiddon who died in 1641: 'Behold a matron yet a
maid', a rather cryptic description referring to the fact that
she was shot by a spurned lover as she left the church with
her husband on her wedding day. Here too lived Jim
Perrott, who knew the moor better than anyone and started
the first Dartmoor letterbox at Cranmere Pool.

The parish climbs to Kes Tor rock with hut circles, stone
rows and kists scattered about the moor. Many of the farms
are mentioned in the Domesday Book. Lower down the
river is Fingle Bridge, on each side of which stand
Cranbrook and Prestonbury Iron Age forts on hill tops. A

fortress of another kind is **Castle Drogo**, the twentieth-century granite palace, the last castle to be built in England, and designed by Sir Edwin Lutyens for Julius Drewe, who made his fortune from the Home and Colonial stores. It now belongs to the National Trust, but the family have a flat above the public rooms with bare walls, huge granite arches and beautiful tapestries.

The megalithic burial dolmen, **Spinster's Rock** (Archaeological Sites) at Shilstone Farm should be seen. The Spinsters were apparently not unmarried ladies, but skittish lady spinners, said to dance on this spot. Prince Charles has a favourite hotel in the area, where the food is said to be fit for princes.

Nearby Gidleigh is worth a visit, just two and a half miles from Chagford, with steep hills running down to lively brown streams. The church and castle form the main part of the hamlet, the latter a small Norman keep surrounded by low walls now ruined, but made into a garden, and said to have been the home in Saxon days of King Harold's mother Gytha. Fernworthy Reservoir, a haunted place where an old farm and clapper bridge were submerged to provide water, is located on the edge of **Fernworthy Forest** (Woodland) which is a good spot for a picnic.

Christow Map 2 Ac

Standing on the hillside of the lovely Teign valley, nearby are the reservoirs of Tottiford and Kennick, supplying Torquay with water, and fishermen with good sport. In the same parish, Canonteign, a Domesday manor has been lovingly restored. When Sir Edward Pellew bought the manors of Christow and Canonteign he built Canonteign House, 1812, in a beautiful timbered park nearby. He was the first Viscount Exmouth, a brilliant naval commander, winning honour for his bombardment of Algiers. He is buried at Christow. There were formerly silver, lead, copper and manganese mines in the parish. An abandoned

C

lead mine can be seen near Old Canonteign; there was talk
lately of re-opening this.

Nicholas Busell was shot at Christow by Parliamentary
troops when he refused to yield the keys of the church.

The pub is called The Artichoke for no good reason.
Arthur Marshall, the lovable television personality lives
here and is much involved in village life about which he has
written. Once the railway ran along the valley, and even the
spanking Cornish Riviera Express was known to use the
route in an emergency when the coastal line was flooded. At
one time too, Teign House Races were held here, known as
pony flapping, but they were illegally set up for several
ponies ran twice in one hour.

Chudleigh see Newton Abbot

Clovelly Map 1 Ab

This unique village, really a cleft in the coast on the bed of
an old waterway, is best approached from the east via
Hobby Drive, one of the most beautiful coast roads in
Britain, created over a period of years by the owners of
Clovelly Court, the Carys, who used the labour of
unemployed soldiers at the end of the Napoleonic Wars.

Soon you see the steep stepped cobbled street with
cottages on either side. It owes its present day magical
enchantment to the 'Queen of Clovelly', Christine Hamlyn,
who died in 1936. There has been a village here for
centuries, for during the Iron Age Clovelly Dykes was a
fortress at the top of the hill where the manor, church and
rectory now stand. Some of the pews in the church still
have little projecting seats at the end for the poor
children and apprentices. Near the pulpit is an hour glass
for timing the sermon.

Clovelly became popular as a result of Charles Kingsley's
Westward Ho! He spent much of his boyhood here, and
apart from the donkeys, who now only carry goods and not
people, it hasn't changed much since his day. It was known
as one of the safest harbours on the treacherous North

C

Devon coast, the original jetty being built in the twelfth century, even the bollards on the quay are said to be upended canons from the Spanish Armada. There are a few families in the area said to be descendents of the sailors saved from the wreck of a Spanish galleon. Ships brought in limestone and the kiln can still be seen at the back of the harbour. The first lifeboat in Clovelly was the *Alexander* and later came the *Matilda Boetefeur* in 1870.

The Clovelly Cannibals who lived in the caves were terrifying murderers, who were eventually burnt alive. The village is closed to wheeled traffic, but Land Rovers use a back road. At the bottom of the hill is the Red Lion, the New Inn and shops halfway up the street. When you have climbed this, a path leads to Gallantry Bower, an almost sheer cliff with glorious views towards Lundy.

Clovelly

C

Colyton Map 4 Ba

This peaceful village dates back to Saxon times, parts of the
vicarage to 1529. Here you can ride on the world's only
surviving open-topped tram to Seaton. There are lovely
walks, too, among the combes with their network of
medieval lanes linking farms, some of which are
ancient, carrying the suffix 'Hayne' or 'Hay' meaning
enclosure. Some became 'mansions' in the sixteenth to
eighteenth centuries and are interesting examples of the
homes of small squires characteristic of their period.

The church of St Andrew is worth a visit because of the
many tombs and monuments to the Courtenays and
Yonges. The parish registers from 1538 are perfectly
preserved and have been printed.

Visitors are welcome to visit **J. & F.J. Baker & Co. Ltd**
(Local Industry), the only oak-bark tannery in England.

Combe Martin Map 1 Ba

The long village street runs for one and a half miles to the
bay, under which are said to be silver and lead mine
workings, whose products were sold to help finance the
Hundred Years' War. The Pack of Cards Inn was built in
the eighteenth century by George Ley who won money
by playing cards. The village is surrounded by National
Trust land with exciting footpaths leading to the headlands
of Little and Great Hangman. On the outskirts is
Buzzacott Manor (Gardens) with its Woolly Monkey
Park. At Higher Leigh Manor are **The Monkey
Sanctuary** (Zoos), gardens and a model railway. There is
also a **Motor Cycle Collection** (Museums) packed with
motor cycle memorabilia.

Crediton Map 4 Aa

This is the famous birthplace of St Boniface in A.D. 680.
The town was founded on the woollen trade, but as with so
many other Devon towns, suffered severely from fire in

C

1743. Holy Cross Church is large and sprawling, built in
red sandstone, and behind the font is a little door which
leads to the Governor's Room which once housed an
ancient library, now removed to Exeter. There is a fantastic
memorial to Sir Redvers Buller who relieved Ladysmith
in the South African War. Next to the church is the
thirteenth-century Chapter House with a Civil War
armoury.

Croyde   Map 1 Ab

In the parish of Croyde, Georgeham is a village of thatched
cottages, one of which was once the home of Henry
Williamson. There is first class surfing and beaches with
rock pools. **The Gem Rock and Shell Museum** houses a
collection of rough cut and polished gems from all over the
world. One mile to the north is Baggy Point which belongs
to the National Trust commanding marvellous views.

Cullompton   Map 2 Ab

Once full of frustrated drivers, this town is now bypassed
by dual carriageways. It was badly damaged by fire in 1839
and the stream through the main street helped to keep the
town clean in the fourteenth century. There are two
handsome houses, Walronds and the Manor House, now a
hotel, both dated 1603. The latter has an elaborate shell
arched doorway, built during the wool boom, as was the
red sandstone church of St Andrew's with decorations in
Beer stone. The Golgotha, an ancient wood carving of
skulls and bones and rocks, is preserved in the church.

Nearby Uffculme, five miles to the northeast, has a
wooden shambles or market area in the square which dates
from the fourteenth century. By the river, to the south of
the village, is Coldharbour Museum and **Coldharbour
Mill**, a working museum of the woollen and worsted
industry run by the Coldharbour Mill Trust. The old
watermill and steam engine are still operating and visitors
can see cloth produced as it was in Victorian times. There

D

is a perfect picnic area in the Culm valley.

To the south of Cullompton is Bradninch. The town has a long history, and stands above the valley of the river Culm, its main street is wide and tree lined. In the twelfth century it was held as an honour or barony with the Earldom of Cornwall by Reginald, the natural son of Henry I, and in 1337 it was absorbed into the Duchy of Cornwall, to which it still belongs. In 1208 King John granted the burgesses the liberties and free customs enjoyed by the city of Exeter with a Saturday market and a four day fair. By the late eighteenth century it was sinking almost into oblivion, but was saved by the establishment of paper mills on the river Culm, whose water was ideal for manufacturing. John Dewdney produced the first glazed writing paper in England in the 1840s and supplied the catalogue paper for the Great Exhibition in 1851. The Hele Mills still flourish and produce high grade paper.

The town was the H.Q. of King Charles's army during the Civil War on 27 July 1644, when the king slept at the Manor House. In October 1645 the town was the H.Q. of Fairfax, but history does not relate where he slept. The parish church, known as St Disen has a sixteenth-century rood screen extending right across the chancel. The Royal coat of arms below the tower is of Edward VIII, one of the rather sad few mementoes we have of his short reign.

Dartington   Map 3 Bb

Dartington is a combination of history, money, but above all, idealism; a self-financing rural community, the dream of Leonard Elmhirst and his American wife, Dorothy Whitney Straight. They bought the estate in 1925 and established the Trust in 1931. Leonard had met Tagore and gone to Bengal with him to set up an Institute of Rural Reconstruction, hence Dartington. The idealism of the Elmhirsts could be said to be a blueprint for the welfare state, for many of the men and women who laid the foundations of post war Britain, came first of all to Dartington to observe, and went away with a vision of a better world. However, for many years they were looked upon with great suspicion by the locals with their talks of communism and free love.

The Trust was first started by founding a co-educational school and now encompasses many activities, including a model farm and dairy, textile mills, shops, building, electrical and forestry firms. The body controls the enlarged progressive school and the College of Arts, offering full time courses in music and drama, also short residential courses in various subjects. The Amadeus String Quartet was formed here, whilst Henry Moore and the potter Bernard Leach taught at the Arts Centre. The Trust not only brought the Ballets Joos to Dartington, but in 1936 they introduced apple juice as a drink to Britain. In 1944 the Trust opened the Cattle Breeding Centre making artificial insemination available to hundreds of farmers in the county who didn't want to keep their own bulls.

Dartington Hall (Gardens), built in 1388, by John Holland, half brother of King Richard II, was said to be

Dartington Hall

D

the most spectacular medieval mansion in Devon, with a quadrangle that has hardly changed over the centuries, and a great central hall with a hammer-beam roof. The Champernowne family lived here from 1559 until the present century, but owing to losses brought about by agricultural recession, the estate was broken up and sold to the Elmhirsts. For 600 years or more the house has been occupied, retaining an air of continuity and tranquillity which envelops the gardens. Dartington is a distillation of the magic of Devon, partly because of the unique peace of its gardens, whose trees, contours, lawns and flowering shrubs create shadows and shapes which bring endless delight to the eye. In the centre of the gardens is the tilting yard, its terraces crowned by Spanish chestnuts at least 400 years old. At the bottom of the glade is Henry Moore's figure of a reclining woman, where he put it in 1947. He wrote that he wanted the figure to have 'a quiet stillness and sense of permanence, as though it would stay there forever – as though it had come to terms with the world and could get over the largest care and losses.' Certainly it is a wonderful place to re-charge your batteries. Also, don't miss the enchanting bronze donkey by Willi Soukop or the 12 tall yew Apostles round the tiltyard.

In the village at Shinner's Bridge is the Cider Press with shops selling local crafts, glass and pottery, and the well-known vegetarian restaurant 'Cranks'. Two hundred yards to the east is the tweed mill. Their world famous glass is made at Great Torrington.

Every year new ventures, new branches of activity are generated, and Dartington could be described as the most ancient, yet the most modern of places, impossible to adequately convey in a short space. Whatever else you overlook, don't miss Dartington.

Dartmoor   Map 3 Ba

Dartmoor (National Parks) is granite country, spanning an area of over 300 square miles in the heart of Devon and stretching from Okehampton in the north to Ivybridge in the south, Ashburton in the east to Lydford in the west. Tin and copper were mined here, it is the source of 14 rivers, and part of its character is dominated by a sinister prison. It is called The Last Wilderness, a document of life since the early Bronze Age, a wild land where ancient rights are preserved and hill farmers still graze cattle, sheep and ponies as they did in the thirteenth century.

There is barren moor at Cranmere and Duck's Pool; at Swincombe and Fox Tor Mire in contrast lush woodland, gorges and fast streams similar to those at Lydford Gorge and **Becky Falls** (Country Parks). There are peat bogs and ponies, not wild, but owned by Dartmoor 'Commoners' who mark and brand during the annual drifts when the animals are rounded up. There are enormous granite outcrops like Hound Tor, Hay Tor and Bowerman's Nose, close to Wingstone Farm where John Galsworthy wrote much of his *Forsyte Saga*. There is the Dewer Stone rock not far from Shaugh Bridge, which is a good place for rock climbing, but look out for the devil and his Whisht

Black Hill, Dartmoor

D

Hounds. There is the site of an old gunpowder factory at Cherry Brook on the Moretonhampstead road, and the stone circle ruins of a once highly important fortified Bronze Age village at Grimspound where 24 hut circles are surrounded by a boundary wall. There are clapper bridges which once carried packhorses with their loads of peat, tin, silver, arsenic and wool. It can be a dangerous place which is best explored with someone who knows it well.

The two main roads from Tavistock to Ashburton, and Plymouth to Moretonhampstead, cut the moor into quarters linking Two Bridges and Princetown whose prison was built by French prisoners during the Napoleonic Wars. At Crockern Tor the Stannary Parliament met in support of the tin miners, forming an early and powerful trade union and a law unto itself. Many of the blowing houses the miners used still remain. Look for **Wistman's Wood** with its stunted and twisted scrub oaks, haunted by adders and ghosts.

The fine clapper bridge at Postbridge is well known. Once the main stone was removed by a man and used to

View from Hexworthy, Dartmoor

D

dam the stream to keep his ducks from straying. Later it was restored, according to the locals, upside down. To the northwest is the **Warren House Inn** (Industrial Archaeology) where a peat fire has been burning continuously for over 130 years. Above all, Dartmoor is a place steeped in folklore, suspicion and hauntings, spiced with such stories as that of Kitty Jay. This poor little workhouse girl came to be a kitchen maid and hanged herself in a barn at Canna farm because the son of the house had seduced her and she was pregnant. There are always flowers on her grave, but no-one is ever seen placing them there. Wart charmers and witches can still be met, people even become pixie led, like poor Jan Coo who was called by the voice of the river Dart below Rowbrook Farm one dimpsy evening, and was never seen again. There are hamlets and remote farms going back to Domesday with no gas, no electricity and no piped water. Near Postbridge there is a mysterious road where unexplained accidents occur, when hairy hands seize the steering wheel, where UFOs hover and scare the police. You either fall in love with it or loathe it. This is Dartmoor, of which a man once wrote while walking across it, 'I am alone. I am King. I have all this.'

Dartmouth Map 4 Ab

This must be one of the most dramatically situated towns in Devon built on a steep wooded valley overlooking the river Dart. Twin castles guard the entrance to the sheltered haven from any wind that blows. Dartmouth has always been a first-class defensive port, but there is also a magic no other river can offer. It has been called the English Rhine where Anchor Stone replaces Lorelei Rock, but the river Dart is too English to be compared with a German river, for along its banks, in its meadows, among the buildings that line it, great events in our history are enshrined in memory. Queen Victoria wrote of Dartmouth in her diary: '20 August 1846. It was thought best to give up Lynmouth and put into that beautiful Dartmouth and we accordingly

D

did so in pouring rain, the deck swimming with water and all of us with umbrellas, the children being most anxious to see everything. Notwithstanding the rain this place is lovely with its wooded rocks and castles at the entrance.'

The castles were built between 1488 and 1502 and a chain known as 'Jawbones' stretched at night from **Dartmouth Castle** to its twin on the Kingswear side. Kingswear castle was converted to a dwelling in the last century and today belongs to Sir Frederick Bennett M.P. The church of St Petrock's beside Dartmouth castle is mentioned as early as 1192, whilst the present building dates from 1641 and is still in use during the summer for weddings, christenings and funerals, the bells carrying their sound with sweet purity across the water to the town on a summer evening. A spy for the Spanish Government in 1599 said the town was not walled, but that the mountains were its walls.

The most famous of the town's merchants who braved the seas was John Hawley, said to be the inspiration for Chaucer's 'Shipman' in the *Canterbury Tales*. The Crusaders of 1147 and 1190 left for Jerusalem from here and over the years it has been the assembly port for the departure of vessels to battles in every corner of the world, the boats of the first Colonial Expedition under Sir Humphrey Gilbert, the first of the great East Indiamen, and on D-Day, 480 vessels bound for the Normandy beaches.

From the seventeenth century the town's trade with Newfoundland became the main source of prosperity. Many of the buildings date back to the Civil War and earlier, such as **Agincourt House** (Other Historic Buildings) and the beautiful Butterwalk's seventeenth-century houses. No. 6 is said to be where Charles II held court and is now the **Borough Museum** with its original ceiling and wainscotting. You can climb up through National Trust property to Gallant's Bower which was once a beacon station where a small dip at the top protected the fire from the wind as smoke and flames gave warning of attack.

Leading families in the town were the Holdsworths and Newmans, whose descendents are still prominent in the county, but Dartmouth's most famous son was Thomas Newcomen born in 1661, an ironmonger by trade, his fame commemorated by a memorial in Coronation Park. He invented the Atmospheric Engine from which a new age of steam power developed, destined to change the face of industry throughout the world.

In Higher Street stands the Cherub Pub, said to be the oldest and sole surviving medieval house in the town erected about 1380. Dartmouth too is the home of the massive Britannia Royal Naval Training College, built in 1905 to the design of Sir Aston Webb, replacing the two wooden training ships moored off Sandquay, *The Hindustan* and *Britannia*. The Royal Regatta began in 1840 and is still held in August. The 'station' which has no railway and no track is used by a passenger ferry; there are two car ferries and many boat trips up river to Totnes. During the Second World War the U.S. Army took over Dartmouth in preparation for D-Day and battles were

Dartmouth Castle

D

rehearsed along the beaches at Slapton. The buildings have attracted many film makers such as the B.B.C. series *The Onedin Line* when the ship *The Charlotte Rhodes* was moored in the river. Bayard's Cove is a cobbled courtyard from where the *Mayflower* and *Speedwell* set off on 31 July 1620. There is still some commercial shipping with timber ships from the Baltic going up to Totnes. Naval ships and submarines visit the College, where King George VI, the Duke of Edinburgh, Prince Charles and Prince Andrew trained. In recent years hundreds of small sailing craft have used the port with two marinas to serve them. Such people as Chay Blyth and Rod and Naomi James have all set off from Dartmouth. On Anzac Street is situated the eccentric **Henley Museum**, a local man's personal collection. **Dartmouth Museum** has an exhibition of model ships, the market square is used every Friday, and the Castle Hotel even has a ghost. The Royal Devon Yacht Club and Dartmouth Sailing Club are based in the town and there are opportunities for diving.

Nearby Dittisham on the banks of the river Dart, is a mass of blossom in the spring as if snow has fallen, and among the trees the houses seem to be tumbling down to the water's edge. Its chief claim to fame is of course its plum orchards. Some call the village 'Ditsam' but even the locals are in two minds over the pronunciation. The church of St George is fifteenth and early sixteenth century, built of local slate, with a famous pulpit, carved of stone with figures, fruit and foliage all in good repair and which somehow survived the Civil War. An offshore rock named the Anchor Stone is said to be where Sir Walter Raleigh retreated from his nearby residence and the scolding women of his household to smoke his pipe. There is a passenger ferry to Greenway Quay run by Roy Andrews, and at one time there was one for cars and cattle, but that has long gone. Both Agatha Christie and Richard Dimbleby had homes here by the river Dart.

D

Dawlish Map 4 Ab

Dawlish was originally a small fishing village but in 1803
The Lawn, with its chestnut trees was laid down. Through
the town runs Dawlish Water, resplendent with its black
swans and ornamental bridges. It has a long beach and
promenade with tunnels through the red cliffs for Brunel's
railway line, which runs from Exeter to Newton Abbot past
the Parson and Clerk rocks. Jane Austen and Charles
Dickens both stayed here, the latter made it Nicholas
Nickleby's birthplace. There are two houses designed by
Nash, Stonelands and Luscombe Castle. There is a
Dawlish Museum containing Victorian dolls and other
fascinating bric-a-brac. Dawlish Warren, two miles up the
coast is a camping and caravan site with a golf course and
the **Railway Museum** and model railway.

Dittisham see Dartmouth

Drewsteignton Map 3 Ba

The thatched Drewe Arms still retains all the
characteristics of a typical Dartmoor Inn of a 100 years ago,
no doubt mostly due to Mrs Mudge, or Aunt Mabel, who
has been host here for over 60 years. You can still get a pint
of beer with taste and bite, and draught cider. It stands at
one side of the square of thatched cottages near the
fifteenth-century granite-built Holy Trinity church, which,
together with the churchyard, is beautifully kept. Entering
the churchyard through a roofed lych-gate you pass a
granite cottage, once a refuge for tramps and mendicants,
but now belonging to the church, having been donated by
public subscription in 1931 in memory of a church-warden
named William Ponsford, last squire of the parish.

A notice above the church door reads: 'Please keep this
door closed to prevent birds entering the church'. There is
an unusual memorial worked in tapestry, to those who
served in the First World War; it is to those who died and
those who survived. Beside the door is a huge magnolia

D

bush, covered in May with creamy blossom like a waiting bride.

James Meadow Rendel, who became a famous engineer, was born here, though the exact date is unknown. For a meal that is different try Miro's Restaurant where great joints of rosemary smothered lamb are cooked on an open spit in a barn. In the restaurant Miro and his wife, Sandra Pupavac, hold Yugoslav evenings, the food cooked by mine host who studied philosophy in his native Dalmatia.

Dunchideock Map 4 Aa

This name is Celtic and means the wooded fort or camp, probably referring to the nearby earthworks at Cotley Castle. The village is buried among the foothills of Haldon and in the church of St Michael is a mural monument to General Stringer Lawrence, 1697, the 'father' of the Indian Army who succeeded Clive of India as Commander-in-Chief, and was reputed to have brought the Koh-i-nor diamond to England. His epitaph is written by the poetess and reformer, Hannah More, but Stringer left his fortune to Sir Robert Palk of Haldon House, who erected a triangular tower in his memory, with a statue and inscription in Persian. It stands on the summit of the hills above, known as Haldon Belvedere, and a landmark for many miles. Marconi was a regular visitor to the village and it is said his first primitive message was transmitted from here. The village is also famous for its legendary treacle mines. There are many explanations for these, some dating back to 1537. They are open to the public every two years when a fete takes place in the ground of Dunchideock House.

Dunkeswell Map 2 Bc

The village lies on the Blackdown plateau. The church of St Nicholas has a Norman font with one of the earliest representations of an elephant. The Abbey, two miles north, is a hamlet centred round a tiny village green with a pump, but the greatest attraction is the airfield which, during the Second World War, was home to the American forces, loud with the roar of Liberators and Catalinas going on missions against U boats. One of the most distinguished personalities at the base was Lieutenant Joseph Kennedy Jnr., elder brother of John who later became President of the U.S.A. and was assassinated. Joseph was killed during an experimental mission named 'Anvil'. Perhaps this changed the whole course of American history. There is now a flying club, facilities for gliding and sky diving. The club is privately owned, but everyone is welcome to the bar and restaurant, and to watch the Rallye planes taking off and landing with pupils and members. There is a visitors' book full of nostalgic memories of American pilots who were stationed here during the Second World War. In the village the pub, the Royal Oak, is run by Peter Cairns who does aerial photography and charter work. His cooking is superb, especially his chips.

Dunsford   Map 2 Ac

A Teign Valley village with beautiful whitewashed cob and thatch cottages, and some examples of sixteenth-century moorstone buildings. St Mary's church contains the Fulford tomb with one of their helmets hung above. The family's house, two and a half miles northwest of the village, was a Domesday Manor; the family was first recorded here in the time of Richard I and is the only one left in Devon who can claim an uninterrupted descent in the male line since that date. They have distinguished themselves as soldiers from the time of the Crusades. The house was garrisoned for the King in the Civil War, and besieged by Fairfax; two redoubts from that period are still in the grounds. The house is one of the most interesting in Devon, completed about 1534 with some remodelling carried out during the reign of William and Mary, but the Tudor quadrangle is untouched. They were the last family in England to employ a jester. Don't miss **Dunsford & Meadhaydown Wood Nature Reserve** and Steps Bridge.

E

Ermington see Yealmpton

Exeter Map 2 Ac

Saxons, Normans, Romans, and German bombers have all
left their mark on this most beautiful city, named Isca
Dumnoniorum by the Romans. They gave it its essential
character, which can still be sensed in the atmosphere
among part of the city walls they built, fragments of which
still stand.

There are beautiful gardens such as in Southernhay,
surrounded by exquisite Georgian buildings; but perhaps
the history of the city, like so many others, is recorded and
reflected mostly in its churches and pubs, and of course in
this case, in **Exeter Cathedral** (Church Buildings),
started by Bishop Leofric. It was originally a small Saxon
minster, a Norman cathedral being built between 1112 and
1137. Catherine of Aragon stayed in the Deanery on her
first night in England. The Cathedral still stands in all its
glory, despite a direct hit during the Second World War,
surrounded by a green close where Richard Hooker sits,
kept company by pigeons, and office and shop workers
eating their lunch time sandwiches. Inside there are three
main visual experiences, and in addition a tour of the roof
can be made, via steep steps, low doors and narrow
passageways, where even the lead for repairs is prepared.
Inside, first of all, is the view down the nave, then the
quire, and finally the walk round the chantry chapels.
Pillars and roof are grooved and vaulted, the Beer stone is
of a soft grey colour. High up one side is the minstrels'
gallery where cheerful stone angels play many and varied
instruments. It is still used for carol concerts, and to hear
the pure voices of the choristers from the Cathedral School
sing is an experience never to be forgotten. Princess
Henrietta, daughter of Charles I, was born in Exeter while
the city was under siege in 1644 by the Roundheads, and
christened in the Cathedral.

The six medieval churches which still remain are one of
the city's chief beauties, for few of them have a normal

plan as they had to fit into the land available. Sometimes the chancel is at an odd angle to the nave, and the pulpits are tucked into towers. St Martin's is one such lovely church on the corner of the Close; in St Catherine's street, just beyond, are the ruins of St Catherine's Almshouses and chapel, which stood here from 1450 to 1942, and provided shelter for 13 poor men of the city. At No. 7 Cathedral Yard is the Devon and Exeter Institute, originally a Tudor gatehouse; at the rear of No. 16 is a Roman well.

The Bishop's Palace stands behind the Chapter House, which houses the Cathedral Library and amongst other precious possessions The Exeter Book which holds the largest collection of Anglo Saxon poems in existence; also the Exeter Domesday Book of 1086. Opposite the Cloister is the Cathedral Choir School. The Royal Clarence Hotel faces the Cathedral, opened in 1768 and called simply The Hotel, until the Royal Duke stayed there in 1808. Nelson, too, was a visitor giving a reception on 15 January 1801. No. 1 Cathedral Close is Mol's Coffee House, built in 1596,

Mol's House, Exeter

E

where the merchants used to gather, and Drake, Frobisher and Hawkins were said to be visitors here. Just up St Martin's Lane is the Ship Inn, said to be frequented by Sir Francis Drake, of which he wrote 'Nexte to mine own shippe I do most love that old Shippe in Exon.'

Under the grass of the Close, a Roman military bath house was situated and also a sports complex. This was excavated in 1971, but it was not possible to leave it open, so the remains were protected with sand, and re-covered.

In 1086 the Normans built **Rougemont Castle**, only the red sand-stone gate remains, but the city soon became the main centre for trade in the southwest, its harbour could easily handle the small sea going vessels. Then in 1290 the Countess of Devon, in a fit of pique, built a weir known as Countess Wear below the city, and the river silted up. So Topsham began to develop as Exeter's outlet to the sea. The Shipping canal was built in 1564 and restored the city as a port, and it is amusing to see small freighters gliding through what appear to be simply water meadows on their way to and from Exeter. Further down the canal towards the estuary, is the Turf Inn on Double Locks, said to be England's oldest pub, built in conjunction with a canal, and with no road access.

Underground Passages (Archaeological Sites) run below the main streets, probably fresh water conduits built during the middle ages, though some may be part Roman. They are high and narrow, and rather spooky to walk through, forming a network under the old city. Many crumbling entrances can be seen in various places, but they can be entered through Princesshay. They were used until the eighteenth century when piped water began to be laid.

It would take weeks to explore all the old buildings in the city, but **The Guildhall** (Other Historic Buildings) is worth a visit. It has stood here since the twelfth century, the oldest Court of Justice in Britain. The upper storey juts over the pavement, its front dating from 1592. The present hall was built in 1330 and remodelled in 1468; there is also a very cosy Mayor's Parlour upstairs. The city has had a mayor since the thirteenth century, not long after the first mayor of London. There have been several lady mayors, always referred to as 'Mr Mayor'.

Just beyond the Guildhall is Parliament Street, the narrowest street in the world. At the bottom of West Street, opposite St Mary Steps, a narrow lane opens which is Stepcote Hill with worn shallow steps up the right hand side. This was once a main thoroughfare leading to the West Gate, and here too, stands the fourteenth-century timber framed house, 'The House that Moved' having been brought to its present site when the road was widened.

One of the remaining manor houses is Cowick Barton, built in 1540 on an 'E' plan; it is now a pub. The White Hart in South Street is a fourteenth-century hostelry, once a rendezvous for carriers with pack horses. Here, down an old well, a carpenter died whilst carrying out repairs, as did his would be rescuer. A third person was actually revived, and told of the strange odour in the well, 'enough to take a man's breath away'. Much of the ground floor is fifteenth century, and some parts even older. There is a beautiful wine room with an early English stone fireplace, an unusual medieval doorway, and evidence of the stables where Cromwell rested his horses. A wonderfully prolific wisteria gives the entrance passage a lovely twilight aura, and for some reason the whole atmosphere of the place brings to mind the words of T. S. Eliot in *Preludes:* 'The winter evening settles down with smell of steaks in passageways, Six o'clock, The burnt ends of smokey days...'

One of the first Municipal Gardens to be laid out in the country was at Northernhay in 1621. In 1743 the Royal Devon and Exeter Hospital was started at the east end of Southernhay. In 1790 on a site then outside the city, the prison was begun, perhaps most famous in fairly recent years as the place where they tried unsuccessfully to hang John 'Babbacombe' Lee three times.

Down on the Quay stands the **Customs House** (Other Historic Buildings) built in 1681, and still in first class condition with fine plaster ceilings. The **Maritime Museum** is housed in beautifully preserved old warehouses with a rich, and ever growing collection of boats from all

E

over the world, some actually afloat. They include a Danish tug, a Fijian proa, a state barge from the film *A Man for All Seasons*. Incidentally, Robert Bolt, who wrote that play, lived for a while in an old manor house not far from Totnes. This really is one of the most imaginative and romantic museums in the country, and not just for small boys. At the nearby Prospect Inn you can sit with a pint and watch the world go by.

The University lies in a campus to the north of the city, and somehow exudes an American feel, perhaps because of the space. The Northcott Theatre is part of the complex, with one of the best theatre buildings in the country. Inside is a steeply raked auditorium with a good relationship between actor and audience. In fact, Exeter is by no means just a city of old traditions, for two of the most modern radio stations are situated on St. David's Hill.

In Queen Street the **Royal Albert Memorial Museum** was built in 1865 and more recently, the redbrick Guildhall precinct for shoppers, whose main entrance is formed by an enormous cream painted classical façade with Doric columns. In the centre a lovely surprise awaits you, for there is a tiny church, little St Pancras, just a nave and chancel built of rough blocks of Heavitree stone. The inscription on the bell says: 'Although I am small I am heard over a great distance.' Services are still held in what was a building first erected in the twelfth century, although its dedication indicates a much earlier church.

In Fore Street it is said you can buy anything from Nazi war souvenirs to naughty nick nacks. These shops are still largely family businesses. Leading off Fore Street is Mint Street with **St Nicholas' Priory** (Church Buildings), the last surviving complete fifteenth-century monastic guest house, run now by the Exeter Museum Service.

Finally, Alphington must be mentioned, though three miles from Exeter. It is now part of the city, and it was where Charles Dickens rented Mile End Cottage, which still stands. His parents stayed there in 1839, but the writer spent much time in the Turk's Head by the Guildhall, where the 'Fat Boy' and Martin Chuzzlewit were 'discovered'.

Just north of Exeter is Brampford Speke, a beautiful village of cob and thatch dating from the late sixteenth to the early nineteenth century. George Gissing wrote thus: 'I have discovered a village called Brampford Speke on the river Exe which I think seriously is the most perfect I ever saw. One imagines that some Lord of the Manor must exert himself to keep it in a picturesque state.' Nearby, Upton Pyne is equally attractive. In the churchyard is the grave of Lord Iddesleigh who, as Stafford Northcote was Gladstone's secretary, and later, Chancellor of the Exchequer. The ancient Devon family of Northcotes trace their settlement in the county as far back as the Norman Conquest. The first Lord Northcote was Governor of Bombay and later of Australia. Their home was at Pynes, a great redbrick mansion in a wooded park overlooking the river Exe.

Exmoor Map 2 Aa

Although Devon has only one third share in the total expanse of Exmoor, it must be mentioned, as the area running roughly from Molland in the south to the coast at County Gate to Combe Martin, along 14 miles of magnificent coastline, to the inland village of North Molton. Within this area there are lovely contrasts of towering cliffs, rich farmland, woodland, stream and heather moorland.

Inside the Devon border too are Lynton and Lynmouth, often known as Little Switzerland. Lynton is a small Victorian town; Lynmouth has a narrow street running nearly parallel to the river Lyn, down to the harbour, a medley of fuschia, roses, colour-washed cottages against the background of the river. Poets and writers have spent time here; Hazlitt stayed with Coleridge in the early nineteenth century, the latter living in a cottage which can still be seen, and Shelley too lived here for a time. The **Exmoor Brass Rubbing Centre** (Unusual Outings) welcomes anyone who would like to spend a happy half hour making their own rubbings under friendly guidance.

E

There is a fascinating water powered **Cliff Railway** donated by Sir George Newnes, the publisher who lived here, plus the **Lyn & Exmoor Museum** and an ancient smithy **Lynton Smithy** (Museums).

In the past year a national award has gone to Mr Ben Halliday's 1,550 acre Glenthorne Estate along the coastal cliffs between Lynton and Countisbury for improved footpaths around the cliff side verge of the estate, opening up breathtaking walks and vistas to the public.

A mile away is the Valley of the Rocks where Castle Rock has a unique feature in the shape of the White Lady which if viewed from the road looks like a woman in a tall hat and apron. A herd of wild goats roams here, living off bilberries, gorse, heather and often the vegetables in the Lynton gardens! It is said over a period of time their hooves have adapted to the rough surface of the rocks on which they move with such agility.

Lynmouth is a perfect starting point for walking along the wooded valley of the East Lyn to **Watersmeet** (Country Parks). Not far inland is Brendon Common, at one point the road crosses a stone bridge, giving walkers an ideal starting point for a walk into the combe where the stream runs into Badgworthy Water, the Carver Doone territory immortalised by R.D. Blackmore. From Cuzzacombe Common and Cuzzacombe Gate, enjoy the breathtaking views of the Bristol Channel, and at night the lighthouses of Hartland and Lundy. On Molland and Anstey Spurs the red deer are much in evidence and hunting is a tradition here, carrying its mixed emotions.

In 1952 tragedy struck when torrential flood waters brought huge boulders crashing into the town of Lynmouth. Thirty-four people died on that terrible night and ninety houses were destroyed. Now the river bed has been widened and it is difficult to visualise the scene. Those who lived through the night tell of the terrifying roar of the waters amid complete darkness as power and light were cut off instantly.

Lee Abbey, one and half miles west of Lynton, is such in name only, being built about 1850, but worth a visit as the whole atmosphere makes you feel as if characters from the *Prisoner of Zenda* may ride by at any moment.

While at Lynton it is worth calling at Trentishoe because the tiny hamlet consists only of a couple of farms and the church, but it is a wonderful centre for exploring the north Devon coastline. The little church of St. Peter's has a musicians' gallery with a hole cut in the parapet, apparently for the local farmer's double bass. No wonder this was a centre for smuggling, only half a mile from the sea. Heddon's Mouth visible on a clear day is a thickly wooded combe leading to a beach with an old lime kiln where lime was brought from Wales.

Exmouth   Map 4 Aa

Before you enter Exmouth, turn off the A377 two miles from the town, and visit **A La Ronde** (Historic Homes) in Summer Lane. It was built in 1798 by Misses Jane and Mary Parminter. The rooms radiate from a central octagonal hall and sixty feet above can be seen the shell gallery. Eight rooms lead from each other on the outside of the hall; the drawing room is completely decorated with feathers and pictures made of seaweed. In some incredible manner the Parminters seem to have combined the intricate glory of San Vitale of Ravenna, which they had visited, with a country cottage. You can eat and drink in the kitchen, in a Victorian atmosphere, where a bygone age has been recaptured. One remarkable relic is a 'drizzler', a small instrument used to pick the gold thread from gowns before they were passed on to the servants, also a very early flushing lavatory. Nearby is tiny Point in View chapel with four almshouses for single women; the Misses Parminter were, perhaps, early pioneers of Women's Lib.

And so to Exmouth, the oldest seaside town in Devon, grown from the two ancient parishes of Littleham and Withycombe Raleigh. The manor of Littleham belonged to the Rolles from the seventeeth century onwards, and they

G

did much to develop the town as a watering place. Exmouth, with its long sandy beaches, is a real family resort, and the first of the 'sand beach' towns along the South Devon coast.

The Beacon has some fashionable and historic houses including No. 6 once occupied by Lady Nelson in 1820. Lady Byron and her daughter spent the year of 1828 at Chapman's Beacon Hotel, now No. 19. Franz Liszt performed at the Beacon Hotel in 1840, now the Manor Hotel. Perhaps the most notorious resident in 1802 was Mary Ann Clark, actress, and mistress of the Duke of York, who lived at Manchester House. She published , and was damned.

There is a charming old world atmosphere about the place. The small harbour and docks are at the western end of the esplanade. Two miles east of the town is the **Country Life Museum** with agricultural machinery, and working steam engines.

Georgeham   see Croyde

Great Torrington   Map 1 Bb

Park at the entrance to this market town, sited on a hill dropping down to the river Torridge, and from the Bideford side, walk along the east slope, where you will see some of the most beautiful views of rolling Devon. It has been a borough since the twelfth century, and the market square would do credit to a town ten times its size. The Town Hall houses **Torrington Museum** and opposite the churchyard is eighteenth century Palmer House where Sir Joshua Reynolds and Dr Johnson stayed. Perhaps one of its major claims to fame in the past was in 1646 when 200 Royalist prisoners held in the church were blown up.

Today **Dartington Glass** (Local Industry) has brought it thousands of visitors, and employment. The factory was founded in 1966 by the Dartington Hall Trustees with skilled labour from Scandinavia, but today a workforce of 200 comprises only a small handful from there, the rest are locals. It takes ten years to train a blower to the exacting standard of Master, and it was a proud experience for the Dartington management when two of their locally trained men secured Master Blower posts in Sweden, surely the ultimate in bearing coals to Newcastle. The experiment is an unqualified success, for the factory has been absorbed into the community life of the region, and some Swedes have married local girls. The high quality of the Dartington glass enjoys an international reputation, and a special welcome is extended to visitors. Last year over 100,000 people toured the works. A small charge is made, and best quality glassware can be bought at very reasonable prices.

Haccombe Map 4 Ab

Haccombe is set in rolling parkland with great stretches of meadows and, for Devon, very few hedges. It has one of the most perfect Early English churches still existent, pinkish grey in colour, and built by Sir Stephen de Haccombe after his return from the Crusades in 1233 and dedicated to St Blaise.

It contains beautiful tombs, brasses, stained-glass and floor tiles. The most striking of the figures is made of alabaster, and thought to commemorate Edward, the eldest child and only son of Sir Hugh and Lady Phillipa Courtenay. He probably died at Oxford aged 16.

The medieval tiles on the floor include 27 different designs, most of which are locally made, but a few of the blue ones may have been brought back by pilgrims from Santiago di Compostella. Don't miss the one and a half horse-shoes nailed on the door. They record the bet made between a Carew of Haccombe and a Champernowne of Dartington as to who could swim his horse furthest into the sea at Torquay. They had their cranks in those days too. It was won by Carew who nailed his horse's shoe to the door.

The Coombe Cellars pub was a noted smuggling centre in the early nineteenth century, famous in later years for cockles and Devon cream teas. Brandy was regularly smuggled from the beach across the fields; if the excise men were about, then the kegs were hidden under water, weighed down with sandbags, and tied to a raft until the coast was clear. There is a ghost here too. In 1968 Margaret Marshall, a barmaid in the pub, woke each night to the sensation of being strangled. No one listened to her 'fancies', until the publican, Jim Harvey, went to a sale and brought back a picture of a woman being strangled by a burglar in the very room where Margaret slept. Odd things still happen here.

Hallsands and Beesands Map 4 Ac

For centuries Hallsands and Beesands were fishing villages. At Hallsands there were more than 100 people living in cottages built on rocks above a shingle bank. Gradually, during 1897, this was eroded by dredging for material to use in building an extension to the Naval Dockyard at Devonport.

Despite protests and predictions by the locals, ignored as always by authority, over 650,000 tons of gravel were dredged from the sea bed. In 1903 houses were undermined, and part of the road through the village collapsed. In January 1917 there were violent storms, and in one night, 29 houses were completely destroyed. The villagers escaped with their lives by some miracle. Eventually they were all re-housed, all except for Elizabeth Prettejohn who lived on in the one inhabitable house with her 20 hens and four cats until her death in 1964. Now only the ruins of walls and fireplaces remain as witness; the whole atmosphere, gull haunted, desolate and sad.

A chapel was recorded in the village in 1506, and it is difficult to believe that a road ran between the church, cottages and the sea. There were originally more buildings on the sea side, including a grocer, post office, a Seamens' Mission where lectures and concerts were held, the London Inn whose title deed went back to 1784, where tourists came from Torquay in pleasure steamers. You can still see where the houses used to be by the slots cut out of the rock to make masonry footings.

There are one or two of the survivors still living in the
row of cottages built in 1924 where they were re-housed.
One told how she remembered the night of the storm; she
was 17, her father came home from fishing and went to the
kitchen to wash, as he did so, 'the walls fell down and the
floor caved in, the sea came down the chimney'. It is a
miracle that no one drowned.

Just above stands Trouts Hotel, now holiday flats, but
once a hotel built by the hands of the formidable Trout
sisters, who even piped spring water and made over 8,000
concrete blocks to build the house. The tranquil
atmosphere and good food attracted famous and
distinguished guests from all over the world. The sisters
though tough as the male fishermen, were no old fashioned
stick-in-the-muds, for Trouts Hotel was one of the first to
have a television set in the area. Cousin Jim still lives in one
of the 'new' houses; his brother Percy had been with Ella
Trout when she saved the life of a seaman during the First
World War, for which she got the O.B.E.

Beesands is a short walk over the cliffs, an unspoilt
fishing village, and **Start Point Lighthouse** should be
visited if only to see how brass should be kept.

Harford Map 3 Bb

This is the gateway to some of the most beautiful parts of
Dartmoor, along the upper valley of the river Erme. Here
can be found one of the densest concentrations of hut
circles and remains of the Bronze Age, also many lovely old
farmhouses with big mossy outbuildings. The late fifteenth-
century church is of moorstone, and has an altar tomb, that
of Thomas Williams who died in 1566. He was born at
Stowford in this parish and became Speaker of the House
of Commons in 1563. The manor house, now a farmhouse,
half a mile west of the church, was the seat of Colonel
Thomas Chudleigh, father of Elizabeth Chudleigh, the
notorious Duchess of Kingston between 1720 and 1788.
The incredibly beautiful Elizabeth was born here, and
when the Earl of Bath was at a shooting party in the

vicinity, he was so taken with her that he obtained the
position for her as Maid of Honour to Augusta, Princess of
Wales. Elizabeth, at a masquerade, appeared almost nude as
Iphigenia at Somerset House. The Princess was not
amused. Later, Elizabeth was proved guilty of bigamy,
however she claimed Benefit of Peerage, escaped prison,
and took to travelling abroad. She bought a mansion which
she named Chudleigh near St Petersburg in Russia. She
died in Paris in 1788.

Hartland   Map 1 Ab

Hartland is a small town with an immense parish covering
over 17,900 acres, and occupying the peninsula in the
extreme northwest corner of Devon. It commands some of
the most impressive scenery in England and Wales with
superb seascapes, and it is quite overwhelming to realise
there is no land between this coast and America. Inland the
scenery becomes very Cornish in character, with white
farmhouses dotted about in grey landscape which is still
remote, withdrawn and buzzard haunted.

The small market town itself has many pretty Georgian
houses, and the church of St Nectan has been called one of
the glories of North Devon, dating from 1350. It replaces a
building erected by King Harold's mother, Gytha, as a
landmark for ships since its fifteenth-century tower is one
of the highest in Devon. The rood screen is exquisitely
carved. This is one of the Devon parishes where one could
happily spend a week exploring, preferably in the spring. A
mile further west is Hartland Quay which has a long and
colourful history, going back before the days of Elizabeth I.
Because of the remoteness of the parish, and the difficulties
of travel overland, it was Hartland's key to the outside
world for nearly three centuries. The day to day life of
many families revolved around the place, relieved
occasionally by the excitements of war, wrecks and storms.
The Quay was most probably built by William Abbott in
the closing decades of the sixteenth century. In the late
eighteenth century lime, coal, slate, deal planks, and the

nails to fix them, all arrived here, but no shipping has been able to use the Quay since the destruction of the harbour last century in successive storms. The **Hartland Quay Museum** records many of the wrecks in the area. There are magnificent walks to the Cornish border taking in the 70 feet high waterfall at Speke's Mill Mouth. Three miles to the north is Hartland Point with a lighthouse at its foot, which is open to the public in good weather during the summer.

Thomas Oatway, driver of the mail service to Bideford, first converted the old buildings on the Quay into a hotel, ideal for lovers of the wilds of Devon who came in ever increasing numbers when the railway reached westward in the late 1850s. By 1911 the Hartland Quay Hotel was well and truly on the tourist map. In 1940 a sea mine blew off the roof, but after repairs had been carried out, the 'Monkey Club', a girls' boarding school, evacuated from Pont Street in London, took it over, also occupying Hartland Abbey.

Generations of coastguards and their families have lived in the Quay cottages; in 1914 the coastguard was called up, and the lookout manned by civilians until 1920. In the major review in 1931, inevitable change was brought about, and within a year the old station closed down, the duties being transferred to Hartland Point.

Holne Map 3 Bb

Near here the river Dart is crossed by two medieval bridges, the present Holne bridge being built after the destruction of an earlier one by a flood in 1413. The church of St Mary was originally cruciform, built in 1300, with a fine screen and much detailed work. Charles Kingsley was born at the vicarage 12 June 1819 while his father was curate in charge. The Vicarage was rebuilt in 1832 and stands a little way outside the village, approached through a white gate by an old tithe barn, the gate bearing the name

Glebe House. The font where he was christened has gone, the present one being erected in 1827; the booklet about the church states: 'the old one has unfortunately been lost!'

Dr Ramsay, once Archbishop of Canterbury, stayed many times at the Church House Inn so he could walk in the area. The Ram Roast a feast with pagan undertones was once the big event of the summer, held on old Midsummer Day. The Holne Revels included pony racing and other sports, all now forgotten. Kingsley said of the village, 'O what a scene . . . and in the far east, wooded glens, fertile meadows . . . through the rich country some spur of granite hill . . . each with its tor like a ruined castle at the top. I was alone with God and the hills, the Dart winding down a thousand feet below . . . I could only pray'. One wonders if he got the inspiration for his famous *Water Babies* from here.

Honiton   Map 2 Bc

Honiton was of course an important stopping place for the coaches running from London to Exeter, and in modern times, once famous for its traffic jams, though now thankfully, bypassed, and thus remaining unspoiled. The Roman High Street is long and wide with lovely Georgian houses.

St Paul's church is early Victorian with Norman decoration. The old parish church of St Michael's calls for a steep climb; it was badly gutted by fire inside in 1911, but has been well rebuilt. Thomas Marwood, the father of the man who built Marwood, was physician to Queen Elizabeth I and in 1592 cured her favourite courtier, the Earl of Essex, who had been given up as a hopeless case. There is a memorial to him in the church here.

This is one of the earliest towns in Devon to link itself with one of our E.E.C. partners, twinning itself with Mezidon-Canon in the Calvados region. Many exchange visits are organised between the local schools and their French counterparts, as well as visits by the Carnival Committee, football clubs, musicians, police, farmers and many more. The valley is worth driving around, dotted with old farms linked by narrow, winding lanes.

Allhallows Museum is more of a living museum with demonstrations in lace-making and crafts, talks on local history, also a shop and special entertainments for children. The main building is some 750-years-old, but the interior has now been designed to be both attractive and interesting with new exhibits brought in each year, so the returning visitor need never be bored. It is run as an independent registered charity entirely staffed by volunteers, and their enthusiasm really does reflect in a lively and bright place for the whole family to spend some time.

There is also the famous Honiton Pottery where visitors are welcome to wander through the workrooms and see the pottery being made; hand throwing and hand painting are in progress most of the time. Originally only functional items such as bread pans and baking dishes were made, but in 1918 a new owner changed the policy and began making decorative pieces with a style of their own.

Copper Castle, a castellated toll house, on the Exeter Road is worth looking at, many of these have been destroyed in the West country.

Hope   Map 3 Bc

This village was aptly named as it gave hope to generations of shipwrecked seamen. It was once a flourishing fishing settlement, and having no estuary, its sons grew up skilled in the handling of boats off beaches. Fame came mostly from its lobsters and crabs, its wrecks and its lovely cob cottages. Sadly now, only one man earns his living by fishing, and in summer the beaches are crowded with sun worshippers. The cottages at Inner Hope are worth a visit, standing round a small square, crisply white and pink and cream, under thatched roofs like bristling brows. Cob of course is really a term for sophisticated clay or mud, a mixture of soil, pebbles, straw, water and cow dung and hair, the walls being built up in layers two feet thick, like a cake, and left to dry before the next layer is begun. Usually about three feet thick, the walls are more delightfully warm and waterproof to live within than many modern buildings, providing their feet and head are kept dry.

Whilst here, walk to Bolt Head via Bolt Tail, taking in some of England's wildest and most exciting coastal scenery. Along this five mile stretch some of the most fearful wrecks, many unrecorded, have occurred. One of the first mentioned was that of the *San Pedro el Major*, a hospital ship from the Armada, on which the local wreckers were soon working. The *Ramillies*, after which a local cove is named, was wrecked on 15 February 1760 with over 700 people drowned. The Captain of the Marines went mad and strode up and down the deck of his sinking ship, singing. During the Second World War, the *Louis Shied*, and the *Tanjandoen* were wrecked the same night. The most dramatic of all wrecks however, must be the last of the square riggers on 25 April 1936, when the barque *Herzogin Cecilie*, carrying a cargo of Australian wheat, went down off the Ham Stone at Soar Mill Cove, and local farmers had a ball charging for parking on the cliff tops.

Ilfracombe Map 1 Ba

This is another of those fishing ports which was rather fading into insignificance during the time of Napoleon, but flourished again in the late nineteenth century. It is an excellent starting place for excursions onto Exmoor. A somewhat Victorian atmosphere is still presented, with many delightful public gardens. In common with many parts of the North Devon coast, the cliff scenery is its main attraction. The oldest part of the town is near the harbour with its long quay and fishermen's cottages, whose inner harbour affords a haven for small craft, with an old pier on the seaward side. At the time of writing, the boat, *The Polar Bear*, still leaves here for Lundy, but there is some talk of transferring it elsewhere.

To the west of the pier is Lantern Hill crowned by St Nicholas Chapel, a votive chapel for fishermen, used since the Reformation as a lighthouse. This is one of the three vantage points for looking at the wonderful views all round the town, the others being Capstone and Hillsborough Hills. Lee, often called Fuschia Valley because they grow wild in profusion there, is one of the prettiest places in the area, about three miles from Ilfracombe. Two miles west of Lee is Bullpoint Lighthouse, first lit in 1879. Perhaps the most fascinating place in the area however is **Chambercombe Manor** (Historic Homes) formerly the manor house of Ilfracombe. Lady Jane Grey is said to have slept in the room above the hall when visiting the owners, the Champernownes into whose ownership it came soon after the Norman Conquest. A secret chamber was discovered in 1865 in the form of a furnished bedroom containing the skeleton of a woman whose ghost is said to haunt the manor. According to legend she was Kate Oatway, daughter of the 'Wrecker' of Chambercombe; another relates that after the wreck of a Spanish vessel in Hele Bay, a half conscious girl was found stranded on the beach, and married her rescuer, the son of the local 'Wrecker'. The story ended with the drowning of her own daughter in a similar episode years later, whose ghost now haunts the manor. So you pays your money and takes your choice. There is also a private oratory and a kitchen with an enormous 800-year-old cider press.

   Ilfracombe Museum boasts a collection ranging from Cromwellian helmets and Victoriana to butterflies and fossils.

Instow see Appledore

Ivybridge Map 3 Bb

This town was made a civil parish in 1894, the church being built in 1882, but there was once a chapel there in 1402. It is said to have taken its name from an ancient bridge covered with an ivy creeper, although it was first recorded in 1280 as Ponte Ederoso. High above the east bank of the river Erme is Stowford Lodge, a Domesday manor, now a conference centre for the Royal Agricultural

K

Society. Below is Stowford Paper Mill, which in 1785 used the power of the Erme and its pure water for papermaking. William Dunsterville started up business in that year, and the same mill went through various ownerships, producing hand-made paper until 1837 when a 48 inch Fourdriner machine was installed. In 1849 John Allen, a Plymouth malster, bought the mills as a speculative enterprise and during the 1860s put in two 72 inch machines; with such mechanisation the mills went from strength to strength, soon employing more than 200 people. For many years in fact all the paper used for British postage stamps was made in Ivybridge. Today they are still in operation under the direction of Wiggins Teape.

In 1848 Brunel's railway reached Ivybridge, and the stone and timber viaduct across the valley was built, now draped romantically in ivy. William Cotton, a friend of Sir Joshua Reynolds, lived at the mansion named Highlands, and his unique collection of prints, drawings and bronzes is now in Plymouth Art Gallery.

Today Ivybridge is undergoing a crisis of identity. The District Council has allowed the building of a superstore development at Lee Mill; this, along with the demolition of the nineteenth and twentieth-century buildings in the town centre to make a car park, has changed the whole atmosphere. It was to be the first stage of a new town centre development, but after more than four years not a brick has been laid.

Kenn Map 4 Aa

Hereabouts everything seems to be dyed with the red of the earth itself, even the cattle. There are two villages, Kenn and Kennford. The whole area is luxuriantly wooded, with many ancient houses, including Haldon House, once the most notable house in the Devon countryside. Started in 1735 by Sir George Chudleigh, it was then bought in 1770 by Robert Palk, who enlarged the timbered park. He built the Haldon Belvedere as a memorial to his friend, Stringer Lawrence already mentioned under Dunchideock.

The family lived here until 1892. The house now has practically disappeared.

The church of St Andrew is also built of deep-red sandstone from nearby Trehill quarry; it is early fourteenth century, and in 1889 the rood figures, carved at Oberammergau, were added, the first rood in fact to be restored since the Reformation. The paintings of the saints in the lower panels were created in about 1550, and are particularly interesting as the males are to the north of the central doorway, the females to the south. Is this evidence of the early days of male chauvinism?

Kenton Map 4 Aa

Situated in the typically rich rolling Devon countryside, not far from the river Exe estuary, with great dark trees against late summer fields of rippling golden corn, the church of All Saints has an exterior of local red stone with decorations in Beer stone and decorated with many images, including one of a lady with a horned headdress, Joan of Navarre, and a bearded man said to be Henry IV.

Oxton Manor house, nearby, was built in 1781 in a setting of almost tropical luxuriance. There is a lake crossed by a romantic Victorian iron bridge; the house has a Greek Doric porch and it all seems so far from traffic and cities that one expects to see Grecian ladies, or even Isadora Duncan, flitting through the trees and shrubs. The estate probably dates from the twelfth century and has belonged to many different Exeter merchants such as Wilford, Hurst and Martin, who loved this style of estates. Eventually it belonged to the Rev. John Swete who built the existing house in 1789 and laid out much of the beautiful grounds; it then became a girls' school, but has now been converted into flats.

Although it is difficult to visualise now, Kenton was once a port on the river, but various reclamation projects have prevented the high tides reaching this area. If you really want to get to know this village, read *Kenton Memories*, a collection of local recollections. One amusing anecdote is

K

told of the cobbler who went to church so he could examine the soles and heels of his fellow villagers when they knelt to pray, and establish who needed repairs, giving the cold shoulder to those who had visited his rival.

Kingsbridge Map 3 Bc

The main street, Fore Street, runs steeply up from the estuary. Before the car park was built, when the upper end of the estuary was filled in, the quays were busy with packet steamers and the paddle steamer which ran regularly from Salcombe, berthed here, while fishing boats bobbed at anchor. The estuary's medieval trade was with the wine growing region of southwest France, and schooners such as *The Fanny* were built at Dodbrooke in 1850. William Date learned the craft of shipbuilding at Salcombe, and in about 1840 started to build ships on his own account at Kingsbridge. Bill Bond, once the owner of the famous Crabshell Inn on the quay, descendant of the original families in this area, tells how the mould of the Kingsbridge clippers still exists in the offices of Charles Head. 'In those days they didn't draw designs, they made moulds...' These ships carried cargoes of every sort all over the world and back to this Devon port.

The coming of the steel ships put an end to Kingsbridge as a prominent port, and it is now a holiday centre for the area, remaining relatively unspoilt with its many inns, at one time famous for the local White Ale with a mystical ingredient called 'grout'.

Walking up Fore Street one must recall the words of the song 'An Old Fashioned Town' written by W.H. Squire of Celeste Octet fame, who attended Kingsbridge Grammar School. In that song he wrote of '...an old fashioned house in an old fashioned street that runs up and now down...' Fore Street.

Kingsbridge has many famous sons, including John Wolcot, later to be known as Peter Pindar the satirical versifier. Thomas Crispin born in 1608 made his fortune, like many others, from cloth in Exeter and a plaque over the Grammar School door commemorates its building in 1670 at his expense. A more recent celebrity, Leslie Thomas, author of *The Virgin Soldiers* was at an orphanage in the town as a child; but most famous of all is William Cookworthy after whom the Museum is named and who made the first true porcelain in England.

The **Cookworthy Museum** is a must, really astonishing for a town this size, with exhibits illustrating the development of the clay industry, and a huge collection of other items from the South Hams, of which Kingsbridge has been called the metropolis, for it is the market town and capital of the area. On show are the famous Lidstone stoves and ranges, exported all over the world, a maritime section recalling the thriving shipbuilding era in great detail, and a selection of clothes from the past. In the Farm Gallery a notice reads: 'The South Hams measured its corn in sacks, and its land in farthings unlike anywhere else in Devon. It had its own breed of cattle and its own breed of sheep, and also its own variety of apple – the white sour, famous for its cider.' In a way this epitomises the whole atmosphere of the South Hams. The word 'Hams' means a settlement or clearing, usually royally owned, Ham being the old English word for low lying meadow or enclosed pasture.

This beautiful part of Devon is still largely unspoiled, and amidst its maze of high banked lanes, starred and perfumed with primroses and white violets in the spring, one is transported back in time to farms and hamlets tucked away among woods and fields. Before the Second World War it was said that life in the South Hams was a hundred years behind the times.

Returning to Kingsbridge, the name is said to come from the fact that a Saxon king on reaching Dodbrooke during his travels, could not cross the stream, so a volunteer from one of the local families waded across the river Dod with the king on his back. A charter was granted to King Aethelwold in A.D. 846 for a large part of the South Hams area. It was mentioned twice in the Anglo Saxon charter of A.D. 962; later the town belonged to Buckfast Abbey, and in 1219 the Abbot granted it a market, to which farmers

K

from all around still come.

There are many eighteenth-century houses, some slate-hung in the local style. The Town Hall is early Victorian with a tower and an unusual ball clock dated 1875, on a curious curved neck. Just beyond is the Shambles, a covered arcade supported by granite pillars built in 1585, but in 1796, when the volume of wheeled traffic was increasing, the old wooden market building in the middle of Fore Street impeded it and the present Shambles was built for the butchers on the site of an old corn market.

Behind the Shambles is St Edmund's church, dating from the thirteenth to fifteenth centuries, with the well known slab outside bearing the epitaph of Robert Phillips:

> 'Here lie I at the chancel door,
> Here lie I because I'm poor,
> The further in the more you pay
> Here lie I as warm as they'

He died in 1798, a cooper by trade, but also the local whipping boy, who was a scapegoat for punishment, charging a penny a time.

Before the church was built the people of Kingsbridge had to carry their dead up 'a high mountain' to Churchstow two miles away. The most important house in the area is Bowringsleigh at West Alvington. A Tudor and Jacobean building among the oaks and beeches of a glorious park. It had been established even before the Bowrings lived there in 1332; the last family to own it were the Ilberts who bought it in 1696.

Opposite the Shambles stands the King's Arms from whence coaches and carriers wagons set out. Although we think our roads today are dangerous, in the nineteenth century they had serious coach accidents, and no wonder when one reads of the tricks they got up to trying to race each other and cut seconds off their time, tipping over, slashing, passing and repassing with much blowing of coaching horns or sounding of the 'yard of tin' by the bugles on rival coaches.

At the time of writing, great controversy rages as to

whether or not the historic old Crabshell Inn on the quay should be pulled down to make way for yet more holiday flats.

To the northwest of Kingsbridge is Aveton Gifford, pronounced Awton Jifford, a truly one street Devon village. St. Andrew's church was badly damaged by a hit and run bomber during the Second World War. There is a wonderful walk along the river Avon estuary, with a tidal road leading from the village to Ringmore and Bigbury, which is covered at high tide, so that driving along it is always tinged with excitement. It is called the Sticks because of the poles which mark out the hard road from the mud, which is about four feet deep. Halfway to the sea, this gives way to a firm, golden sand at low tide. In the village itself, on the Kingsbridge side, is a medieval causeway nearly three quarters of a mile long. The river here also contains an ancient salmon trap.

Kingston   Map 3 Bc

This charming little South Hams village, a mile from the river Avon, with only a population of just over 200, boasts both the possession of its own fire engine, and a first class pub with facilities for all the family at some of the most reasonable prices in Devon. The sixteenth-century Dolphin, has not only the normal bar, but opposite stand the old stables with a tallet above, converted into a restaurant, and also a large garden with tables for food. The bottom storey of the stabling was originally used for packhorses and donkeys, storing the fish they brought from the river. Above that, the tallet stored grain and hay.

This is an unspoilt village and some of the local television and radio personalities who live here can be seen at the bar. The church of St James the Less is next door, built of local slate, mainly early fourteenth century and probably the monks who built it had some kind of rest home where the pub now stands.

L

Lewtrenchard   Map 3 Aa

The most interesting part of Lewtrenchard is Lew House
dating back to 1620, once the home of Rev. Baring-Gould,
but originally bought by his family in 1625. A ghost of one
of his ancestors is said to haunt the house still. He not only
wrote many books, and the hymn 'Onward Christian
Soldiers', but also collected the old folk songs and stories of
Devon. He was rector here for 43 years, his life spanning
from 1834-1924, when the old world he knew was starting
to change. He added a ballroom to the house, possibly to
hold dances in an effort to introduce his eight daughters to
suitors. In a way it could be said he was the last of
the'Squarsons'. He was also very keen on church
preservation; St Peter's is full of memorials to the Baring-
Gould family. This preoccupation with preservation started
in early childhood when his grandfather destroyed the
church rood screen in 1833, but young Sabine picked up
the pieces and had it re-constructed in 1899.

Lundy   Map 1 Aa

Not Lundy Island please, as the name itself incorporates
the word, coming from the Norse 'Lunde', meaning a
puffin, and 'ey' or 'y', an island.

How can one describe the magic of this Kingdom of
Heaven, as it was once named after the Heaven family who
owned it from 1836 to 1918. In 1965 Felix Gade, the agent
for so many years, wrote in reply to a query: 'This island is
now jointly owned by the surviving children of the late Mr
Martin Coles-Harman. Mr Albion Harman is Lord of the
Manor of Lundy. Puffins still nest here, but in greatly
reduced numbers, 20 years ago there were about 1,000
pairs, now only 50. Peregrines have not nested here
successfully for the past four years, the falcon was found
dead two years ago. She had a lethal quantity of hydro
carbons residue in her system. Dogs are not admitted, nor
guns, rifles, bows and arrows or catapults allowed. The
Marisco Tavern opens at 12 noon to 1.30 p.m. and from 6
p.m. till midnight . . .' In those halcyon days the rent of a
cottage was 24 shillings a night.

Islands are always tempting, fascinating, and this one, 20 miles off the north coast of Devon is no exception, just three miles long, one mile wide and no cars. It has a central moorland plateau and treacherous 400 feet cliffs where only recently a young girl birdwatcher was killed. **Lundy's** (Country Parks) history goes back into the mists of time when probably the Vikings used it as a temporary base for their raids on the mainland. Later the notorious Norman pirate family of Marisco, preyed on boats in the Bristol Channel. Over the years it has had many owners, including the Civil War General, Sir Bevil Grenville. In William and Mary's time the French invaded by means of a trick similar to the Wooden Horse of Troy, saying they wanted to bury their dead captain. They brought a heavy coffin ashore which proved to be full of guns and swords, with which they took over the island. In 1747 Thomas Benson, M.P. for Barnstaple leased it, and diverted the American bound convict ships to use the 'passengers' as slave labour in the quarries. In 1834 W. H. Heaven bought it for 9,400 guineas. In 1968 Albion Harman, a member of the family who then owned it, died, and a crisis arose. The island was put up for sale by auction. After many alarms and much heartsearching, the National Trust acquired it with the help of a fairy god-father in the shape of Jack Hayward, a millionaire living in the Bahamas who made a gift of £150,000 towards it. So, Lundy will always remain Lundy. The National Trust leases it to the Landmark Trust. On 6 July 1966 Jack Hayward visited Lundy, and Felix Gade presented him with a scroll of thanks signed by each of the residents.   Thankfully the island is today still unspoiled, although your arrival there may be slightly hazardous. Usually the boat stands a little way off while a tender ferries you to the landing stage beneath Rat Island, one of the few remaining homes of the aboriginal black rat, now almost extinguished by the brown variety.

Quarries have been in existence on the island for years and the granite has been used for many famous buildings, including the Charing Cross Hotel and the Victoria Embankment. There was once a mill, also a golf course,

L

which had a very short life through lack of members. There was too, for a period, an air service, and during the Second World War the Air Ministry used the air-field, but that petered out, although there are helicopter landing pads near both lighthouses.

For such a small area, there is much to be seen with 400 varieties of flora recorded, including the famous Lundy cabbage. Unspectacular it may be, but naturalists have come from the four corners of the earth to see it. Over 400 different types of birds can be seen including puffins, fulmars, kittiwakes and peregrines. It is a well-known retreat for seals, wild goats and ponies. Most people don't realise that a unique herd of ponies have lived here for over 50 years. Mr Martin Coles-Harman brought 42 in foal ponies from the New Forest in 1928, and a Welsh Arab stallion. Later a pure white stallion was introduced. From the original stock, a mild tempered and hardy children's pony has emerged. The herd is acknowledged by the National Pony Society and these can be purchased if so desired. Three kinds of deer were introduced in 1927, and also a flock of Soay sheep. There are no snakes on Lundy, but an enormous rabbit population. Now a new attempt is to be made to modernise the farming pattern. The chief problem is getting the stock to market, embarking them alone is a headache, and once, during the 15 mile sea trip to the mainland, a ferocious Galloway bull ran amok in the boat's hold. Now 100 Exmoor horn ewes are to be added to the existing flock, also Simon, the five-year-old Galloway bull is to be replaced by the more convenient method of artificial insemination.

There is a long history of wrecks on the rocky beaches; perhaps most famous was the battleship *Montagu* in 1906, when she hit the rocks in fog and was totally lost. There have also been aeroplane crashes during the Second World War, two German and one English.

There is a ruined castle to see, also a disused lighthouse built in 1819 which was often found to be obscured by fog, and was replaced in 1897 by the two existing lights at either end of the island. Shutter Rock on the southwest point of the island is where Charles Kingsley caused Don Guzman's ship to be wrecked in *Westward Ho!* However, what really strikes the visitor is the strange sense of space, in spite of the smallness of the island. At night the feeling is that of being completely surrounded by lights, both those of the ships in the Bristol Channel and the towns and villages along the coast. In spring the wild rhododendrons are a sight, and the pink thrift like a carpet, all part of the magic that is Lundy. There are other interests such as a hotel, self-catering cottages, a store, a souvenir shop, and of course a pub. Inevitably the Marisco Tavern, in spite of licensing hours, never seems to be closed whatever time one arrives.

Lustleigh Map 3 Ba

This picture book village is reached by winding lanes and has traditional rose covered, thatched cottages clustered round a village green, with a stream running through into the woodland, and magnificent walks through Lustleigh Cleave. The church of St John the Baptist is chiefly remarkable for its rood screen bearing the pomegranate badge of Catherine of Aragon. The Rev. William Davy, born in 1743, was a curate at Lustleigh for many years and printed at the rectory on a press made by himself, 26 volumes of *The System of Divinity*, described by the Bishop of Exeter as a 'trifle'. He was also a pioneer of rural education and in 1825 opened a school in the churchyard. He endowed it with the rent of a meadow, and its tablet confirms that it was 'Built by public subscription and endowed with Lewton Meadow in Moreton for supporting a school forever by the Rev. William Davy, curate of this parish'.

Just across the stream is Wreyland where Cecil Torr wrote the three volumes of *Small Talk at Wreyland*, quoting family letters and personal observations, one of the most charming books of the period about Dartmoor. His aim was to preserve the wealth of local knowledge still retained by the older people in the area whose lives may have been narrow, but who themselves were full of interest.

L

It was one of the first villages to be discovered by the tourist just before the First World War when tourists came by branch-line railway for holidays. The coming of the railway itself had been traumatic, for people were certain the sparks from the engine would fire the thatched roofs. Mothers feared that their daughters would be seduced by the rough navvies working on the track, while the worst they did was raid the hen roosts for eggs. By then however, village time went by the station clock, no longer by the rooks going home, or the cows waiting to be milked by the gate. This is everyone's mental vision of a Devon village and should not be missed.

Lydford   Map 3 Ba

The parish covers 50,000 acres; the earliest documented Dartmoor tracks are the paths which led to Lydford where all the people had to bury their dead until Bishop Bronescombe gave permission for those in the eastern part

Denham Bridge on the river Tavy

of the moor to use Widecombe church. Even in the 1930s this custom of taking bodies across the moor by horse and cart was still in use. In 1198 the 'Parliament' of the tinners used to meet at Crockern Tor in the heart of the moor, and it was in the grim keep of Lydford Prison that sentenced miners were held or hanged, and the poet Browne wrote in 1644, 'I oft have heard of Lydford Law, How in the morn they hang and draw.' During the reign of Henry VIII, Lydford Prison was described as 'One of the most contagious and detestable places within this realme.' Sir Richard Grenville was governor during the Civil War, and Judge Jeffreys is said to have presided in its courts. The last execution took place in 1650, the man was hanged in chains and left to swing, his body daubed with pitch for preservation.

Once it had its own mint during the reign of Ethelred II and there are coins in Scandinavian museums from Lydford to show the success of the Danish raiders.

The White Lady Waterfall, Lydford Gorge

L

St Petrock's church was built on the site of an early oratory. In the churchyard there are many old gravestones in good condition, one to George Routleigh, a master clockmaker in the nineteenth century, which reads, '... wound up in hopes of being taken in hand by his master, and of being thoroughly cleaned and repaired and set a-going in the world to come'. To the west is **Lydford Gorge** (Country Parks) where the river descends for two miles over potholes; the Devil's Cauldron is well named, and there is a spectacular 90 feet high waterfall called the White Lady.

Around here lived the Gubbins, mentioned in *Westward Ho!* In the seventeenth century they lived in holes in the ground, from which they crawled to burn, rob and terrorise the neighbourhood.

Lympstone   Map 4 Aa

This remains an unspoilt and virtually uncommercialised village on the estuary of the river Exe, with rich smells of seaweed and mud therefrom. It appears in Domesday Book as Leustona. It has a good pub with first class seafood on offer. The villas and cottages dated about 1800 have great character. Few fishermen operate from here today, apart from seine netting for salmon. Winkles, mussels, cockles and crabs are gathered from the shore. It has its store of smuggling stories and many of the cottages near the river have spaces in adjoining roofs where contraband could be passed from home to home while the prevention officer was enticed in the opposite direction. There is little traffic through the narrow streets where you get occasional glimpses of gardens with flowering tubs. There is an Italian sytle clock in memory of Mrs Peters, who was good to the poor. Back on the main road is the famous camp and training ground for the marines.

Lynmouth   see Exmoor

Lynton   see Exmoor

Mamhead Map 4 Aa

As is so often the case, a casual glance here might not at first show an area full of interesting history. Before talking of that, take a walk through the Haldon Forest and then go to the Old Stable for a meal, preferably Sunday lunch, or even just a snack. Here is true English cooking at its very best, like our grannies used to produce, with no gimmicks, and at an astonishingly reasonable price.

Mamhead is a small parish on the eastern flank of the Haldon Hills, and the park said to be landscaped by Capability Brown, really is beautiful, though somewhat overgrown now, its original beauty can still be seen. Under a yew tree in the churchyard, James Boswell swore never to become drunk again. He was a friend of William Temple, great grandfather of Archbishop William Temple. Lady Gasgoine Nightingale was struck by lightning whilst walking in this park, and died in her husband's arms. Although she was laid to rest in Westminster Abbey, her ghost still haunts the grounds.

The Valley of the Rocks, Lynton

M

There is a fine obelisk which can be reached from the car park on Haldon. It was put there in 1742 by Thomas Belle, and is made of Portland stone as a shipping aid for the English Channel. Robert Adam was employed to design Mamhead House for the Earl of Lisburne: orange trees were grown in the Orangery in 1833, and this still stands as a residence. Mamhead House was rebuilt in 1828 and is now a special school. It made the architect, Anthony Salvin, famous. From here Sir Peter Balle first saw through his telescope that Saturn had more than one ring. During the Second World War the cellars were used to store such valuables as the Bishop's Throne from Exeter Cathedral. A bomb fell on the exact spot in the cathedral where it had stood. Thomas Balle in 1686 was the first person in England to raise trees from acorns. Nearby Ashcombe Tower was once the home of Sir Ralph Rayner, among the first men to enter Berlin with the English troops and go into Hitler's bunker, from where he smuggled a telephone which had belonged to Adolf. Nearby too is Haldon racecourse, said to be the oldest racecourse in England where horses have galloped since the reign of Queen Anne.

Manaton   Map 3 Ba

This unspoilt Dartmoor village has a green flanked by trees. John Galsworthy lived in Wingstone Farm nearby, during the First World War, and would probably have made a permanent home there if his wife Amy, had not disliked country life. He took a great interest in Dartmoor Prison and through his writing, particularly in the play *Justice*, eventually, in September 1909, persuaded Winston Churchill who was then Home Secretary to reduce the severity of solitary confinement to a maximum of three months. He wrote much of the *Forsyte Saga* here. From this sixteenth-century farm can be seen Bowerman's Nose, a pile of granite rocks named after Mr Bowerman, turned to stone by local witches. Nearby is Becky or **Becka Falls** (Country Parks) where there is a cafe and souvenir shop, but if you wish, you can get away from this among the trees where you can wander and listen to the brook in its haste to reach the river Bovey. Nearby also is **Grimspound** (Archaeological Sites), a well preserved Bronze Age settlement, in the form of an enclosed village with the remains of 24 huts clearly to be seen, traces of stone beds and cooking stones.

The church was damaged by lightning on 13 December 1779, and restored in 1865. The yew tree on the right of the lych-gate is 300-years-old. If you look carefully, you will see faces in the twisted branches and trunk. In 1920 some of the agricultural workers formed a branch of the National Agricultural Workers' Union, the first this side of the moor, portraying the kind of courage which once made the West Country the place where so many rebellions might be hatched.

Marldon   Map 4 Ab

Here is one of the best examples of a fortified manor house in the county, namely early fourteenth-century Compton Castle, built by Geoffrey Gilbert who had married a Compton heiress. You come upon it suddenly and without warning as you drive along a narrow country lane, somehow the last building you expect to see. The solar and cellar still remain, also some foundations of the great hall, and much of the second building period in 1450. Further changes were made about 1520. **Compton Castle** (Historic Homes) now belongs to the National Trust, but Commander Gilbert and his wife still live here. It was the home of Sir Humphrey Gilbert, the explorer, until 1800, when it was sold, but Commander Gilbert bought it back and lovingly restored it to its present beauty.

In complete contrast, near Marldon, is a first class museum run by personality Keith Fordyce, **Torbay, Trains, Robes, Roses and Aircraft**. Here is an Aircraft Museum, a Model Railway, a collection of period costumes, and a garden created to the memory of Kenneth More. There is a licensed cafeteria, a woodland picnic area, kennels for your dogs and a play-ground for the children.

Even a P.O.W. camp is reproduced with life-like models in uniform, an escape tunnel and the glider from Colditz. Since a recent visit to America, Keith has re-organised the whole area and you can spend the day, whatever the weather, without the most demanding youngster, or grown up, becoming bored.

Meavy see Yelverton

Modbury Map 3 Bb

Here is another typical hill-town like Kingsbridge, with two lovely main streets bordered on either side by Georgian and Victorian houses. In the centre of the town Broad Street, Church Street and Brownston Street meet; cattle were sold in Broad Street up until 1940. Many of the eighteenth and nineteenth-century houses were the homes of the rich local wool merchants. There are two inns, the sixteenth-century half timbered Exeter Inn and the White Hart. The Champernownes were Lords of the Manor from the time of Edward II until 1770. They lived in Court House at the top of Church Street, but only a few traces remain of the house. It suffered badly in the Civil War. Parliamentary troops were billetted in the church, and defaced many of the effigies by hacking off their feet. St George's has had many ups and downs, at one time Eton became its benefactor.

The houses in Brownston Street have a lovely variety of styles, Old Traine House, an Elizabethan mansion was replaced by New Traine House with an impressive nineteenth-century pillared facade. Tall, three storeyed Brick House was once a hat factory in the nineteenth-century. Walk up the ridgeway where South Hams' farmers used to drive their cattle to the moor to save their precious lower grass fields for hay. They probably took the same route as the Bronze Age Beaker people. You get the feeling as you stand between the widely spaced hedges of the past, of people who walked there, along the northern boundary of the parish. Try to get a copy of John Rogers' little booklet *In the Life of a Country Thatcher*, a microcosm of the past in this area.

Moretonhampstead   Map 3 Ba

Marking the gateway to Dartmoor, the name of the town is often contracted to Moreton, for it was originally just that, meaning a moor farm. The churchyard has many graves of French officers who were prisoners during the Napoleonic Wars and died here while on parole from Princetown. Most spectacular was General Rochambeau, Commander-in-Chief at San Domingo, who capitulated in 1803. To celebrate news of a French victory on land or sea, he would parade the streets in full dress uniform, a free show which much endeared him to the people who were officially his enemies.

George Parker Bidder, the 'Calculating boy' was born here in 1806, whose genius fascinated the Rev. Davy who endowed the school at Lustleigh. He used to fire questions at him, dumbfounded by a boy who could find the cube root of 304, 821, and 217 instantly. Bidder built the Victoria Docks in London and helped Stephenson to build the London to Birmingham railway. Unfortunately Bidder's birthplace was destroyed by fire in 1926.

There is a rather attractive Market Square with seventeenth and eighteenth-century houses around, and the White Hart Inn. At the end of Cross Street are the almshouses built in 1637 which have a very medieval appearance, probably because of their rather crudely turned pillars. Near them once stood the old elm, called the Dancing Tree, where in 1801 a platform was erected for open air drinking and dancing. It was blown down in a gale on 10 September 1903 and a copper beech planted in its place.

In Cross Street is **Mearsdon Manor** (Art Galleries), a thirteenth-century house with an eleventh-century doorway, now an art gallery with a bird sanctuary in the garden. It houses mostly paintings of wild life and Dartmoor; well worth a visit. The town is of course a

M

marvellous centre for walking on some of the wildest parts
of Dartmoor, and also nearby is Manor House Hotel with
its beautiful golf course.

Mortehoe   Map 1 Aa

Its chief claim to fame is the treacherous Morte Point,
where five ships were wrecked in 1852, along with many
others down the centuries. Bull Point is in this parish with
a lighthouse which was first lit in 1879, and operates a
powerful fog signal to warn vessels from this deadly coast.
It is an attractive village worth a visit, with a farm in the
middle as well as a church and an inn. The church of St
Mary Magdalene was built between the twelfth and
fourteenth centuries, incorporating local slate, and with
three Norman doorways. The carved bench ends are really
beautiful, and the tomb chest to William de Tracy should
be seen. Damage Barton, one mile to the northwest is a
lovely example of an old Devon barton where the Tudor
farmhouse and its small walled garden face into the yard.

   Half a mile down the coast is the resort of Woolacombe,
whose vast sandy beach has earned the town a reputation
for being a fine surfing centre.

Morwellham Quay   Map 4 Ab

The Duke of Bedford created a five mile drive from
Endsleigh on the river Tamar to the river port of
Morwellham. In 1803 an amazing engineering feat took
place when the Tavistock Canal was taken from the river in
the centre of the town to run four miles to **Morwellham
Quay** (Museums), building a two mile long tunnel in the
middle to take the canal under Morwell Down, the
tunnellers working from each side of the hill and meeting
exactly in the middle. Here for a hundred years the lively
port of Morwellham, the busiest inland port west of Exeter,
handled the ore rushed from the Duke's mines, for in 1844
copper was discovered on his land at Blanchdown, and the
Devon Great Consols mine was opened. By the mid-1850s

it was one of the most productive mines in the world along with others at Morwellham. Shares bought at £1 rocketed to £200, but by the end of the century the boom was over. However, during the years it worked, a complex system of extraction and transport was evolved. The river Tamar is navigable as far as Morwellham and ships used to bring lime up to it from Plymouth to be used in the fields. New big quays were built for the three-masted boats that took away the ore, which was brought to the quays by trucks along a network of railways.

The Dartington Amenities Research Centre re-opened the port in June 1970 as a recreation and research centre. They removed silt and rubbish from the quays and now there are museums, trails, dray rides to Endsleigh, and a tramway trip into the re-opened George and Charlotte mine. The Great Dock, the raised railway, the blacksmiths and copper shops have been restored, there are even plans to restart mining. Morwellham's well worth a visit.

Newton Abbot   Map 4 Ab

This used to be a delightful, warm and friendly market town, where Victorian buildings stood amidst shady plane trees, and farmers from the surrounding area brought their cattle. However the 'planners' have put an end to all that with a shopping precinct and covered market stalls under a multi-storey car park which resembles a prison building. The town streets now have very few old family stores, which have been replaced by chain and multiple stores, estate agents and building societies. However, even the planners cannot take away the past history of the town.

Flint tools used by Neolithic men were found at Berry's Wood Hill Fort near **Bradley Manor** (Historic Homes), itself a fine old house built in 1419, well preserved with a great hall, a chapel and kitchen. Milton Down Camp has been proved to date back to the first century B.C. and Roman coins have been dug up in the vicinity. Another very old site is Castle Dyke at Highweek where a house in the village contains a Norman arch leading to Highweek

N

Hill, revealing the remains of a Norman castle.

Two small settlements, Shireborne Newton and Newton Bushel which became Newton Abbot, grew up on either side of the river Lemon which runs through the town to join the river Teign on its way to the sea. Although the town existed in the twelfth century, there is not much really pre-Victorian building in the town itself except for St Leonard's Tower in the centre where William of Orange was declared king, the old half timbered shop nearby, and Forde House built in 1610 by Sir Richard Reynell, member of a well-known local family, and where Charles I once stayed. The Mackrell Almshouses are also well preserved and inhabited. All Saints church at Highweek stands on a hill, as does St Mary's Wolborough, which has a Norman font with seventeenth-century monuments to the Reynell family. St Luke's at Milber, although perhaps not the most beautiful, must be the most interesting by virtue of the fact that it was built as the result of a dream that the Rev. Keble Martin, author of *The Concise British Flora in Colour*, had in 1931.

There are numerous pubs in the town, some bearing names reminiscent of the days when men waited in them to hear news of the fishing fleets going to Newfoundland. There were many spin offs from there in the town, such as the mill just outside at Holbeam or Hobbim, where knives and hooks were made, as well as edge tools famous all over Devon. This was one of the last of the hammer mills whose 'works' have been preserved in the South Kensington Science Museum. There were also woollen and leather mills on the river Lemon, such as Bradley Mills run for generations by the Vicary family, and a factory where rope was made, the premises are still known as Rope Walk. Granite used for constructing London Bridge as well as many other famous buildings, was brought from **Haytor Quarry** (Industrial Archaeology) down a specially made railway to a canal, both built by the Templars of Stover.

The merchants and residents of the town have always been generous and public spirited with many of the amenities provided on a voluntary basis. Among these were

the original hospital donated by Squire Scratton of Ogwell, who also gave piped water free to the entire village; Baker's Park, the swimming pool and community centre; the library donated by Passmore Edwards who came from humble origins to be the owner of a publishing house.

From 1846 when many of the yellow brick terraced houses were built, and the solid middle class villas, it was essentially a railway town. John Lethbridge perfected the first diving machine in 1715 in his back garden. William Yeo was the first noncomformist preacher in the area. He had to address his flock in a pit in Bradley Woods for fear of persecution. This still exists and is known as Puritan's Pit or sometimes Devil's Pit.

The river Lemon caused bad flooding with much damage and some loss of life in the years 1853, 1894, 1938 and 1979. A dam has now been built above the town at enormous expense, said to be an assurance against future floods.

Bradley Manor, Newton Abbot

N

Newton Abbot had one of the first cider works, Henleys, founded in1791; beer was brewed also in 1843 by two brewers, named Palk and Pinsent. Malt is still prepared for such firms as Guinness and Whitbread, by Tuckers, a family firm established over 150 years ago.

George Templar founded the first cricket club in Devon at Teigngrace, of which the famous Parson Jack Russell was a member. At the house called Sandford Orleigh lived Sir Samuel Baker in 1875; he discovered the source of the river Nile, and his friend, General Gordon, stayed with him there before setting out for Khartoum.

The two main hotels are the Globe and the Queens; the former was once an old hunting lodge and still retains much of the atmosphere of a bygone age, with present day amenities. There is first class National Hunt racing at **Newton Abbot Racecourse** (Horseracing), at which the crime writer, Dick Francis can often be seen, and a famous Agricultural College founded by local men. Newton Abbot is a wonderful centre from which to explore Dartmoor and the beaches of the South Devon Coast, surrounded by green hills and woods, many of which are visible at the ends of the town's streets.

Three miles to the north is Chudleigh, an old market town largely destroyed by fire in either 1807 or 1810, the history books differ. It was a staging point for coaches and has some attractive old inns. In the Bishop Lacey can be seen the charred beam where the great fire ended. There is an old mill with a water wheel which has been restored and is now a craft centre well worth a visit.

There are beautiful walks round Chudleigh Rocks with limestone cliffs popular with climbers, also many caves in the area where prehistoric man once lived where pottery, charcoal and flint tools have been found.

To the south is **Ugbrooke House** (Historic Homes) and park belonging to Lord Clifford with an Iron Age Fort, Castle Dyke, and a grove of beech trees known as Dryden's Walk. He was a close friend of the first Lord Clifford and often visited Ugbrooke. It is said he completed his translation of Virgil while staying here.

Two very old parishes, East and West Ogwell, near Newton Abbot, joined in 1881. East Ogwell has a cruciform church, St Bartholomew, with the tomb of Richard Reynell, Sheriff of Devon, who died 1855. Holbeam, or Hobbim to the locals, was a Domesday Manor and the home of the Holbeams for at least 12 generations. The original mill stands as a residence. West Ogwell consists of farms and one big house, once the home of the benevolent Squire Scratton who gave so much to Newton Abbot. It is now a convent; standing in the park beside it is a beautiful little church, dedication unknown, with an early unaltered cruciform plan with high box pews, and a small one for a child, also an open fireplace for squire to warm his coat tails: It is said by Sir John Betjeman to be one of the most beautiful little churches of its kind in England, and probably sited where Druids once worshipped.

Northam See Appledore

Okehampton

Included in this parish is the highest point of Dartmoor, High Willhays 2,039 feet high. From Yes Tor, 2,028 feet high, is one of the best views over Devon, reaching as far as Bodmin Moor. The first settlement founded by Baldwin de Brionne about 1086, stands between the East and West Okement rivers, with a bad reputation for endless queues of traffic, and consequently under a long standing and bitter dispute over a by-pass.

The town itself is not very exciting, the best building being the town hall, erected as a dwelling house by John Northmore in 1685, and converted in 1821. Somehow the atmosphere of the northern part of Dartmoor creeps into this town making it a little cold and desolate. The Georgian White Hart Inn, Fore Street, is a pleasant old coaching inn. All that is left of the fifteenth-century church after a fire in 1842 is the tower, the present building has windows by William Morris. Beside the river, south of the town, are the

O

ruins of the really spectacular **Okehampton Castle**, stark
against the sky. The Normans built the keep, which became
the basis of a castle much enlarged in 1370. The chapel is
very impressive, although probably a French prisoner of
war on parole may have thought differently, for he
scratched on a stone, early graffiti: 'Hic V – fuit captivus
belli'.

Of course there is a ghost in the form of Lady
Howard, said to have survived four husbands, all of whom
she probably murdered. Eventually she was burned as a
witch on Gibbet Hill, and her ghost made to bring grass
from Okehampton Castle to Tavistock, where she once
lived at Fitzford House. She rides each night in a coach
drawn by a headless horse driven by a headless coachman
with a black hound running alongside. On the return
journey it carries in its mouth, one blade of grass.

In the area of Okehampton, a man could buy a wife up
until the end of the eighteenth century. Anne Frise was
sold by her husband for two shillings and sixpence.
Okehampton & District Museum of Dartmoor Life
shows how people lived and worked in the past. On the
Saturday after Christmas the 'giglet market' is held,
mentioned in the Domesday Book, and so called from the
privilege of self introduction to any spinsters who might
attract a single man's attention, given by an ancient charter
to bachelors. It seems that in one way and another the area
must have been full of male chauvinist pigs. The maidens
who hoped to be courted were the 'giglets'.

Three miles from Okehampton is Sticklepath, and here
the **Finch Foundry** (Industrial Archaeology) Trust and
Finch Foundry Museum of Rural Industry are open all
the year. Behind is the Quaker Burial Ground, for many
Friends from here went to found the settlement of
Pennsylvania, and it was the Quakers who first welcomed
Wesley to the village.

South Zeal is a mile away with the lovely Oxenham Arms
built in the latter part of the twelfth century by lay monks.
After the Dissolution, it became a Dower House of the
Burgoynes, whose heiress took it to the Oxenham family,

O

and was first licensed in 1477. Many novelists have featured it in their books including Eden Phillpotts in *The Beacon*, and Baring Gould in *John Herring*. In *Westward Ho!* there is much about the Oxenham family. Don't miss the monolith in the wall of the small bar, which was shaped by man 5,000 years ago; it is thought that the monastic builders set their house round this, and however deeply people dig, they have never reached its foundation. A very good Folk Festival with such people as Bob Cann performing, is held here in August.

Ottery St Mary   Map 4 Ba

Perhaps its chief claim to fame is that it produced the only real literary genius to come out of Devon, Samuel Taylor Coleridge, poet and philosopher, most famous for *The Rhyme of the Ancient Mariner*. His father, John Coleridge, born in 1719, was vicar of Ottery and master of the Grammar School. Ottery is also the Clavering St Mary of *Pendennis* by Thackeray, who used to stay at Larkbeare nearby.

The Church of St Mary, Ottery St Mary

Great fires swept through the town in 1767 and 1866. St Mary's church is really beautiful and said to be modelled on Exeter Cathedral by Bishop Grandisson. The fourteenth-century clock is one of the oldest in England, and the spire has a weathercock which used to whistle in the wind. There is a fine pulpit and gilded wooden eagle lectern in the Lady Chapel; the fourteenth-century roof has a superb ceiling, while the Dorset Aisle of 1520 has been likened to a breaking wave.

The town has some lovely Georgian houses. By the river is a relic of the Industrial Revolution, the Serge Factory, dating from 1788-90. Don't miss **Cadhay House** (Historic Home) one mile to the north, a Tudor mansion built by John Haydon with its quadrangle known as the Court of Kings, or Sovereigns, with chequered stonework, and small statues of Henry VIII and his three children.

Paignton Map 4 Ab

Many people think of Paignton as a rather uninteresting suburb of Torquay. Nothing could be further from the truth. It was probably started by the Saxons founding a village half a mile inland, and so like many other watering places on this coast, really only sprang to life in Victorian times with the coming of the railway.

It has a marvellous sandy beach, an 800 feet pier, 75 acres of one of the best **Zoological & Botanic Gardens** (Zoos), in the county, many parks and an aquarium. The harbour is quite charming and is always seething with activity, as there is a windsurfing school here. Paignton became famous for its very special sweet cabbages, which were sent all over the county.

One of the 'musts' however is a visit to **Oldway** (Historic Homes). There are 115 rooms, built for the Singer sewing machine millionaire. The house cost him £100,000 in 1874. He nicknamed it 'The Wigwam'. In 1914 the family gave it up and the town bought it eventually in 1945 for £45,000. There is a hall of mirrors, a marble staircase where two enormous brass figures sit in niches, Italian gardens, a café, bowling greens, tennis courts and behind the building, Bishop Copplestone's Folly.

The parish of St John has the remains of the twelfth-century church, although it was almost entirely rebuilt in red sandstone in the early fifteenth century. Next to the church is the Coverdale Tower, all that remains of the old Bishop of Exeter's palace.

On the promenade stands the modern Festival Hall where concerts and variety concerts are held; nearby, on the promenade is the imposing pillared facade of the Paignton Club, which has recently celebrated its centenary. With its pier, the green grass, brightly coloured bathing chalets and sparkling lights, there is nothing dull about Paignton.

Peter Tavy   Map 3 Aa

The church here is fifteenth century, and a screen in the tower arch was made from a pew 500-years-old. A memorial on the wall tells of the five daughters of Michael Eveleigh, rector in the seventeenth century, who all died before they were two-years-old. The Peter Tavy Inn is seventeenth century, and there is also the Elephant's Nest where you can sit and drink while you admire the view. Two streams meet at Hillbridge, and a mine leat runs off to Mary Tavy, (the mining village which saw the copper strike,) leading to the building of Morwellham Canal and Quays. Many abandoned mines can be seen in the area including the Devon Friendship and **Wheal Betsy** (Industrial Archaeology). Willsworthy was a Saxon farmstead, the sixteenth century farmhouse originally included a chapter. Other remote farmsteads are Wapsworthy 1230, and Baggator 1238, of great interest to any student of English Peasant building. There are many hut circles and other evidence of Bronze Age settlement, particularly on Standon Down where there is an unenclosed village.

Pilton   see Barnstaple

P

Plymouth   Map 3 Ab

When Exeter was founded by the Romans, Plymouth
was still non existent. There were various settlements
nearby such as Mount Batten and Stonehouse, but the
Romans only passed through the area, and it was not until
the Saxon invasion that Plymouth started to emerge. Sutton
was only a fishing village (exporting Dartmoor tin),
overshadowed by Plymouth Prior, which was the main
centre of population until the middle of the fourteenth
century. Then the river Plym silted up because of tin
streaming waste, and Plympton lost its trade to Sutton.
Eventually Plymouth prospered and grew, despite many
invasions from France and Spain.

In 1528 William Hawkins became the first Englishman to
trade across the Atlantic. He brought back with him a
native chief from Brazil, the first true American to set foot
on English soil. In 1562 one of the Hawkins sons started
the English trade in black slavery. In 1572 Drake sailed
from Plymouth to Nombre de Dios, and then in 1577
embarked on the voyage which developed into the
circumnavigation of the world. In April 1581 he was
knighted on board his ship; **The Golden Hind Replica**
(Unusual Outings) can be seen in Brixham Harbour.

During the next decades, Plymouth witnessed two more
events of national importance, namely the defeat of the
Spanish Armada in 1588, and the sailing of the Pilgrim
Fathers in 1620. The first transatlantic flight landed safely
at Plymouth, in 1919, and in 1967 Sir Francis Chichester
returned from his single handed circumnavigation of the
globe.

Plymouth has been a naval station for centuries, but it
has never had first class facilities for repairing men-o'-war.
King William changed all that in 1691 when he authorised
work to begin on the first dock, which expanded through
the eighteenth century and became known as Plymouth
Dock. In January 1824 it became Devonport. Stonehouse
too was 'growing up', where several military establishments
were situated, and also the commercial docks at Millbay. In

1914 it was agreed to amalgamate all three places, Stonehouse, Devonport and Plymouth. The latter was granted city status in 1928. In 1967 the boundary was again extended to take in Plympton, and now Plymouth is the largest city west of Bristol. Because of its naval importance, it was a major target for German bombing in the Second World War; 1,000 people were killed, 5,000 injured, 70,000 houses damaged or destroyed. However, some of the oldest parts were not hit and the city has been rebuilt and redeveloped, giving a sense of spaciousness with wide and windy streets. It stretches from west to east across the peninsula between the estuaries of the rivers Tamar and Plym.

The construction of the breakwater two miles from the Hoe was started in 1811 by Rennie, though not finished until the 1840s, it gave the port one of the longest and safest harbours in England. It is 1,700 yards long, and three and a half million tons of stone lie beneath your feet as you stand on it. At the western end is the lighthouse begun in 1833; in 1845 the beacon which stands at the other end, was erected. The Hoe is still the great central point of Plymouth, where people gather, including of course Drake with his famous game of bowls, for great occasions, both of joy and sorrow. Here stands Drake's statue and there is a memorial to commemorate the sailors who died in the wars of this century, namely the Armada memorial and Smeaton's Lighthouse Tower, brought from the Eddystone reef, 14 miles out in the Channel, when the present **Smeaton's Tower** (Other Historic Buildings), and fourth lighthouse, was erected in 1882. In 1698 the first lighthouse in the world was built on Eddystone reef. It was made of wood, and destroyed by a storm in 1703, the second one by fire in 1755. Sadly now, the light is automatic, but on clear days you can see the stump of the old lighthouse beside the present one. Drake's Island which is just off shore was once a prison, later a military fortress, and now a youth adventure centre.

At the eastern end of the Hoe is the **Royal Citadel** (Other Historic Buildings), the most important historic building left in Plymouth; the foundation of the present

P

building, which can still be seen, was laid in 1666 by John Grenville, Governor of the town. The main gateway dated 1670 is one of the best examples of baroque architecture in this country, wrongly attributed to Wren, and in fact the work of Sir Thomas Fitz. King Charles II visited the town twice, especially to inspect the Citadel. East of the Hoe, and built around Sutton harbour, is the Barbican, the city's historic quarter. Here the streets are still truly medieval, and many of the buildings 300 to 500-years-old. The fish quay is still used by trawlers and the Pilgrim Fathers sailed from the Mayflower Steps nearby. Island House is where they stayed before leaving, the list of names of those who sailed is nailed to the wall, minus the women. This is a crowded area yet it retains a magical feeling of the past, particularly New Street which is narrow and Elizabethan, where the upper stories of some of the houses stick out over the street. The back yards were once gardens. No. 32, **Elizabethan House** (Historic Homes), a typical example, was the house of a merchant or sea captain, a passage leads from front to back straight into the garden. A maze of tunnels existed under the old streets, leading to caves beneath the cliffs where contraband was brought to be hidden.

In Southside Street stands **Black Friar's Distillery** (Other Historic Buildings), once a fourteenth-century Dominican Priory, and still intact after more than five centuries. The original monastic refectory has a roof like an upturned boat and dates back to 1425. Records reveal that in 1793 the family firm of Coates and Co. was making Plymouth Gin and has done so ever since.

The **Merchant's House** (Other Historic Buildings) in St Andrew's Street is sixteenth century, half timbered with limestone, built by William Parker, a privateer who raided the Spanish fleet and became rich on the proceeds. He was made Mayor in 1601. The house has been so beautifully restored that standing in the rooms today it is not at all hard to imagine that if a member of the Parker family entered the house they would immediately recognise their home. Now it is run as a branch of the Plymouth City

Museum and Art Gallery, and is well worth a visit.

To the west of the Sound is **Mount Edgcumbe** (Country Parks), technically in Cornwall; to the east is Mount Batten, the R.A.F. station where T.E. Lawrence, Lawrence of Arabia, author of *The Seven Pillars of Wisdom*, posed as Aircraftsman Shaw, later to be killed in a motor cycle accident. The regional Meteorological Office is located here, manned round the clock, and modern technology is very much in evidence. Another famous citizen of Plymouth, Viscount Astor, was elected M.P. in 1910 for a Plymouth constituency. In 1918 he succeeded to his father's title, but his wife Nancy, fought and won his vacant Commons' seat, which she held for 25 years.

The new shopping centre has been entirely rebuilt since the Second World War. An early decision had to be taken to devise a totally new street pattern. Plymouth's centre has been one of the most congested in Britain, and they planned a shopping centre for the motorcar age. The axis of the new centre was Armada Way, a wide tree lined avenue stretching from the railway station to the war memorial on Plymouth Hoe. The re-building began in March 1947, a plaque commemorates the event.

The 1943 plan for Plymouth was drawn up in two years by Abercrombie and Paton Watson. Forty years later, new proposals are in the air with sites for two new riverside parks, eight recreational footpaths, 16 new areas of public open space, four district parks and ten new local parks; the central shopping area of the city is to become a pedestrian precinct, with schemes also for two suburban shopping centres.

The parish church of St Andrew's was one of those destroyed and only the shell remained. The day after the bombing a notice had been hung above the door bearing the one word 'Resurgam', I will rise again. It did. At the end of the Royal Parade are the bombed ruins of another church, left as a memorial of the bombing. **Prysten House** (Museum) off Royal Parade was formerly a priest's house built in 1490, now housing exhibits from the Mayflower expedition.

P

A famous modern son of Plymouth is Wayne Sleep the dancer who became a soloist with the Royal Ballet at 22 years of age, and three years later their principal dancer. This brings us inevitably to the Theatre Royal, opened in May 1982 by Princess Margaret. The first Theatre Royal had been built by John Foulson in 1811, the city's famous Regency architect who designed and built so much of the city; it was demolished in 1937. In 1970 the vacant land between the Civic Centre and Derry's Cross at the end of Royal Parade was chosen for the site. It contains not one but two separate theatres, and the larger has a movable ceiling which can change the seating capacity from 700 to 1,300. The second, The Drum, seats 250 people. This was the largest theatre to be built in regional Britain in the last 30 years.

Devonport Docks are still the navy's major port; views of them can be obtained from the Tamar Ferry, also from here is a good view of the two bridges which join Devon to Cornwall over the river. It took ten years to build the rail bridge, designed by Isambard Kingdom Brunel, one of the engineering feats of the Victorian Age. Sadly, when Prince Albert opened the bridge in 1859, Brunel was a very sick man. Beside it now stands the Tamar Toll Bridge. These docks are the largest ship repair complex in West Europe and they cover more than 300 acres, including Britain's biggest and most up to date nuclear submarine complex. It was from this dockyard that most of the historic events of the Falklands campaign were carried out. The huge Task Force, Operation Corporate, sailed from here, and at the time all the local shops were scoured for huge supplies of razor blades, other toilet requisites, and men's clothing. Marks & Spencer were divested of hundreds of pairs of men's underpants. The streets here seem to seethe with life, people have an air of independence, perhaps due to the docks which have guaranteed work for so many generations.

It may be rather surprising that a number of farms continue to thrive and prosper inside the city's boundaries. At Staddiscombe at the southern tip of the city, is

Courtgates, a mixed farm referred to in the Domesday Book. Even the most dedicated urbanite needs sometimes to find a green retreat, and Plymouth is fortunate in having many open spaces and parks, apart from delightful little pockets of shrubs and trees tucked away.

One of the places not to be missed is **Saltram** (Historic Homes), one of three mansions still kept up in Devon, the others being Powderham and **Castle Hill** (Gardens). Saltram lies between Plympton and Plymstock, once the home of the Parker family, who took the title of Lord of Borington, and then Earl of Morley. The Tudor and Stuart buildings were enlarged into the present mid-eighteenth-century mansion, and seem to welcome visitors, being beautifully maintained by the National Trust. Somehow it is as if the family were about to return from a shopping expedition. Even clean towels are ready for use. There is a fine collection of paintings, including some by Joshua Reynolds who was a friend of the family and a frequent visitor.

Plymouth is one of the best sporting centres for sailing, windsurfing, swimming, tennis, golf, deep sea fishing and coastal walks. It has given its name to some forty towns scattered all over the world, what greater proof of the deep affection it holds in the hearts of the people who know it.

Portlemouth   see Salcombe

Postbridge   Map 3Bb

Once an important place for tinners, but now just a string of cottages, the village's claim to fame is its clapper bridge. It is the best example on **Dartmoor** (National Parks) 42 feet long, standing seven feet above the East Dart river, and definitely one of the most photographed sites of the moor. Some claim it is Bronze Age, but others that it only dates from the thirteenth century, designed for pack horses. In 1820 it was partly destroyed by a young man who wanted the stones to stop his ducks going downstream and was then restored in 1880 by workmen from the granite quarries at Merrivale and said by locals to be wrongly

P

replaced, the stones being 'foreback behind'. Nearby is the
Warren Inn where a peat fire has burned continuously for
over 130 years and where, when the inmates became
snowed in, anyone who died was salted down in the big
granite pig trough. In the early nineteenth century it stood
on the opposite side of the road when Jonas Coaker, born at
Postbridge, builder of stone walls and poet, owned,
pulled down and rebuilt it on the present site. Vitifer and
other tin and copper mines are nearby, and the miners once
cut four plots of land in the outline of the four aces which
can still be seen. The cards were dropped by Jan Reynolds
of Widecombe when the devil flew over Vitifer with his
soul after the great storm. At Archerton, near Postbridge,
the Hairy Hands appear to cause unexplained accidents.

Clapper Bridge, Postbridge

P

Powderham Map 4 Aa

At the time of writing the beautiful castle here is to let. It is
one of the county's finest mansions and has been in the
Courtenay family since 1377 when Sir Philip Courtenay
began the buildings as a fortified manor house rather than
as a true castle, and until the eighteenth century the river
Exe spread its waters almost to the east walls of the house.
During the Civil War it was garrisoned for the King.
Fairfax sent a party to attack on 14 December 1645. They
met with strong resistance, so the troops took the church
instead, but the castle had to surrender a few weeks later on
25 January 1646. Afterwards many improvements were
made, the chapel and library built, and an embankment
made along the river Exe to stop the land being flooded.
The Belvedere was built and many trees planted in the
park. The rooms are beautifully furnished, the domed
music room was designed by James Wyatt, and in the ante
room there is a window above the fireplace instead of a
chimney. This was covered by a small sliding mirror at
night; a flue was built to one side to draw the smoke.
There are some gorgeous paintings. In the painting of
Frances Finch, Viscountess Courtenay, by Hudson, the
satin of the dress is so lifelike you could put out your hand
and feel its soft shiny texture. Hudson was a great West
Country painter, Reynold's drawing master, but it has been
said someone else painted his satins. There is a herd of deer
in the park and also in Pigeon Vale a cottage converted
from an old dovecote.

Princetown Map 3 Bb

In the parish of Lydford, where the remains of that other
grim prison stand is Princetown, 1,400 feet above sea level,
and said to be the highest inhabited town in England with
nearly 90 inches of rain a year. Sir Thomas Tyrwhitt, Lord
of the Stannaries, started it all when he improved part of
the Moor which he named Tor Royal, half a mile southeast
of Princetown where he built a house in 1798, near his
granite quarries. He also built the road from Tavistock to

P

Princetown, and suggested providing a prison to house the captives of the American and Napoleonic Wars who had become too numerous for the prisons and hulks at Plymouth.

The name Princetown comes from the fact that the Prince of Wales of the day gave it to him; he holds the lands of the Duchy of Cornwall to which parts of the Moor belong. The prison was built in 1806 at a cost of £130,000 and at one time between 7,000 and 9,000 prisoners were crammed in there. A small town grew up, and two large inns were built, for many of the prisoners of war had prize money due to them, forging notes which they passed off in the great daily market held in the prison.

When the prisoners left, the town nearly died, but the railway came in 1823 bringing back life to the quarries. The prison itself was empty until 1850 when it became a place for prisoners serving long term sentences.

Escapees do not last long on the Moors. The first attempt was on 10 December 1850, by John Broderick, John Thompson and Charles Webster. Eventually Thompson was arrested in Ashburton; Broderick and Webster were challenged by a constable on the road to London. Broderick was seized, but Webster escaped and was never recaptured. Most Moor people were sympathetic to the inmates of this grim prison, but sympathy got smothered by fright as soon as the alarm bell sounded. Doors were barred and guns loaded.

Eventually a model farm was set up for the prisoners to work. Care for the animals had a curious effect on some of the hardened criminals, who showed great gentleness with a mare in foal as men born in cities suddenly became shepherds.

The Plume of Feathers Inn stood here before the prison was built. St Michael's church was constructed by French prisoners, some of the inside decoration being financed by American widows whose husbands had died in the prison. There is little of the original interior for Americans to see, for a fire in 1868 gutted much of it, but still they come every year; some are descendents of the men whose only crime had been to honour the wrong flag. Nearby at North Hessary Tor soars the mast of the B.B.C.

Dozens of books have been written about this great tomb of the living. It is an eerie place, the main street wide and somehow reminiscent of a Western Frontier town in an old film. One of the most interesting old buildings is the Duchy Hotel, now the Prison Officers' Mess, to which recently Prince Charles paid a visit and other members of the Royal family have visited in the past, notably King George V and Queen Mary, and such famous people as Baring Gould, Eden Phillpotts and William Crossing, also Edward VIII when Prince of Wales.

Mr Raymond of Paignton, whose father was Principal Officer at the prison when he was born in 1900, remembers eating good meals there attended by a waiter. He was also a choir boy with many memories of bitter winters, but with a gentle sense of humour he remarks, 'the four tar blackened cottages standing in a field off the Two Bridges road were called New London.'

When you stand under the prison walls you do feel as if the whole heart of England has ceased to beat. There is a bleak inner silence.

Ringmore see Shaldon

Saltram see Plymouth

Salcombe Map 3 Bc

After the Second World War this became a lotus eating area for men returning from the hell they had known, with gratuities to spend and borrowed time which they had not expected. They took up lobster and crab fishing, which appeared an idyllic way of life but most of them were soon disillusioned. Others bought luxury boats for charter, cafés, and restaurants as life became one perpetual summer and Salcombe lent itself favourably to idleness and enjoyment.

The climate is one of the mildest in England, where

S

oranges and lemons grow out of doors. The estuary is crowded with boats and the roads with cars, but it is an ideal place to learn to sail as it is so safe. The estuary runs up to Kingsbridge through some of the most beautiful countryside in Devon with meadows and trees sweeping down to the water, small sandy coves where you hear nothing but the everlasting rhythm of the tides, and secret creeks crowded with bird life.

It is no wonder such people as the author Paul Gallico had a house here, that members of the current popular bands and the Crazy Gang spent holidays in one of the hotels kept by an ex member of Show Biz, that Norman Long of B.B.C. fame had the Bolt Head Hotel, built of wood in Norwegian style by Captain Trinick.

On North Sands is Salcombe Castle or Fort Charles, a battered shell of its old self standing on a rock, half surrounded by sea, telling the story of far off unhappy days. It was built in the reign of Henry VIII against French and Spanish marauders, renamed Fort Charles and garrisoned with sufficient strength to withstand a four month siege through the spring of 1646.

Through the ages the harbour has been thronged with vessels, many built in the Salcombe yards. In the middle of the nineteenth century there were as many as 98 schooners working the port, bringing in every kind of merchandise from cocoa to hides, oils, wine and silk. The air of the little town must have smelled of pitch, tar and wood shavings, and been loud with the sounds of axe, saw and hammer. Today it is again one of the most popular harbours for the modern sailor in South Devon, although the type of craft is hardly comparable with the beautiful three-masted schooners. However if you close your eyes you can imagine the streets full of swaggering seamen with their salt and sun burned faces, their long hair and tasselled caps, with gold rings in their ears; not much has changed, except now they own their own boats and don't just man them.

It was here Tennyson looked out from the deck of the yacht *Sunbeam* and wrote his poem of farewell, *Crossing the Bar*.

The lifeboat must be one of the most interesting integral parts of Salcombe; the station itself was established in 1869 and in 1870 a lifeboat house was built. In 1916 came the greatest tragedy of all when on 27 October the *William and Emma* was launched in a furious gale to go to the assistance of the *Western Lass*, a schooner which had gone ashore at Lannacombe Bay. In spite of almost insurmountable difficulties, the Coxswain, Sam Distin, got the boat out over the sand bar at the mouth of the estuary. In the meantime the Prawle rocket company had saved the schooner's crew, but in those days there was no way of letting the lifeboat crew know, and they went on into the stormy dark autumn dawn. When they reached the wreck they realised what had happened and turned for home. As they approached the harbour mouth a huge wave caught them, the boat capsized and only two men survived, Distin and Johnson.

The present boat is the *Baltic Exchange*, said to be the best kept lifeboat afloat. The station record includes nearly 400 launches with over 300 lives saved. Bill Budgett, the

Salcombe

S

Secretary, tells how one boat, the *Alfred and Clara*, was sent to Guernsey as a replacement during the Second World War, when the island was captured by the Germans. They kept the lifeboat, the only R.N.L.I. one to be taken by the enemy.

Of course there is a history of piracy and smuggling in the bays and inlets, of horses and donkeys with muffled hooves, and 'watch the wall, my darling, as the gentlemen go by'. In fact, in 1607, the Justices complained that sometimes seamen raided the town in gangs 200 strong, they were often said to murder each other and bury the bodies in the sand.

There is a very good **Maritime & Local History Museum** on the Island Quay. The most famous house is The Moult on the hill between North and South Sands, built in 1764 by John Hawkins and once occupied by Froude, the historian. There are boutiques and restaurants, and high up on the hillside, Sharpitor Gardens, and **Overbecks Museum**, both well worth the climb if only for the blissful peace. There is no bridge across the estuary, but a ferry has run across from the quay by the Ferry Inn since forever. On the other side are some of the best beaches in the area, notably Fisherman's Cove, Millbay, and behind it a valley, in spring filled with beautiful flowers. No wonder people compare Salcombe with the Côte d'Azur.

Strangely enough East Portlemouth was a more important place than Salcombe in Medieval times. It is recorded in the Domesday Book as belonging to Judhel, Baron of Totnes. It sent five ships and 96 men to join the fleet, which took 10,000 English longbowmen to victory for Edward III at Crécy in 1346. Prawle Point on the coast just round the corner, with its offshore rock, the Island, is the southernmost point of Devon. Just beyond is one of the most superb bays, an anchorage for swimming, with a perfect coastal path above, covered with wild flowers through the seasons ranging from bluebells to thrift, and squill, wild thyme and stonecrop. From the hillside below Portlemouth Parish church is one of the most beautiful estuary views in

England. There is the story of the rector here who from his
pulpit, faltered in his sermon one stormy Sunday, then
stopped altogether, tearing off his surplice and crying to the
congregation, 'My brethren, there is a wreck on the Bar!
But let us all start fair!' for in the sixteenth and seventeenth
centuries this was a paradise for pirates and wreckers, being
almost inaccessible from the land.

Salcombe Regis Map 2 Bc

This lovely little village nestles in its own combe, protected
on all sides except from the sea, and owing its royal name
to the fact that it was originally a manor of Alfred the
Great, given by his grandson to the monastery founded in
Exeter.

Before you go down into the village from the Sidmouth
road, look at the thorn tree which stands with a plaque
stating that a thorn has stood there since Saxon times to
mark the boundary between cultivated fields and common
land.

On top of the hill stands the Norman Lockyer
Observatory concerned with the chemistry of the stars. The
church of St Peter has an eagle lectern dating from the
fifteenth century carved from one block of wood. Thorn is
an old farmhouse whose land was farmed by the Hooper
family for 400 years since 1355. At Dunscombe are the
remains of a former mansion once occupied by a branch of
the Drakes of Ashe, also disused quarries, some of whose
stones went into the building of Exeter Cathedral in the
fourteenth century.

Shaldon Map 4 Ab

Ringmore and Shaldon make up the parish of St Nicholas,
annexed to Teignmouth in 1881, with a ferry and bridge
connecting them. The first wooden bridge was designed
and built by Roger Hopkins in 1827, it was 1,632 feet long
with 34 arches and had some kind of drawbridge in the
centre. In 1838 it was found to be full of shipworm and was

S

closed until 1840. The toll house, which still stands at one end, collected money for building the bridge as well as road tax.

The Ness Rock rises steeply above, a bright red sandstone headland. Ness House dating from Regency times stands here, the thatched buildings supposed to be part of a tithe barn, said to be given to Nell Gwyn by Charles II. The tunnel to the beach was probably used at one time as a carriageway to a belvedere which overlooked the beach as well as by smugglers.

Shaldon village is enchanting with its late Georgian houses, especially in Fore Street and the Strand. One house called Magnolia with its lovely intricate cast-iron verandah built about the middle of the nineteenth century is particularly attractive. Once old sea dogs of all shapes and sizes came here for their final anchorage, which is obvious from the white flagstaffs and figureheads among the rocks with a profusion of flowers tumbling over walls and fences. The whole village has a Regency air even today and a complete absence of town planning. It has resulted in a lovely tumble of streets, cottages and gardens transporting the visitor back to the golden days of the eighteenth century.

By 1690 Ringmore was said to be a thriving hamlet. The small circular window in the thatched cottage beside Ringmore church is known as the Wreckers' Window, used to lure ships on to the Ness rocks with a lighted lantern. Once a gibbet stood on top of the hill between Shaldon and Stokeinteignhead. Hunters' Lodge at the end of the bridge was built in the Gothic style about 1650 as a hunting lodge for the Carews.

Shebbear Map 1 Ac

Stand beneath the old oak and admire the oval shaped stone weighing at least a ton. Discarded by the Devil on a flight from hell to torment the people on earth, the 'Devil's Stone' is the focal point of a traditional village ceremony celebrated on the night of 5 November. The locals meet in the village pub, aptly named 'The Devil's Stone', the church bells are rung, then, led by the vicar, the villagers advance carrying poles, and crowbars, strong enough to wedge under one side of the boulder. Slowly the stone is levered up on edge and turned right over to the accompaniment of shouts from the villagers. If this ritual was not honoured each year, crops would fail, cattle would die, and the prosperity of one and all would be in jeopardy for the next year. The church of St Michael is 800-years-old with a Norman door; the pub is seventeenth century. Nearby is a Theological College and two miles northeast of the village, **Alscott Farm Museum** with a collection of old ploughs, tractors and other farm equipment.

To the northwest of Shebbear at West Putford is the famous **Gnome Reserve** (Unusual Outings) where over 1,000 gnomes and pixies can be seen in a picturesque woodland setting.

Sheepstor Map 3 Bb

This lovely peaceful village is set below towering granite tors, near the very attractive Burrator Reservoir built in 1891 and enlarged in 1928, covering 150 acres, and supplying Plymouth with its water. In the rocks is a pixie cave, a granite chamber which at one time was capable of holding several people, but eventually the stones shifted. In 1909 Crossing wrote: 'It is not advisable to enter it...' It was said that one of the Elford family took refuge here during the Civil War and painted pictures on the walls.

In the churchyard lie the remains of the White Rajah of Sarawak, Sir James Brooke, under a large lump of Aberdeen Granite. He retired to Burrator House and died there in 1868. The grave of his nephew, Sir Charles Brooke, is also in the churchyard. The fascinating story of these men is told on a plaque just inside the church. Charles Vyner Brooke was the best known of the rajahs, and the last; his daughters were the 'princesses' of whom Princess Pearl the wife of Harry Roy, the dance band leader was the most famous. Another married an all-in-wrestler,

S

and the third an American army officer. The Ranee wrote a fascinating book about her life in Sarawak entitled *Queen of the Headhunters*, in which she remarks: 'I have had eight sons-in-law, and never remember which of my daughters has been married to whom, as they changed husbands so often.'

There is a lovely tomb in the church to Elizabeth Elford who died in 1641, lying on a bed with her baby in her arms, and kneeling beside, three daughters. Over the door of the church is a carving, once a sundial in the form of a skull with bones in its mouth over a charged hour glass. Out of its eye sockets and jaws sprout ears of grain, symbolising life out of death.

Sidmouth Map 4 Ba

This town gives the feeling that Alice in Wonderland may suddenly appear, freshly scrubbed in a white pinny; the very air is sparkling. Ronnie Delderfield the famous novelist lived at a house called The Gazebo, and it was as a result of spending so much time walking in the area, and his love for Devon, that inspired his great books ranging from *The Dreaming Suburb* to *To Serve Them All My Days*. He also wrote much about Napoleon upon whom he was an expert, and was fascinated by the fact that French prisoners had worked on the river Otter. He also 'buried' Benn Gunn in a kind of sequel he wrote to Stevenson's *Treasure Island*, in the village of East Budleigh. As a result many tourists call upon him to be shown the 'grave'.

The shingle beach did not attract the Victorians, so the railway came late to the town. However the wealthy residents built very ornate houses, many of which are now hotels. Queen Victoria was brought here as a baby by her father the Duke of Kent. They stayed at Woolbrook Cottage, now the Royal Glen Hotel. It was said that a boy, shooting at birds, fired a pellet which broke the window of the room where the baby lay, and grazed her dress. The Duke died in Sidmouth in 1820.

The sea wall was built in 1835, and the esplanade, which is the only description one could use to describe this lovely wide Victorian promenade, has houses dating from 1837, still retaining a delightful period air, the nineteenth-century atmosphere preserved. Until the harbour silted up in 1450, this was an important port.

The best beach is one called Jacob's ladder, located round a small hill. There is a county standard cricket ground, laid out in 1820 and at one time the Grand Duchess Helen of Russia stayed in a house which overlooked it. Nearby is the famous **Donkey Sanctuary** (Unusual Outings), open to the public. There is a first class Folk Festival in August with singers and dancers from all over the world.

Silverton   Map 4 Aa

This is one of the oldest villages in Devon, and an important settlement before the Norman Conquest. Fore Street and High Street have beautiful thatch and cob cottages with tall chimneys known as 'Hall Houses', built during the reign of Henry VII and Henry VIII. Now two storeys high, they originally had no floor division and the fire was in the middle of each room.

You could walk around the lanes and fields here for days in the rich, soft countryside. The church of St Mary is mostly fifteenth century; in 1863 someone removed the old screen, which was probably Jacobean and chopped it up for firewood. One mile east of the village is Silverton Park where the Earl of Egremont built a large mansion, of which nothing remains except a classical looking façade which was the stable block. The house itself was based on a version of the east front of Buckingham Palace with 187 rooms, 150 cellars, and 230 marble mantel-pieces. The doorknobs were made of amber and one of the baths was cut from a solid block of marble. The Earl died without an heir, and by November 1901 the mansion was derelict; it was then blown up. Apart from the stables, all that remains is an underpass, known as the 'Deep Cut' to locals.

S

Among the village industries in the past were weaving, farming and paper making, the Silverton Mill still makes paper beside the river Culm.

Slapton   Map 4 Ac

Have a look at **Slapton Ley Nature Reserve** first, for this encompasses a fairly unique freshwater lake separated from the sea by a raised bank of sand and shingle. Probably stabilised about 3,000 years ago, the lake is said to be about 1,000-years-old. Here grows the yellow horned poppy, sea radish, sea carrot, restharrow, sea campion and many other plants. The reeds were once used for thatching. If you stand on the little bridge that leads to the village you can see beds of flags and bog bean. Here is the stopping place for birds migrating in spring and autumn, a choice spot for the Field Centre to study the flora and fauna. Over 233 bird species have been recorded, including gulls, terns, grebes, gannets, and the Arctic skua. Ducks, swans and geese congregate on the roadside to be fed. As you stand there in the hush of the evening, enshrouded by the timeless hills and sand, you could be forgiven for imagining Excalibur itself arising; such is the magic spell it weaves. Slapton Ley has however seen much action and violence in its time, from early battles between the English and French, with clouds of arrows whistling through the air, and stones thrown by the wives of English bowmen, to the present century with the rehearsal for the invasion of Normandy on D-Day by the Americans. Live ammunition and bombs were used, for on 13 November 1943 the inhabitants of this area were told to make immediate plans to evacuate their homes in six weeks. This strategy covered an area in the form of a triangle from the coast to the hillside village of Blackawton at its apex, absorbing seven parishes, 180 farms, 750 families, and 3,000 people. They had to move everything from the turnips in the fields to the corn in the ricks. Some died, some committed suicide, some never returned, many homes were destroyed. People in the rest of England had no idea of this occurrence, and all that is left now to remind us is the memorial which stands halfway along the road where the Royal Sands Hotel once stood; erected not to the dead, but as a gesture of thanks to the living from the U.S.A.

Inland is the village of Slapton with old narrow streets and thatched cottages. The church of St James the Great has stood there for over 650 years. Inside the main porch is a sanctuary ring, for the canon law provided sanctuary for a limited time for any criminal who could elude his pursuers and reach a consecrated place. It sufficed if he could touch the ring. In 1372 Sir Guy de Brien founded a Chantry for four chaplains, the ruins of which can still be seen, standing in the garden of Chantry House, which has a delightful iron bridge crossing the road leading to a secret garden on the other side. In summer it is festooned with sweetly perfumed wisteria.

South of Slapton is Torcross, part of the area evacuated during the Second World War for the Americans to use as a rehearsal ground for D-Day. In 1979 it was almost destroyed by terrible gales. A man called Laurie Emberson, who lived in the village, wrote an account of the storm, *The Torcross Disaster*. It is a story of complete dedication by one man to save his village by forcing the authorities to build an adequate defence against the sea. Not only is it an example to anyone trying to fight bureaucracy, but his descriptions of the night of the storm are quite brilliant, and it is almost impossible to believe as you stand looking at the tranquil sea on a warm summer afternoon. He says, '. . . a tell tale hairline crack in the sea road appeared . . . and disappeared into the rocks . . . the first big wave came crashing in . . . then the gurgling rush of green water poured down the sides of the houses . . . darkness had fallen and it was still an hour and a quarter before high tide . . .' Now you can see the completed wall for which he fought.

South Molton Map 1 Bb

This always seems a very cheery little market town with many Georgian and Victorian houses. Originally it was an

S

Anglo Saxon settlement, owing its later prosperity to the wool trade, its position on the route of coaches passing through it, and its nearness to the iron and copper mines of North Molton. In the middle of Broad Street is the Medical Hall with an iron verandah and heavy columns. In the Guildhall, which hangs over the pavement in a series of arches, is **The South Molton Museum** of local history which includes some of the oldest fire-fighting equipment in Devon much needed during the eighteenth century when so many of the Devon towns seemed to catch fire.

The church of St Mary Magdalene is fifteenth century, reached through a lovely iron gateway and avenues of trees, a kind of secret green place. The stone carving inside is beautiful. Hugh Squier built and endowed the Grammar School.

The **Quince Honey Farm** housing wild Exmoor honey bees in their natural habitat is well worth a visit.

West of South Molton is Chittlehampton and the **Cobbaton Combat Vehicles Museum** with a private collection of Second World War vehicles and equipment. The fine church, famous for the height of its tower, is dedicated to St Urith or Hieritha, a Celtic saint martyred by the parishioners who cut her into pieces with their scythes. The well at the end of the village is said to be the spot where this occurred.

Visitors to Highbullen Hotel at nearby Chittlehamholt may have a surprise when they order a drink for Sir Laurence Olivier is a regular guest and has been known to serve behind the bar.

Staverton Map 3 Bb

The station here has been beautifully restored as part of the Dart Valley Railway complex, and is often used in films for television. The Sea Trout is a first-class Inn, but the bridge here is its real glory, erected in 1413 with seven arches and little 'refuges' built into the parapet for pedestrians. Like many ancient Devon bridges, it was built by local bishops who sold 'Indulgences', 40 days work on a bridge brought remission of sins. Every year the annual raft race passes underneath in August. Nearby Riverford Farm provides a tour of farm implements and animals, all in working order. The village is famous too for its cider.

Gazing down into the river, it seems the water is almost static, reflecting pink willow herb and green trees, yet the gentleness is deceptive for it can become a menacing torrent as indicated in the story of John Edmonds who, on 17 August 1840, his wedding day, set off with his young bride from Staverton church; as they reached the ford a great wall of water rose and swept them away without warning. Her body was found entangled in the branches of a tree, while his was not discovered for another three weeks. The poor terrified horse struggled in the foaming water and was carried over Totnes weir.

Sticklepath   see Okehampton

Stoke Gabriel   Map 4 Ab

Another lovely village on the banks of the Dart river is Stoke Gabriel. St Mary and St Gabriel church is very old, accompanied by an ancient yew probably 1,500-years-old and rather spooky. Some years ago the squire built a weir so that the upper part of the creek would not be tidal, and you can walk across this at low tide. The Dart Salmon Fishing Authority operates from here keeping a strict surveillance. If you have time, for the sake of historical interest, it is worth spending a few minutes driving up the road towards Berry Pomeroy to see Parliament House, a little thatched cottage, outside which stands a stone stating that William of Orange held his first parliament in England here on Guy Fawkes Day 1688. Before that, John Davis the navigator had been born in 1543 at nearby Sandridge Barton.

More history surrounds the house called Maisonette, standing at the top of the steep lane which runs down to

T

Duncannon Creek. At one time called Stoke Gabriel
House, it was built for a mistress of George IV, who came
all the way from Brighton to visit the lady by post-chaise.
In the tiny creek stand three houses, once the boats coming
up and down river used to stop here for people to come
ashore.

Opposite, two small rivers run into Bow Creek, the river
Wash and the river Harbourne. Here is Tuckenhay, a village
which once handled road stone, had two paper mills, one
making five pound notes, and a corn mill. One of the paper
mills operated until 1960, and has now been made into
holiday flats. There is a delightful pub, The Malsters Arms,
where you can sit and eat or drink whilst watching the
ducks, swans, and people trying to moor their boats. It is a
breathtakingly beautiful spot; in summer the air is heavy
with the perfume of roses and honeysuckle in the hedges.
The passing of time has left the village untouched, even the
remains of the houses where gas was produced in 1806,
cannot spoil the serenity.

Tavistock   Map 3 Ab

The first impression of this town is one of cleanliness,
spaciousness and a sense of order, but perhaps it is most
famous for its Goosey Fair during the second week of
October. Many of the elegant buildings are the work of the
Duke of Bedford in the nineteenth century. This is one of
those parishes in Devon so full of old houses, history and
lovely views, that a week is too little time to spend
exploring. The existing town is the product of its two main
owners namely the Earls and Dukes of Bedford, and
Tavistock Abbey. They created the town but it was the
Russell family who gave the place its character.

In A.D. 974 a hamlet existed with its own chapel, and it
was the establishment of the Abbey which gave impetus to
the village. Centuries later it was still a hive of industry, for
here one of the largest printing presses was set up and a
monk named Don Thomas Ryehard became the first
printer in Devon.

The Russells, later the Earls and Dukes of Bedford, acquired the borough with a vast estate in 1539, and from then on exerted strong political influence.

Tavistock was involved in the tin industry from the twelfth century onwards, and in 1305 it was established as a Stannary Town, where the tin mined in Devon had to be weighed and stamped before being sold. Later, the cloth industry took over; copper mining then reached its peak in the 1860s when the famous Devon Great Consol at Blanchdown was at the peak of production. It was one of the richest copper mines in the world. However, it closed down in 1901. These deserted sites are worth a visit, their beauty desolate and buzzard haunted, pervaded perhaps also by the singing of the ghosts of the bal maidens, who at dawn and dusk, walked along the sides of the Tamar valley to work, hammering the mineral ore into small pieces. It was for the transport of this copper that the canal was built in 1803, taken from the river at the centre of the town to run four miles to Morwellham Quay, passing through a two mile tunnel. The ore was taken from the mines by barge along the canal, the men lying down in the tunnel section and 'walking' along the roof. When the copper ran out, the miners turned to the production of arsenic used to destroy the boll weevil on the American cotton plantations, but even that dried up and it was said there was enough arsenic stored in jars to have killed every living creature on the face of the earth. It is difficult now to appreciate that it was a mining town like Barnsley or Wigan. However the Dukes of Bedford ensured an orderly expansion, building model houses along the Yelverton road for the miners, remodelling the centre of the town in the 1840s, building the Guildhall in Gothic style, and Gothicising the Bedford Hotel, which had been a dwelling house in 1725 built by Jacob Saunders, a rich Presbyterian merchant. The dining room of this delightful hotel is part of the original building.

The Abbey Bridge was built in 1764, and the Vigo Bridge in 1773. Nearby is the Quaker cemetery with clipped cypresses, weeping willows and copper beeches.

T

The Abbey church ran parallel to the existing parish church, with four entrances, three of which survive; Court Gate at the southeast corner of Bedford Square, the building known as Betsy Grimbal's Tower, a nun who was said to be murdered by her monk lover and the others which are within the church tower. In the churchyard there is a tree said to be grown from the bud of the original thorn of Glastonbury which has white blossom in May and at Christmas. In the square are some wooden seats, one bears the inscription as a warning to vandals – 'Never Cut A Friend.'

The Library is the western part of the Old Abbey Gateway; the Chevalier's House in Market Street is said to be where King Charles made his H.Q. during the Civil War. On Friday there is a Pannier Market forming a meeting place for locals from a wide area, and on Creber's Corner in Brook Street stands the shop run by the same family since 1881, which has a mail order section for sending hampers all over the world. Step inside the door and the heady aroma of all the goodies on sale reaches your nostrils from freshly roasted coffee to malt whisky.

Tavistock's most famous son is Sir Francis Drake, born at Crowndale Farm, sadly now destroyed, but his statue stands proudly at the entrance to the town, of which the one on the Hoe is a replica. Of the Bedfords, the best known are probably Lord John Russell, and his grandson, the philosopher Bertrand Russell. Lord John represented Tavistock in Parliament and helped frame the Reform Bill of 1832. He was Prime Minister twice. John Pym born in 1584, was the father of English democracy, and most recently, Michael Heseltine, was the last representative of the Tavistock constituency. Another famous resident was Mrs Bray, wife of the vicar, who wrote about Tavistock in the Victorian era, and corresponded with the poet, Robert Southey. The vicarage has altered little since her time. Nearby Kelly College Public School was founded by Admiral Kelly in 1877 and now admits girls.

T

Teignmouth   Map 4 Ab

Fanny Burney aged 21, wrote in her journal that she was
spending two months of the summer of 1773 with her
young married friend, Maria Rishton, in 'Tingmouth', the
name the locals gave it in those days. She was a keeper of
the robes of Queen Charlotte, chiefly known for her diaries
and letters in 1778 and 1840, and her novels *Evelina* and
Cecilia. Her *Tingmouth Journal* gives a wonderful picture of
those days when Fanny went for a bathe, a new activity,
for Teignmouth was one of the first coastal towns to
become a seaside resort. Keats also stayed here and a
plaque records this at No. 20 Northumberland Place. He
stayed for two months in 1818, but had very mixed feelings
about Devon because of the wet weather. He said: '... the
primroses are out – but you are in!' However he did go to
Dawlish Fair and finished his poem 'Isabella' or 'The Pot
of Basil' in Teignmouth. He also got to know quite a
number of the local girls, including the ones at the bonnet
shop opposite the house where he lodged, but he never
mentions the local poet, Winthrop Mackworth Praed, a
brilliant orator and member of Parliament.

Lady Harriet Silvester too wrote a diary in 1824: 'Sat.
17. Went over to Teignmouth, a small place originally but
much increased by lodging houses and libraries, Ball
Rooms etc. The shore is remarkably good for bathing'. She
also met Luny, the painter and visited the Regatta.

By 1817 it had become a very popular watering place
with 16 bathing machines. In the autumn of 1894 a terrible
storm battered the town, and great slabs of stone were lifted
at the base of Brook Hill over the river. Fears ran high for
the safety of the pier, which had been built in 1860, but it
survived. The town was heavily bombed during the Second
World War when 88 people were killed and 228 houses
damaged, including the Town Hall, the Library and
Hospital. In 1968 Morgan Giles, the last of the
Teignmouth shipyards closed, and in the same year Donald
Crowhurst sailed from the town on his ill-fated voyage.

There have been happier occurrences. In 1975, 200

Tyards off the Church Rocks, Simon Burton, a teenager, discovered a bronze six pounder gun made between the years 1550 and 1650, probably from a Genoese or Florentine Trading Galley. Since then many more artefacts have been brought to light, including more cannon and a large copper cooking pot with bones still inside. Although Simon has not been able to trace the name of the ship, it is thought to have been a Venetian Galley rowed by three hundred slaves, probably wrecked between 1500 and 1520.

The town has a long and bloody history of Danish and French invaders, and was actually burnt twice in 1340 and 1690. The present town is the result of a union between East and West Teignmouth, separated by a stream called the Tame, now covered in and forgotten. The Roman Catholic church is the work of Hansom who also invented the hansom cab. As a port it has a thriving and ever expanding trade, particularly in the shipment of ball clay all over the world brought from the Teign valley. In 1821 George Templer of Stover built the New Quay for the shipment of granite from his Haytor quarries.

The Den, six acres of well-planted gardens, runs parallel with the front and there are all kinds of amenities including the pier, a bowling green, tennis courts, an aquarium and above the town, a golf course. The lagoon known as the Salty lies behind the bar of land at the estuary mouth with fishing and pleasure boats. Here are two good pubs, and Salty Cottage where a boat hull frames the door. Bitton House, built by Viscount Exmouth, with views across the estuary, is now council offices, but the original cannon are still on show. Below the Ness stand the Parson and Clerk rocks where it is said the Devil caused a wicked priest and his clerk to be driven over the cliff and two huge masses of sandstone became their grave monument. Smuggling was rife here too and a windmill high above Penny's Cottage on the Teignmouth to Torquay road acted as a signalling post for them, its sails set in a predetermined position to warn of trouble.

Tiverton Map 2 Ab

Tiverton stands where the rivers Exe and Lowman meet, now a market town, it was once the chief industrial area of Devon, founded by the Saxons around A.D. 650, and later becoming a leading woollen town. It has a Georgian flavour, for many of the houses were burnt down in 1732 and rebuilt, but without doubt the best way to discover the history of the town is to visit its museum, one of the largest and most comprehensive in the west of England.

Tiverton Museum stands in St Andrew's Street. It was started by volunteer enthusiasts in 1960 in two borrowed rooms. In 1977 it received commendation and an award in the National Heritage Museum of the Year competition. Much of the credit must go to the work and enthusiasm of Alderman W.P. Authers, the Curator.

The collection covers almost every aspect of the history and life of the region. Entering the forecourt, you pass an eight feet high undershot water-wheel which, for 100 years,

Holcombe Court, Holcombe Rogus

Tdrove the machinery in the Victorian laundry. Inside there is a section on Blundell's School, known as the Eton of the west and founded in 1599 by Peter Blundell who had very humble beginnings in the wool trade, but died a wealthy bachelor at 80-years-old. The original old school was built in 1604 and it is said some of the roof timbers came from the wrecked ships of the Armada. It moved to the 100 acres it now covers in 1882; many famous people both taught and learned within its walls. Samuel Wesley, brother of John and Charles, was a headmaster; Jan Ridd gives a description of a fight which took place on the grass section known as the Ironing Box in *Lorna Doone*, for the author R.D. Blackmore was a pupil. Bampfylde Moore Carew, son of the rector of Bickleigh and one of the best-known Devon families, later became King of the Beggars. He was also a pupil at Blundell's School, although expelled for hunting when he should have been studying. Parson Jack Russell, Frederick Temple, Archbishop of Canterbury, and Lord Stokes of British Leyland were also past pupils.

In 1816 John Heathcoat, accompanied by 200 of his workers, walked from Loughborough after the Luddites had burnt his factory, to Tiverton where he re-started his business. Many of the present day Tiverton families are descendents of those who walked with him. He invented the first lace-making machine, which is now in the museum; 23 feet long and weighing six tons with more than 10,000 delicate parts, it had one inch clearance at each side on its way through the door. Later Heathcoat invented a second machine on an entirely different principle, and within years there were several hundred of these at Tiverton, driven by the waters of the river Exe. This company made the veiling worn by H.M. the Queen at her marriage, and one hundred years earlier, Queen Adelaide had also given royal patronage to the Heathcoat products.

St Peter's church was built in the fifteenth century by rich wool merchants, John Greenway providing the porch and chapel, and the Almshouses. From the church, turn left into Castle Street, where an old medieval leat flows down the middle. At the end of Newport Street in Bampton

Street is the Old Corn Market where John Wesley preached.

Tiverton is an important manufacturing centre for many other commodities as well as lace, namely brewing, paper making, elastic thread, and many commodities produced within the town from the raw materials right through to the finished article. Five years ago the **English Lace School** (Local Industry) opened to teach the traditional craft of lace-making by hand, the only one of its kind, however it is shortly to move to Rockbeare near Exeter.

Tiverton Castle was started in 1106 in the Norman style, with much building completed by Richard de Redvers, the 1st Earl of Devon, but it was besieged by the Roundheads and mostly destroyed by Fairfax in 1643, whose lucky cannon stroke broke the chain of the drawbridge. However there is a fourteenth-century gatehouse left and also parts of the Tudor mansion.

Many celebrities have been connected with the town, including Thomas Rippon, chief cashier of the Bank of England, and Basil Cameron the conductor; in 1835 the M.P. for the town was Lord Palmerston. The **Grand Western Canal** (Country Parks) has its terminus at Tiverton and the eleven and a half miles of this picturesque waterway are worth visiting. Originally it was intended to reach Topsham, but the coming of the railway caused the owners to abandon the idea; it was used mainly for carrying stone from the quarries near Burlescombe to the terminus at the canal basin by narrow barges pulled by horses, reaching the Somerset border at Holcombe Rogus. The parkland provides a tranquil background for walking, fishing, boating or floating along in the horse drawn barge. There is also a nature reserve, and ample car parking.

Knightshayes Court (Gardens), two miles to the north, is an imposing sandstone building designed in 1868 by William Burges. It is very Victorian both inside and out, the billiard room now a restaurant. It was built for Sir John Heathcoat-Amory M.P., grandson of the mill pioneer, John, and bequeathed eventually to the National Trust in 1973. The gardens are really lovely.

T

Topsham   Map 4 Aa

Although Exeter may now include Topsham within its
boundaries, the town remains an entity in its own right.
Here are lovely side streets and pubs to be explored; the
waterfront on a warm summer evening has a serenity
accentuated by people paddling about in boats, or sitting in
a beer garden at the water's edge. It lies on a promontory of
the east bank of the river Exe where the estuary starts to
open up and the mud flats are a haven for waterfowl. It was
used by the Romans as a coastal port for Exeter, and was
also a shipbuilding town. It traded woollen goods for fruit
and wine, and joined in the Newfoundland fishing trade. In
those days, on the river side of the Strand, stood the quays
and the yards, which are now gardens. Here also are the
beautiful merchants' Dutch houses with their uniquely
curved gables. The Topsham merchants traded in Holland
and brought back not only this fashion in architecture, but
the bricks as ballast. Shell House dates back to 1718 with a
fine scallop shell in the hollow of its doorway. From the
streets you can glimpse the enchanting courtyards, and if
you are lucky enough to be invited inside, you will see
lovely staircases, panelling and plastered ceilings. Some
have underground escape routes for smugglers.

At No. 25 is **Topsham Museum** built up by Dorothy
Holman in the old sail loft on the first floor, herself a
descendent of famous shipbuilders. The Salutation Inn in
Fore Street dates from 1726, the church has a Norman
font, with a wolf bearing an apple in its mouth. The
Passage Inn, slate-hung, has a date stone 1788, but the inn is
much older with a lovely waterside garden.

The death of a woman in Topsham in her late-thirties
has its bearing on literary history, for Mrs Tryphena Gale,
whose husband was a wine merchant in Fore Street, was
Thomas Hardy's cousin.

The town was originally Topa's Ham, so Topsam is
probably the correct pronunciation. At Newport, on the
northern fringe of the village, the D'Urban family achieved
immortality, for Durban in South Africa is named after Sir
Benjamin D'Urban.

The Romans built what is now the Topsham road into Isca Dumnoniorum, or Exeter, to their forum in the tribal capital. The view from the churchyard, which is set on a small cliff overhanging the river, is breathtakingly beautiful when the evening tide is coming in. Here sat George Gissing who wrote *The Private Papers of Henry Ryecroft*.

Torbay see Torquay

Torcross see Slapton

Torquay Map 4 Ab

About 100,000 years ago settlers occupied **Kent's Cavern** (Archaeological Sites) just off the Babbacombe Road, the oldest recognisable human dwellings in Britain, where men took shelter from the cold of the last Ice Age. Implements have been found of paleolithic man, and similar animal bones to those at Buckfastleigh; also the bones of mammoth, cave bears, and sabre toothed tigers. It was inhabited during the Roman occupation, for pieces of pottery have been found belonging to the earliest Iron Age invaders, small groups of peasant farmers known as Iron Age A. There are wonderful collections of these objects to be seen in the Natural History Museum.

Torquay was once the centre for smuggling on the western side of the South Devon coast. A case of wrecking took place at Petitor, St Marychurch. Cows grazing on the cliff tops were decorated at night with lanterns dangling from their horns, and a native called Drake was said to have had a hand in this business. He lived in a little cottage in a hollow of the cliffs. The place is still called Drake's Hole. Rattenbury, one of the best known smugglers, took, on his last expedition in January 1836, two tubs of brandy late one night by cart from Torquay to Newton Bushel, now Newton Abbot. A mile from his goal he was stopped by excise men but escaped. Women joined in this smuggling and one old Torquay woman hawked spirits in a pig's bladder concealed

T

under her cloak round St Marychurch and Market Street.
Thirza Rendle hid a tub in her bed and faked labour when
her home was searched. Also at Babbacombe lived the man
the authorities couldn't hang, John Babbacombe Lee, who
worked for, and killed, Miss Emma Keyse at her home.
Three times the noose was put round his neck; three times
the gallows failed to work.

The town could in fact be called modern, since it is
mostly nineteenth-century. There was only a tiny hamlet
known as Tor Quay in the middle ages, but it wasn't until
the seventeenth and eighteenth centuries when the English
fleet lay in Torbay during the wars with the French that
the fleet anchored long enough for the officers to bring
their wives with them. However, even in 1821 the
population was still only about 2,000, just over 160 years
ago, which today is unbelievable. Doctors in the cities used
to send patients to enjoy this mild climate, particularly
those with consumption as T.B. was then called.

In August 1833 the Duchess of Kent and the young
Victoria called at Torquay, landing at what is now Victoria
Parade. They spent the night at the Royal Hotel, a plaque
recalling this on the front of the building. There was
however a tragedy for a bootmaker tried to present the
princess with a pair of boots, and an over enthusiastic
coastguard was careless with his bayonet, blinding the poor
man. The Duchess, hearing of this, had him sent to
hospital at her own expense, with an annuity for life.
Another plaque shows the house on Harbour Quay where
Elizabeth Barrett Browning stayed. She took a quite
understandable dislike to the place when her brother was
drowned in a boating accident in the bay.

Travelling was made easier when the railway came to
Torquay in 1848, and a couple of years later it won the title
of 'Queen of Watering Places'. By then all the villas and
terraces of houses were starting to extend along the north
shore for about a mile. From a boat in the bay it is clear
that in those days they knew something about planning for
beauty. There are lovely wooded drives and terraces,
carefully following the contours of the hills; two thirds of

the town is rocks, trees and gardens, the whole classically
graceful with white stuccoed houses with big windows,
columned and pilastered, set in wide road-ways. Much of
this is due to the Palk family, and the Carys, who then
owned most of Torquay. Sir Lawrence Palk enlarged and
partly rebuilt the Royal Hotel, as well as starting to build
the inner harbour. Then, as so often happens, the people
with the money who had taken Torquay to their hearts and
spent so much time there, decided to holiday abroad, so in
the 1870s the growth of the town slowed up.

Meanwhile St Marychurch on the north side had started
to grow, and also the village of Cockington, whose name
comes from Cocca's Farm in the Domesday Book. S.H.
Burton in his book on Devon villages, says that many
people think the village and forge date from that time. He
reveals that in 1800 all the buildings, except the church,
were demolished and new ones built in a different position
so that the view from sixteenth-century Cockington Court
set in a lovely park, should not be spoiled. This was the
home of the Carys, and later the Mallocks, but now belongs
to Torquay Corporation. The Drum Inn was designed and
built in 1934, Lutyens being the architect. In 1892
Torquay became a municipal borough and in 1900
absorbed Babbacombe, Chelston, Ilsham, and St
Marychurch. In some ways it has lost its exclusive
Victorian and Edwardian style, but it still retains that
lovely almost Mediterranean feel, exuded by big villas and
shady drives.

Torre Abbey (Museums) was founded in 1196 and the
twelfth-century entrance to the chapter house can still be
seen, incorporating the early fourteenth-century gatehouse
and guest hall. The Spanish Barn still stands, built in the
twelfth century as a 124 feet high tithe barn, where 400
prisoners from the flagship *Neustra Senora del Rosario* of
the Armada fleet were held. The grounds too are beautiful
with a rock garden, rose garden and trial flower beds. The
Clear Span House, which replaced the original Palm House
in 1969, contains plants from all over the world, including
white daturas from Peru, orchids behind a locked cage,

Tbananas, tangerines and papyrus. All the parks are
beautifully kept with wide-open grass spaces. At night the
coloured lights reflecting in the water are a magical sight.
St John's church stands on a remarkable site cut into the
hill with a huge lighted cross on the side. First built in
1823 and added to in 1861, it is said to be haunted by a
past organist. **Babbacombe Model Village** (Unusual
Outings) is worth a visit, set in a steep valley with groups of
models, portraying a church wedding, a farm, a golf course
and many local features with a stream and street lights;
each little home is also lighted inside at night. The model is
a wonderful and enchanting sight. There is also a life-size
cliff railway running down the cliffs to the beach.

Torquay has an aquarium on the harbour, **Aqualand**
(Aquariums), said to be the largest in the southwest, and of
course boasts the five star Imperial Hotel with its
prestigious gastronomic weekends.

Thatcher Rock, Torquay

T

Totnes Map 3 Bb

This must be one of the most beautiful and interesting towns in the whole of Devon, built on a hill rising from the banks of the river Dart, it extends to the suburb of Bridgetown. It is first mentioned during the reign of Edgar in A.D. 959, when coins were minted. There are the remains of the Norman **Totnes Castle** on a mound above the town, rising to 50 feet and crowned with a small circular keep. There are also substantial remains of the old town walls.

The first bridge was built by the time of King John, certainly before 1216, and rebuilt in 1828. There is too, a brand new bridge bypassing the town, built near the site of a temporary structure which the Americans erected to improve their communications with the coastal area before D-Day.

One of the many legends about Totnes relates that Brutus the Trojan was the coloniser of Britain, and Totnes the first place on which he set foot. A granite block can be seen just above No. 15 Fore Street. 'Here I stand and here I rest and this good town shall be called Totnes.' However it is more feasible that this granite boulder was left when the waters of the river Dart flowed at a much higher level during the Ice Age.

One of the leaders of the Norman campaign in the west was Judhael, who was granted the Royal Burgh of Totnes, and many other manors in Devon for his services to William the Conqueror; he settled here and became known as Judhael of Totnes, where he founded a Benedictine Priory.

During the reign of Henry VIII the town was second only to Exeter in wealth. This lasted throughout the Elizabethan Age, but by the 1660s the industrial history of the town was virtually ended. This was due to several reasons, one of which was that they did not move with the times and develop the serge industry.

Walking down Fore Street, you pass the Butterwalk whose name derives from the fact that butter had to be kept

Tin the shade when it was sold in open markets. Many of the lovely old houses down here are slate-hung, like so many in this part of Devon; these are mostly sixteenth and seventeenth-century. The church of St Mary standing on the north side of the street was rebuilt in 1432 with a magnificent rood screen of Beer stone. Behind it stands the Guildhall, the older part of which dates back to 1553. On the other side of the street is the **Elizabethan House Town Museum** with two entrances, one from the street to the old merchant's shop, and down the passage, the door to the house. The well worn staircase is spiralled round a great pole said to be the mast from an Elizabethan ship. There are carved fireplaces and many little closets, all holding lovely treasures from the past, including a pair of carved ivory false teeth. There is also a computer exhibition presented to the Museum by International Computers Ltd. in recognition of Charles Babbage, an old pupil of the Edward VI Grammar School, who is known as the 'Father of the Modern Computer'. The Grammar School, a lovely old Georgian House with Corinthian pillars, was founded in 1533, and granted a charter by Edward VI.

Many people will have forgotten, or have never known, that races used to be held here on Wednesday and Thursday of the first week in September. The racecourse is now an industrial site, but until 1939 tents and marquees were put up there and some 50,000 people were known to attend. The main feature was the Somerset Steeplechase run over four miles, starting near Bourton Hall, now the Chateau Bellevue, and crossing the river. The Kingsbridge Inn is the oldest pub, at the top of the town. A house stood here in A.D. 990 where shepherds would sleep on their feet leaning on their crooks until the gates were opened and they could enter the town with their flocks. In contrast, at the bottom of the town, is the Royal Seven Stars Hotel, the hall a flagged courtyard where the horses once passed through to the stables at the back; it is now covered in and part of the hall of the hotel. The building dates from 1660 or even before. Defoe once stayed here when he was working on his book *A Tour of England*

and Wales published in 1724. He was charged only a shilling by the landlord for a salmon dinner and considered Totnes a very cheap place in which to live. Today, to remind people of the history of the town, Tuesdays during the summer are Elizabethan days when everyone dresses up in period costume.

On the Plains at the bottom of the town is a statue to William John Wills who was the first man to cross the Australian continent with Burke – he died of starvation on the return journey

The river is tidal from Totnes to Dartmouth, and the oblong flat by the west bank of the river leads to the sheds and wharves of the quays. Here boats were built at the time of the Armada, and during the Second World War, minesweepers were built of wood to safeguard them from magnetic mines. DUKWs were also provided for the invasion of Normandy. Ships still bring timber up to the wharves, and the Island is a delightful place to sit and watch the river and the world go by. If you want to see something unusual and interesting, then visit the nearby **Totnes Motor Museum**, an Aladdin's Cave, sited in an old cider store, run by Richard and Trisha Pilkington. Trisha is well-known as a Grand Prix driver in her scarlet Alfa Romeo. There is everything here from the Amphicar, an amphibious beast as happy on land as in the water, to the 1904 Rover 'Car' Tandem tricycle, also 'Wheels', a paradise of models for sale.

There is a certain magic about Totnes, perhaps best described by the author Sean O'Casey who, at the suggestion of George Bernard Shaw, sent his two boys to school in Dartington, and settled in Totnes which he described thus:'Totnes is set out so that its main street sinks slowly down a slender hill in the valley of the Dart...there is nothing sham about Totnes. All its shops are genuine examples of Tudor or Jacobean housing.' There isn't much doubt that Totnes and Devon turned a wild terrorist Marxist into a gentle poet. *Sunset and Evening Star*, the final book of his biography, gives some of the most beautiful descriptions of Devon and of Totnes in particular: 'The town is like a greyhaired lady with a young face sitting calmly ... in an orchard of ageing trees, drowsy with the scent of the apples about to fall but never do...' He died in 1965 and was cremated, his ashes scattered in Golders Green Cemetery, but certain it is his Irish spirit still haunts Totnes.

Two Bridges   Map 3 Bb

The hotel here was originally The Saracen's Head, named later after the two bridges built in 1780 and 1928 over the West Dart river. It is a good base from which to walk and see such places as **Wistman's Wood** (Nature Reserves); 700 hundred yards long, the stunted and misshapen oak trees are said to be 500-years-old, possibly the last remaining part of the primaeval forest that once covered Dartmoor, providing a sacred site for the Druids and very eerie with hidden adders among the boulders.

Two miles up the river Dart is the point where Drake's Devonport leat was taken out and you can follow this for quite a distance. At Huccaby stands the last house to be built in a day on Dartmoor, Jolly Lane Cott, built on Midsummer Day in 1832 by Tom Satterley, an ostler at the pub, and Sally his 18-year-old wife. This brought right of tenure and many perks such as peat, grazing, bracken for bedding and stones for building. They started work at sunrise and had the roof on and the fire lighted by sunset.

Uffculme   see Cullompton

Wembury   Map 3 Ac

The church of St Werburgh has been a landmark on this wild coast since the fourteenth century, the date of the tower; the rest of the building is fifteenth century. In 1683 Sir Warwick Hele built the almshouses with the chapel in the centre where services were held. There is a monument to him in the church with his wife and ten children. The ancestors of the writer Galsworthy came from here, and he describes the church in *Swan Song*. His antecedents can be traced back to the twelfth century and some of them farmed in this parish. Offshore is the Great Mew Stone, and there is a lovely walk from here to Stoke house, about seven miles, with a ferry over the river Yealm en route, and many secluded coves reached only on foot.

Westward Ho! see Appledore

Widecombe-in-the-Moor Map 3 Bb

As you drive down the hill into Widecombe, and wherever you come from it will be down a hill, it is like stepping back in time, for most of the buildings, the fields, the lanes and hedges are much today as they have been for centuries. A typical moorland village with church, inn, church house and smithy at its heart, is surrounded by the cottages and

Widecombe-in-the Moor

W

farms of families who have lived there for generations. There cannot be many corners of the world that have not at least heard the old song of Widecombe Fair and Uncle Tom Cobley, and yet there is so much more to the village than that. In spite of the fact that it is accused of being commercialised, Widecombe preserves its character, but if it had not developed, it would probably have died like so many other moorland villages. Those travellers who are warned off by threats of pixies and painted mugs, miss a close-up of a village which for 700 years has been vital to the life on the eastern moor.

Widecombe lies in the broad valley of the East Webburn. The parish covers nearly 11,000 acres and many of the buildings are not only beautiful but carry fascinating histories. The **Church House** (Church Buildings), built about 1500, now belongs to the National Trust; years ago, when people wanted to attend church, they often had to travel for miles over the Moor, and were glad to be able to rest before the service, for that purpose church councils built such places. It was once an almshouse and also a village school, described by the school mistress in 1884 as: 'so small as to be without accommodation for cleanliness or even decency...' The church, St Pancras, was licensed for baptism and funeral in 1260, known as The Cathedral of the Moor; miners' money helped to pay for it. The date in its history which is outstanding is 21 October 1638 when a freak storm destroyed part of the building, killing four people and injuring 62, mostly by burning. The story is told on a board on the right-hand side of the belfry, written by Richard Hill, the village schoolmaster. The local people knew of course that it was the Devil who visited the church that day in search of Jan Reynolds who had sold him his soul. Lucifer had been seen earlier at the Tavistock Inn at Poundsgate where the beer had sizzled as it went down his throat, and the money he gave the landlord had turned to dried leaves. The Rev. George Lyde was the minister then at Widecombe and in the pulpit at the time. He was unharmed, but one man had 'his head cloven and his brains thrown upon the ground...a dog was whirled about

130

towards the door and fell down stark dead'. To more
pleasant subjects; don't miss the memorial in the form of an
anagram to Mary Elford . . . 'Fear My Lord'.

Another lovely old building in the square is Glebe
House, a sixteenth-century farm during the boom of the tin
mining industry, now a gift shop, retaining the huge open
hearth and bread oven. The smithy can still be seen and is
preserved as a tiny museum with even a man trap on view.
It has all been kept just as it was with hood and anvil in
place; close your eyes and imagine if you can the smell of
the burning hoof as the horse was shod. Just beyond is the
old Saxon well said never to run dry.

The Green is the heart of the village, its proper name
being Butte Park from the days when the bowmen of
England used these places for bow and arrow practice. The
Old Inn dates back to the fourteenth century. In January
1977 it was damaged by fire and firemen from five stations
were needed to control it. Today, perfectly restored, it
offers first class food and drink, a warm welcome and a
benign ghost. The village sign stands on the Green,
showing the legend of Uncle Tom. Simon Northmore
played the role for over two decades at the Annual Fair on
the second Tuesday in September. Did Tom Pearse really
exist? Did all those men really ride the poor old grey mare,
whose name we never knew? The song was first published
in 1880 by W.H. Davies of Kingsbridge, and later in 1889
by Sabine Baring Gould. Despite research the matter
remains unresolved, although there were, and still are,
people with names like Tom Cobley, Jan Stewer, and Bill
Brewer. One of Uncle Tom's descendents is still farming
the same land that his ancestor worked 200 years ago. The
song itself was sung by the Devon Regiment in the South
African War.

The other great character who lived at Widecombe was
Beatrice Chase whose grave is in the churchyard. She lived
at Venton and her house and little chapel can still be seen.
Her real name was Olive Parr, but she wrote under the
pseudonym of Chase and became known as My Lady of the
Moor. Her early books were in the form of reportage and

Y

she wrote in a lively style about the moor, bringing the real Dartmoor to the city people who knew very little about the granite wilderness. She re-discovered Jay's Grave and had it put on the Ordnance Survey Map; she also revived the dying interest in the Fair.

Do not miss the logan stone of Rugglestone above Widecombe, or the lovely old pub which takes its name from the stone where some genuine farmhouse cider can be savoured. Coming down off the high moor in summer on Sundays you hear the sound of the bells across the fields, and at Christmas carols are sung in the church and the people come from as far away as Somerset just to listen.

Woolacombe see Mortehoe

Yealmpton Map 3 Bb

Pronounced 'Yampton', this village is notable for the **Devon Shire Horse Farm** which is well worth a visit, for all the work on the 60 acre farm is done by horses. Wander around the blacksmith's shop. There is a saddler at work, as well as the enchanting little foals, cart rides and Devon teas, but the best and most interesting part is to see these gentle giants ploughing, pulling harrows and bringing in the hay. The Flower family who run it, breed most of their own animals.

In the village don't miss the cottage said to have belonged to Old Mother Hubbard, made famous in nursery rhyme by Miss Sarah Martin who was a sister-in-law of Squire Bastard of nearby Kitley Manor. Kitley Manor dates from the time of Henry VII and near the river are **Kitley Caves** (Unusual Outings) discovered by quarrymen in 1800. The bones of prehistoric animals have been found here and there are some beautiful stalactites and stalacmites in different colours. The church, St Bartholomew, was rebuilt by Butterfield in 1850, and said by Sir John Betjeman to be 'the most amazing Victorian church in Devon'. There is much local marble inside and some memorials to the local squires, rather unfortunately named Bastard.

Nearby Ermington is famous above all for its twisted leaning church spire which looks in imminent danger of collapsing. Inside are beautiful wood carvings giving the impression of a forest filled with living creatures, which is the work of Violet Pinwell daughter of the one time rector and her six sisters. One mile south is **Flete House** (Historic Homes), a rambling mansion built for the millionaire banker H.B. Mildmay with beautiful gardens and many romantic nineteenth-century carriage drives. It is said Queen Victoria spent much time being driven through Devon woods. The house is divided into flats but the main rooms are open to the public.

Yelverton Map 3 Ab

Perhaps the most interesting part of this area is the site of the old Harrowbeer aerodrome, now reverted to moorland from which it sprang. Picnickers sit where dispersal bays once held planes, for here during the Second World War

Buckland Abbey

fighters roared low overhead the only reminder of those days being some of the nearby buildings which are still only single storey, the top half having been demolished to allow for incoming planes.

R.A.F. Harrowbeer was opened on 15 August 1941 and was home for No. 302 Squadron. General Sikorski was a visitor; John Pudney the author was billeted here and left his ration card behind. The airfield was bombed and saw many forced landings. Among the aircraft based here were Blenheim bombers, Spitfires, Hurricanes and old 'Stringbags', Swordfish carrying a torpedo net slung underneath.

In 1943 a crippled Halifax bomber returning from a raid over Germany overshot the runway and ploughed across the road. On 28 May 1944 a Typhoon fighter hit the church tower, killing the pilot. By the middle of the war more than 2,000 people were employed here and 16 different types of aircraft were in use. It was also a centre for air sea rescue work. It closed officially in July 1945, apart from some glider flying and an occasional emergency landing.

You can still see bunkers, stretches of tarmac, and patches of concrete where a water or control tower once stood, now covered by brambles and bracken, but where people spend a summer afternoon, and men once lived, and died.

To the southwest, within the parish of Meavy, at Brisworthy, occurs the earliest actual reference to tin working on Dartmoor in 1168 and nearby Wigford Down is rich in hut circles. There is a partly Norman church, and near it the famous Meavy Oak, claimed to be of the same age, and carefully preserved. It is 27 feet in circumference and seven people once dined inside it. The splendid tree stands on the green by the Inn, a place where both walkers and locals gather, as they have done for centuries. Adjoining St Peter's church are the remains of a manor house where Sir Francis Drake once lived. Nearby at Shaugh Bridge is a good picnic spot, if somewhat crowded in summer.

One and a half miles southwest is **Buckland Abbey**

(Museums), bought by Sir Francis Drake in 1581 with the proceeds of his voyage round the world. Acquired by the National Trust in 1948 it now houses a naval museum exhibiting relics of Drake and Grenville, including the famous Drake's Drum. One of the chief attractions is the magnificent Tithe Barn which is 180 feet long and contains a selection of horse-drawn vehicles. The garden is exquisite.

It is also worth travelling half a mile south to Milton Combe, an unspoilt village with a delightful old pub named 'Who'd have Thought it?'. This was the exclamation of another innkeeper when his rival received a licence to sell spirits.

Map 1

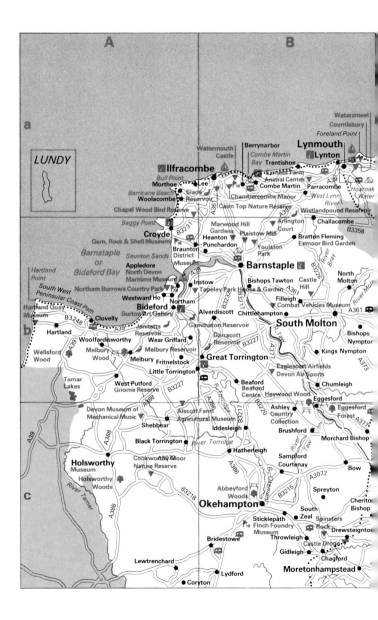

Map 2

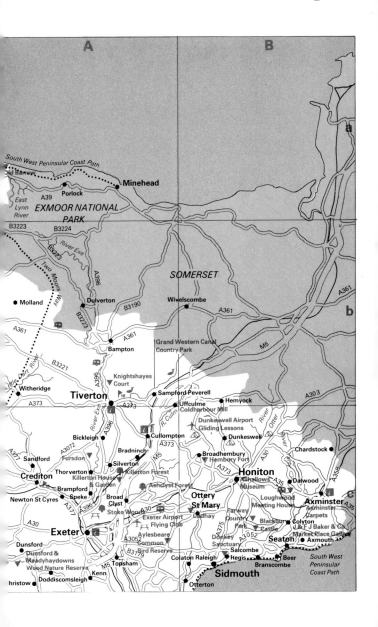

A

B

South West Peninsular Coast Path

Old Barow

Minehead

Porlock

A39

East Lynn River

EXMOOR NATIONAL PARK

B3223

B3224

River Exe

B3223

a

Two Moors Way

● Molland

Dulverton

B3190

● Wivelscombe

SOMERSET

A361

A361

A396

Little Dart River

A361

A303

A361

A396

Bampton

B3221

Knightshayes Court

A396

Witheridge

Tiverton

A373

● Sampford Peverell

Uffculme

Coldharbour Mill

R. Culm

● Hemyock

A361

M5

River Exe

A373

Dunkeswell Airport Gliding Lessons

Dunkeswell

River Otter

A303

Chardstock

A358

b

c

Bickleigh

A3072

Bradninch

A373

Cullompton

Broadhembury

Hembury Fort

A373

Honiton

Allhallows Museum

A35

Dalwood

Axminster

A358

A35

Sandford

Fursden

Thorverton

A377

Silverton

Killerton House & Garden

M5

Killerton Forest

Ashclyst Forest

A30

A375

Loughwood Meeting House

Axminster Carpets

Colyton

Market Place Gall...

Crediton

Brampford Speke

Broad Clyst

Ottery St Mary

Farway Country Park

Blackbury Castle

A30

A377

Newton St Cyres

Stoke Woods

Exeter Airport Flying Club

Cadhay

A3052

A375

A3052

Seaton

● Axmouth

A30

Exeter

Aylesbeare Common

Bird Reserve

Donkey Sanctuary

Salcombe Regis

Beer

Dunsford

B3179

Colaton Raleigh

Branscombe

South West Peninsular Coast Path

Dunsford & Meadyhaydowns Wood Nature Reserve

M5

Topsham

Sidmouth

Kenn

hristow

● Doddiscombsleigh

Otterton

Map 3

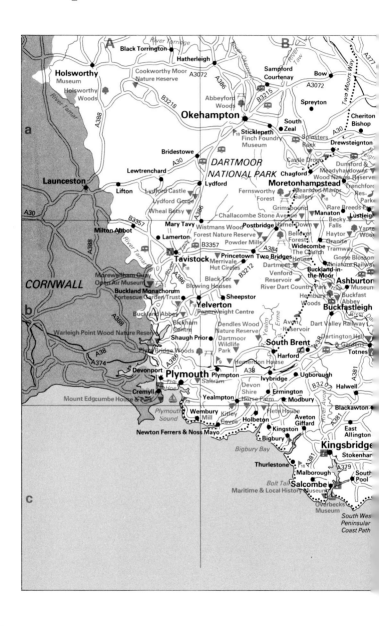

Map 4

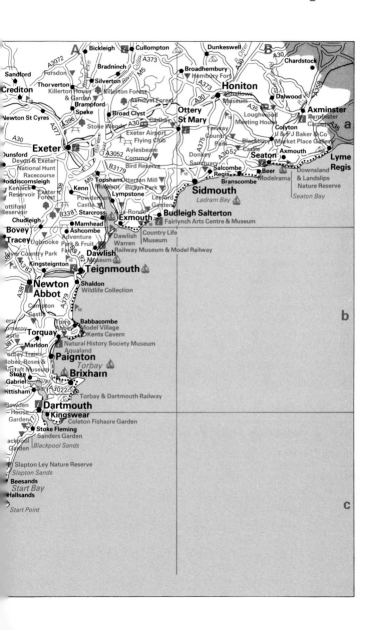

Town Directory

Barnstaple
Map 1 Bb

Garden: Woodside Garden
Museum: St Anne's Chapel Museum
Sports Centre: North Devon
Nearby:
Garden: Marwood Hill garden
Mill: Plaistow Mill
Museum: Braunton District Museum
Nature Reserve: Braunton Barrow
Nature Reserve
Historic Home: Youlston Park
Early Closing: Wednesday
Market day: Friday & Tuesday

Bovey Tracey
Map 4 Ab

Country Park: Parke
Farm: Rare Breeds Farm
Nearby:
Country Park: Stover Country Park
Historic Home: Ugbrooke
Nature Reserve: Yarner Wood
National Nature Reserve
Railway: Gorse Blossom Miniature
Railway Park
Industrial Archaeology: Haytor
Granite Tramway & Quarries

Brixham
Map 4 Ab

Aquarium: Marine Aquarium
Beaches: St Mary's Bay, Shoalstone
Beach
Country Park: Berry Head Country
Park
Museums: British Fisheries Museum,
Brixham Museum
Unusual: Golden Hind Replica
Early Closing: Wednesday

Combe Martin
Map 1 Ba

Beach: Wild Pear Beach
Garden: Buzzacott Manor House
Museum: Motor Cycle Collection
Zoo: Monkey Sanctuary
Nearby:
Historic Home: Arlington Court
Early Closing: Wednesday

Dartmouth
Map 4 Ab

Archaeological Site: Bayards Cove
Castle
Historic Home: The Mansion House
Museum: Dartmouth Museum
Other Historic Building: Agincourt
House
Railway: Torbay & Dartmouth
Railway
Unusual: Newcomen Engine House
Nearby:
Beach: Blackpool Sands
Gardens: Bowden House, Blackpool,
Coleton Fishacre Garden, Sanders
Garden
Early Closing: Wednesday and
Saturday

Exeter

Map 4 Aa

Archaeological Site: Underground Passages
Art Galleries: Spacex Gallery
Castle: Rougemont Castle Ruins
Church Buildings: Exeter Cathedral, St Nicholas Priory
Greyhound Racing: County Ground Stadium
Historic Buildings: Customs House, Guildhall
Museums: Tuckers Hall, Maritime Museum, Rougemont House Museum, Royal Albert Memorial Museum
Railway: Great Exmouth OO Model Railway
Nearby:
Historic Home: Killerton House & Garden
Markets: Pannier, St George's Hall; Horse & Cattle, Fore St
Museum: Topsham Museum, Brunel Atmospheric Railway Museum
Woodland: Ashclyst Forest, Killerton Forest

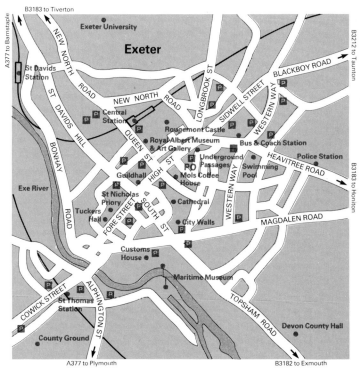

Great Torrington
Map 1 Bb

Garden: Rosemoor Garden Trust
Local Industry: Dartington Glass
Museum: Torrington Museum
Nearby:
Art Gallery: Beaford Centre
Early Closing: Wednesday

Ilfracombe
Map 1 Aa

Museum: Ilfracombe Museum
Mill: Bicclescombe Mill, The Old Corn Mill
Zoo: Wildlife Garden
Nearby:
Beaches: Hele Bay, Raparee Cove, Tunnels Beach Bathing Pool
Unusual: Watermouth Castle
Historic Home: Chambercombe Manor
Early Closing: Thursday

Kingsbridge
Map 3 Bc

Museum: Cookworthy Museum
Railway: Kingsbridge Miniature Railway
Nearby:
Lighthouse: Start Point Lighthouse
Market: Cattle
Museum: Overbecks Museum
Nature Reserve: Slapton Ley Nature Reserve
Early Closing: Thursday

Lynton/Lynmouth
Map 1 Ba

Museum: Lyn & Exmoor Museum
Railway: Cliff Railway
Unusual: Exmoor Brass Rubbing Centre
Nearby:
Archaeological Site: Old Barrow
Beach: Blacklands Beach
Farm: Exmoor Farm Animal Centre
Lighthouse: Foreland Lighthouse
National Park: Exmoor
Other Historic Building: Watersmeet House

Newton Abbot
Map 4 Ab

Historic Home: Bradley Manor
Horseracing: Newton Abbot Racecourse
Sports Centre: Dyrons Sports Centre
Nearby:
Archaeological Site: Hembury Camp
Church Buildings: Buckfast Abbey
Country Park: River Dart Country Park
Markets: Pannier & Cattle, Ponies, Antiques
Museum: Ashburton Museum
Woodland: Hembury Woods
Early Closing: Thursday

Okehampton
Map 3 Ba

Castle: Okehampton Castle
Market: Pannier
Museum: Okehampton Museum of Dartmoor Life
Nearby:
Museum: Finch Foundry Museum
Woodland: Abbeyford Woods
Early Closing: Wednesday

Paignton / Torquay
Map 4 Ab

Aquarium: Aqualand
Archaeological Site: Kent's Cavern
Beaches: Anstey's Cove, Meadfoot, Redgate
Museum: Torre Abbey
Railway: Torbay & Dartmouth Railway
Early Closing: Wednesday

Plymouth
Map 4 Ab

Aquarium: Marine Biological Association
Boat Trip: Millbrook Steamboat Co., Plymouth Boat Cruise Ltd
Museums: City Museum & Art Gallery, Prysten House
Other Historic Buildings: Blackfriars Distillery, Elizabethan House, Guildhall, Merchants House, Royal Citadel, Smeaton
Sports Centres: Kitto Centre, Mayflower Sports Centre
Unusual: Royal Navy Dockyards
Early Closing: Wednesday

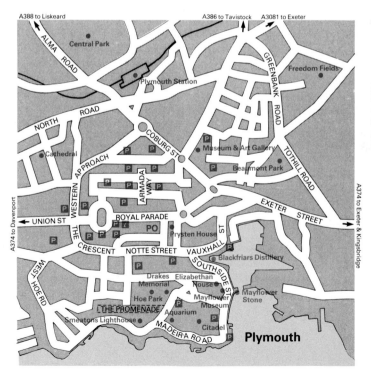

Seaton
Map 2 Bc

Archaeological Site: Blackbury
Castle
Beach: Seaton Hole
Railway: Seaton Electrical Tramway
Sports Centre: Hawkeshyde Motel &
Leisure Centre
Nearby:
Art Gallery: Market Place Gallery
Country Park: Farway Country Park
Nature Reserve: Downland Cliffs &
Landslips Nature Reserve
Unusual: Beer Modelrama
Early Closing: Thursday

Sidmouth
Map 2 Bc

Beach: Western Beach
Museums: Sidmouth Museum, Vin-
tage Toy & Train Museum
Nearby:
Beach: Ladram Bay
Garden: Bicton Park
Mill: Otterton Mill
Museum: Fairlynch Arts Centre &
Museum
Railway: Woodlands Railway
Unusual: The Donkey Sanctuary
Early Closing: Thursday

South Molton
Map 1 Bb

Farm: Quince Honey Farm
Museum: South Molton Museum
Nearby:
Historic Home: Castle House
Museum: Cobbaton Combat Vehicles
Museum
Early Closing: Wednesday

Teignmouth
Map 4 Ab

Aquarium: Aqualand Aquarium
Museum: Teignmouth Museum
Zoo: Shaldon Wildlife Collection
Nearby:
Museum: Dawlish Museum
Early Closing: Thursday

Tiverton
Map 2 Ab

Archaeological Site: Cadbury Castle
Castle: Tiverton Castle
Country Park: Grand Western Canal
Museum: Tiverton Museum
Local Industry: English Lace School
Nearby:
Castle: Bickleigh Castle
Garden: Knightshayes Court
Historic Home: Fursdon House
Mill: Bickleigh Mill
Early Closing: Thursday

Totnes
Map 3 Bb

Castle: Totnes Castle
Historic Building: Guildhall
Market: Panniers
Museums: Devonshire Collection of
Period Costume, Elizabethan House,
Totnes Motor Museum
Railway: Dart Valley Railway
Nearby:
Castle: Berry Pomeroy Castle
Gardens: Dartington Hall & Gardens
Historic Homes: Compton Castle
Museum: Torbay Trains, Robes,
Roses & Aircraft Museum

Leisure A-Z

Details given here have been carefully checked but are subject to change. Last admission can be half an hour before stated closing time.

Symbols: See p 5.
Abbreviations: ch children
ch 16 children to age 16
OAP   old age pensioners
m   mile
N   north
S   south
E   east
W   west

Air Sports

AIR WESTWARD
Map 2 Bc
Luppitt (0404 89) 643
Dunkeswell Aerodrome
Courses: £41 hour, private pilot's licence
Solo and advanced flying courses; modern training aircraft, qualified instructors; superb facilities for light aviation enthusiasts

DEVON AIR SPORTS
Map 1 Bb
Mr Pearson (0271) 78204
Eaglescott Airfield, 4m NW Beaford on B3217
Membership: available for all light aviation enthusiasts and aircraft owners
Courses: gliding Easter-end Sep, 7 days £65 plus flying costs
Trial flights, pilot's licences, parachuting courses, contact Ashreigney (076 93) 213

DEVON & SOMERSET GLIDING CLUB
Map 2 Bc
Chard (046 06) 2151
North Hill Field, Broadhembury
Membership: £55 per year plus £10 joining fee and £1 club share
Courses: 5 day gliding course £80
Visitors & new members always welcome; air experience flights, depending on weather

DUNKESWELL GLIDING CLUB
Map 2 Bc
Exeter (0647) 52249
Dunkeswell Airfield, 5m N Honiton
Membership: £10 joining fee, £55 annual fees, £5 temporary
Courses: 5 day course £80, £40 w/ end course
Clubhouse, social functions; summer courses include expert tuition

EXETER FLYING CLUB LTD
Map 2 Ac
Exeter (0392) 67653
Exeter Airport, 3m E Exeter on A30
Pleasure flights & lessons, telephone for details

Angling

Organisations

NATIONAL FEDERATION OF ANGLERS
Derby (0332) 362000
Halliday House, 2 Wilson St, Derby DE11PG
The governing body of coarse angling in Britain. Membership is through

clubs & associations. 420 such organisations are affiliated, representing some 450,000 coarse anglers.

NATIONAL FEDERATION OF SEA ANGLERS

Uckfield (0825) 3589
General Secretary: R W Page
26 Downsview Cresent, Uckfield, East Sussex TN22 1UB
This is governing body for sea angling in Britain. 800 clubs are affiliated & the federation represents the interests of nearly 2 million sea anglers

SALMON & TROUT ASSOCIATION

01-283 5838
Fishmongers Hall, London Bridge, LondonEC4R 9EL
National body for game fishing, has over70 branches in Britain & over 200,000 members

NATIONAL ANGLERS' COUNCIL

Peterborough (0733) 54084
11 Cowgate, Peterborough PE1 1LZ
Governing body for angling (all types)in England. Runs National Angling Coaching Scheme & a Proficiency Awards Scheme, designed to improve the proficiency of ecology & protection of the water environment

CENTRAL ASSOCIATION OF LONDON & PROVINCIAL ANGLING CLUBS

01-686 3199
9 Kemble Rd, Croydon, Surrey
Members & affiliated clubs can use the waters which the association either owns or rents. They also provide an Anglers'Guide to these waters

Rod Licences

SOUTH WEST WATER AUTHORITY

Exeter (0392) 50861
The rivers and inland waters of Devon are controlled by the South West Water these waters must first obtain an official rod licence. In Devon rod

licences are available from distributors throughout the regions. A list of these locations is available from:
Fisheries Information Office
South West Water, Eastern Area
3-5 Barnfield Road, Exeter, Devon
The office also supplies licences by return post

Permits

Almost all rivers & stillwaters are owned, or leased, by private individuals, angling clubs or local authorities.

Although access is sometimes restricted, often to members of a particular angling club, many private waters offer fishing by permit. These permits are for a day, week or season & are usually available from the angling clubs which control the waters, from bailiffs on the banks or from local tackle shops.

In the following section, **Where to Fish**, the angling clubs, or others,who control particular waters, are listed below each entry. **For the addresses & telephone numbers of club secretaries & details of waters controlled by clubs see** Angling Clubs.

If permits can be obtained elsewhere,this information is also given

Where to Fish

Some of the following information is taken from **The Fishing Handbook**(1983 edition), a comprehensive,annual guide to all angling organisations & locations in Britain & Ireland. It includes a guide to day permit fishing & to sea fishing, a list of angling clubs & a directory of suppliers. Three smaller publications separate information for Coarse Fishing,Game Fishing & Sea Fishing.

For further detalils contact:
Beacon Publishing
Northampton (0604) 407288
Jubilee House, Billing Brook Rd, WestonFavell, Northampton

Coarse Fishing: Rivers

RIVER CLYST
The Clyst rises north of Plymtree and flows in a southwesterly direction, finally entering the river Axe at Topsham
Permits: Exeter & District Angling Association, Exeter Angling Centre, Exeter

RIVER CREEDY
The Creedy rises north of Credition & follows A377 road to its junction with the Exe above Exeter. Trout & some coarse fishing
See also: Game Fishing: Rivers
Permits: Exeter Angling Centre, Exeter (0392) 36404; Newton Abbot Fishing Association

RIVER CULM
The Culm is the longest of the Exe tributaries, the Culm rises on the Eastern side of Devon near Otterhead & flows cross country through Culmstock and Cullompton to join the Exe a short distance above the junction with the Creedy. Trout in the upper reaches & coarse fishing, lower down
See also: Game Fishing: Rivers
Permits: Exeter Angling Centre, Exeter (0392) 36404; Upper Culm Fishing Association; permits also available H M Sanders, The Bakery, Hemyock, Devon (SAE please); also The Old Parsonage Farmhouse, Uffculme (0884) 40205

RIVER EXE

This is Devon's largest river. Rising on Exmoor to the northwest of Exford it continues via Bampton & Tiverton

southwards to Exeter, finally entering the English Channel at Exmouth. In the lower reaches, coarse fishing, including bream & carp are found with grayling up stream.
See also Game Fishing: Rivers
Permits: Newton Abbot Fishing Association; local tackle shops; Exeter Angling Centre; Country Sports, Tiverton (088 42) 4770; T Mortimer, High Banks, Latchmore,Thorverton (0392) 860241; Exeter & District AA; Tiverton & District AA

Stillwaters

ABBROOK POND
Kingsteignton
Permits: Exeter Angling Centre, Exeter (0392) 36404

BUTTLEIGH PONDS
Tiverton
Permits: Tiverton & District AC

BUZZACOTT MANOR LAKE
Combe Martin
Permits: available at lakeside

CHARD POND
Perry St, Chard
Permits: G Bartlett, 20 Fore Street, Chard

CULLOMPTON FISHERY
See: Stout Farm Fishery

DARRACOTT RESERVOIR
Darracott
Coarse fishing for carp, tench, bream, roach and perch
Permits: available from self-service unit on site; day permits from Hon Warden, Mr D Ives

HARCOMBE HOUSE POND
Chudleigh
3 Landscaped reservoirs which are stocked weekly, browns & rainbows in excess of 5lb have been caught here

Permits: day tickets available in advance from estate office, Harcombe House, Chudleigh (0626) 852227

HOME FARM POND
Exeter
Permits: Exeter Angling Centre Exeter (0392) 36404

RACKERHAYES POND
Newton Abbot
Complex of several ponds offering coarse fishing, including carp & bream
Permits: local tackle shops; Newton Abbot Fishing Association; The Anglers' Den, Brixham; Percy Hodge (Sports) Ltd; Drum Sports, Newton Abbot; H Cove Clark & Paignton Sports, Paignton; Fletcher Sports & Tuckermans, Torquay; Blake Sports, Totnes & Exeter Angling Centre, Exeter

SAMPFORD PEVERELL PONDS
Permits: Exeter Angling Centre (0392) 36404; Exeter District AA

SLAPTON LEY
Dartmouth
Situated in a nature reserve; fishing here is from boats. This 200 acre water is noted for the beauty of its rudd. There is also perch, pike & roach
Permits: Slapton Ley Field Centre Kingsbridge (0548) 580466

SQUABMOOR RESERVOIR
Knowle
4.3 acres including roach, rudd, carp, bream and tench
Permits: Knowle Post Office; The Tackle Shop, 20 The Strand, Exmouth; Exeter Angling Centre (0392) 36404; SWWA-information office

STOUT FISHERY
Cullompton
1¼ acre lake with carp and perch
Permits: advanced bookings for permits strongly advised, contact E J Berry, Billingsmoor Farm, near Butterleigh, Cullompton (088 45) 248

STOVER LAKE
Newton Abbot
Situated in Stover Country Park including tench, perch, roach
Permits: available on site; also The County Estates Surveyor, County Hall, Exeter or local tackle shops

VENN POND

Permits: day tickets available from: Rod 'n Reel, Bear St, Barnstaple also E Gate & Sons Ltd, 59 High St, Barnstaple; Barnstaple & District AA

Coarse Fishing: Canals

EXETER CANAL
Offers reasonably mixed coarse fishing with bream, rudd, pike and the occasional tench & carp
Permits: day and week permits available from local tackle dealers or The Bridge Cafe, Countess Wear, Exeter; Exeter & District AA

GRAND WESTERN CANAL
Coarse fishing from Tiverton northeast through Sampford Peverell to Burlscombe. A useful head of tench is the main attraction and there are also roach, perch & pike
Permits: day permits from Country Sports Tackle Shop, Tiverton (088 42) 4770; Council Offices & Post Office, Sampford Peverell

Game Fishing: Rivers

RIVER AVON
Rising on Dartmoor, the Avon, flows for just over 20 miles entering the English Channel via a long narrow

estuary at Bantham. Though the river attracts some salmon, few are caught on rod & line. sea trout are a different story and the best time for them is from late May through to early July. The river also contains brown trout. Fly only is a strict rule in a number of sections. In the estuary bass fishing is highly rated

Permits: Avon Fishing Association (weekly permits only), Loddiswell Post Office; Diptford Post Office; D M Blake, Fore St, Totnes; Molyneux Sports, Fore St, Kingsbridge

RIVER AXE

The Axe rises in Dorset & flows via Axminster, entering the English Channel at Seaton. Salmon, sea trout & trout are the main attraction with occasional sizeable coarse fish, especially roach. Strict regulations are applied by the Water Authority to the methods which may be employed for game fishing

Permits: George Hotel, Axminster (0297) 32209 (available if not required by hotel guests); Ulcombe Farm, Uppottery, Honiton (0404 86) 230; daily tickets, G Bartlett, 20 Fore Street, Chard, Somerset

RIVER BARLE

From Exmoor this river flows through a wooded valley to join the Exe below Dulverton. It offers salmon & trout fishing

Permits: Carnarvon Arms Hotel, Dulverton (0398) 23302; Exmoor Forest Hotel, Simonsbath (0643 83) 341; Tarr Steps Hotel (0643 85) 293

RIVER BOVEY

Rises on Dartmoor and follows a direct southeasterly course to join the right bank of the Teign below Bovey Tracey. It offers similar game fishing to the Teign

Permits: Lower Teign Fishing Association; Percy Hodge (Sports), 104 Queen St, Newton Abbot

RIVER BRAY

Tributary of the river Mole which joins the Taw below South Molton; the Bray offers trout, sea t2out and some salmon

Permits: Little Bray House, Brayford (059 88) 295; Poltimore Arms, North Molton contact: Mrs Hobson; North Molton (059 84) 338 South Molton AC; Gun & Sports Centre, 103 East Street, Molton

RIVER CREEDY

Trout fishing

Permits: Exeter & District Angling Association; Exeter Angling Centre, Exeter (0392) 36404

RIVER CULM

Trout fishing in the upper reaches

Permits: Exeter & District Angling Association; Exeter Angling Centre, Exeter (0392) 36404; Upper Culm FA; H M Sanders, The Bakery, Hemyock (SAE please)

RIVER DART

The Dart begins as two rivers high on Dartmoor. The West Dart rises above Princetown & links with a number of small tributaries before joining with the East Dart, which flows from the other side of Dartmoor, at Dartmeet. From here the Dart flows down via Buckfastleigh and Totnes to enter the English Channel at Dartmouth. It is a game river containing salmon and brown trout. In the lower reaches, the best time for salmon is in spring. Higher up, the salmon fishing improves in September. sea trout fishing is generally at a peak between July and September

Permits: Dart AA; Blakes Sports Shop; Totnes Sports Shop, Buckfastleigh; Percy Hodge Sports, Newton Abbot; Tuckermans Fishing Tackle, Torquay; The Sports Shop, 35/36 Fore St, Buckfastleigh (036 44) 3297; also The Forest Inn, Hexworthy; James Bowden & Son, Chagford; Post Office, Princetown; Post Office, Newton Abbot

EAST & WEST DART

Flows southeast across Dartmoor to join the West Dart at Dartmeet to form the Dart. It is game fishing with chances for the visitor
Permits: Upper Dart Fishing Association; The Sports Shop at Newton Abbot; The Forest Inn, Hexworthy; James Bowden & Sons, Chagford; Princetown Post Office; Postbridge Post Office; Percy Hodge Sports, Newton Abbot

RIVER LITTLE DART

Flowing in from the east, the Little Dart joins the right bank of the Taw just below Eggesford. It offers similar sport to the river Bray
Permits: Fox & Hounds Hotel, Eggesford (076 98) 345

RIVER ERME

Permits: limited permits to members of Anglers' Co-operative, subscription available on site

RIVER EXE

Game fishing in upper & middle reaches, salmon runs best from May-Sept.
Permits: Exeter & District AA; Newton Abbot FA; local tackle shops; Exeter Angling Centre, Exeter (0392) 36404; Country Sports, 9 William St, Tiverton; T Mortimer, High Banks, Latchmore, Thoverton; Tiverton & District AA; Carnarvon Arms Hotel, Dulverton (0398) 23302; also Tiverton & District AA; Country Sports, Tiverton; Hartnoll Country House Hotel, Bolham, Tiverton

RIVER LEW

Rising to the east of Okehampton, the Lew flows north to join the Torridge near Hatherleigh; similar fishing to the Torridge
Permits: The West of England School of Game Angling

RIVER LYN (EAST & WEST)

From Exmoor Forest, the East Lyn flows through Lynmouth, and is joined by the West Lyn just below this well-known Devonshire resort. It is a game river offering sport with salmon, sea trout and brown trout. The most prolific section of the East Lyn is that controlled by the SWWA is lying betwwen Watersmeet & Lynmouth. July onwards is the best time for salmon. The West Lyn is private
Permits: Mrs Stevens, Globe House, Brendon, Lynton; The Warden, Combe Park Lodge, Lynton (059 85) 3586; Hillsford Bridge, Lynton; Mr Hill, The Esplanade, Lynmouth; Mr Parfrey, Stag Hunters Inn, Brendon; Mr Lynn; Ironmongers, High St, Porlock; Angels Corner, Imperial Buildings Castle Hill, Lynton; Mrs Pile, Oakleigh, Tors Road, Lynmouth; Fisheries Office SWWA

RIVER MOLE

Flowing in from the east, the Mole, joins the Taw a short distance below its junction with the Little Dart. It offers trout, sea trout & salmon
Permits: South Molton Angling Centre; Fortescue Arms Hotel; AW Youings, Garramarsh, Queens Nympton (076) 97360; The Rising Sun Hotel, Lynmouth; Rockford Inn, Brendon; Doone Valley, Riding Stables, Malmshead, Brendon

RIVER OKEMENT

Rising on Dartmoor, this river flows north through Okehampton to join the Torridge on its right bank below Hatherleigh. It is rated best for trout
Permits: Hill Barton Farm, Mr Pennington, Okehampton (0837) 2454; West of England School of Game Angling

RIVER OTTER

Rising in northeast Devon, the Otter flows south via Honiton & Ottery St Mary to enter the English Channel through a long, narrow estuary at Budleigh Salterton. Best noted for its trout fishing, there is also some sea trout, fly only tends to be the rule in the upper reaches. The estuary is highly rated for mullet

Permits: free fishing (1 April-Sept) for anglers holding SWWA rod licences; Venn Ottery Barton Hotel; Mr C P May, Bridge House, Weston, Honiton (0404) 2738; Reception, Deer Park Hotel, Weston, Honiton (0404) 2064; Mr J R D B Oswell, Combe House Hotel, Gittisham, Honiton

RIVER TAW

Rising on Dartmoor, the Taw takes a northerly course, turning northwest just below Eggesford before flowing on through Umberleigh to enter its estuary at Barnstaple. Best known as a game river the Taw also contains coarse fish (mostly roach & dace) in its lower reaches. In addition to trout, there are sea trout & salmon. The main salmon run is in spring from March to May sea trout begin moving strongly from July onwards. The estuary offers excellant mullet fishing

Permits: Barnstaple & District A A; Barnstaple tackle shops; Fox & Hounds Hotel, Chumleigh (076 98) 345; R Drayton, 46 Gardens Row, Bow (036 33) 417; The Barton, North Tawton (0837 82) 230; Mr French, Davencourt, Sticklepath (0837 84) 325; Fortescue Arms Hotel, Umberleigh (076 98) 214; The Rising Sun Hotel, Umberleigh, (076 96) 447 (subject to hotel bookings)

RIVER TEIGN

Another of the rivers which drains Dartmoor, the Teign's course adopts a broad estuary arc from Chagford swinging back to enter its estuary 30 miles from its source at Newton Abbot. It offers good fishing including trout, sea trout and salmon. The best time is in spring with peak times for migratory fish early April-June

Permits: Upper Teign; The Anglers Rest; Upper Teign Fishing Association; Fingle Bridge, Drewsteignton; Lower Teign Fishing Association, Lower Teign; Percy Hodge Sports, 104 Queen St, Newton Abbot; Bowdens, the Square, Chagford; Drum Sports, Courtenay, Newton Abbot; The Mill End Hotel, Sandy Park; Clifford Bridge Caravan Park, Clifford Bridge; Exeter Angling Centre

RIVER TORRIDGE

Rising northwest Devon, a few miles inland from Clovelly. It then flows southeast to Sheepwash where it turns back in a northwesterly direction, its course resembling a half-circle before it enters the estuary above Torrington at Bideford. A typical Devonshire game river, the Torridge contains trout and also attracts runs of salmon and sea trout. Salmon are most likely in late spring (April-May) while the sea trout run gains impetus from July onwards

Permits: Group Cpt Norron Smith, Little Warham, Beaford (080 53) 317; Union Inn, Dolton (080 54) 244; Woodford Bridge Hotel, Milton Damerel (040 26) 252; Lower Torridge Fisheries, Appledore (0237 23) 126; Half Moon Inn, Beaworthy (0409 23) 376; The West of England School of Angling; A Hooper, Post Office, Riverdale, Wear Giffard, Bideford (023 72) 2479; D Ives, Town Mills Hotel, Torrington

Stillwaters: Game Fishing

AVON DAM

50 acres, brown trout SWWA Natural trout fishing, no permits required

BELLBROOK VALLEY TROUT FISHERY
Oakford
5 large ponds, rainbows & wild browns
Day Permits: contact J Braithwaite, Oakford, Tiverton (039 85) 292

DARRACOTT RESERVOIR
2.6 acres
Rainbow fish permitted all year
Permits: from self-service unit on site

EAST BATSWORTHY FISHERIES
Rackenford, near Tiverton
2 lakes of 1½ acres, rainbow trout
Permits: day permits available, Contact: Mr Gardner, Rackenford (088 488) 278 advance booking advisable

EXE VALLEY FISHERY
Dulverton
2 small lakes, brown and rainbow trout
Permits: half day permits (advance booking advisable), contact: Exe Valley Fishery, Dulverton (0398) 23328

FERNWORTHY RESERVOIR
Chagford, stocked trout fishing (fly only)
Permits: day & evening permits available from self-service unit on site

GAMMATON RESERVOIR
Bideford
4.6 acres & 4.4 acres brown and rainbow trout
Permits: day tickets available from Petherick's Tackle Shop, High St, Bideford

JENNETS RESERVOIR
Bideford
Same as above

KENNICK RESERVOIR
Trout fishing permitted (fly only) weather permitting, near Bovey Tracey, Devon
Permits: day & evening permits available from self-service unit on site

SLADE RESERVOIR
Ilfracombe
Natural trout & some coarse
Permits: day permits from self-service unit on site; Slade Post Office, Lee Rd, Slade, Ilfracombe (0271) 62257

SPURTHAM FISHERY
Uppottery, near Honiton
3 one acre lakes, rainbow trout from Spurtham Farm, Uppottery
Permits: day & evening permits available (advance bookings advisable)
Uppotery (0404 86) 209

SQUABMOOR RESERVOIR
Near east Budleigh, mixed trout
Permits: Knowle Post Office; The Tackle Shop, 20 The Strand, Exmouth; Exeter Angling Centre, City Arcade, Fore Street, Exeter; SWWA - Information Centre

STAFFORD MOOR FISHERY
Dolton, Winkleigh
2 lakes producing a considerable number of big trout, biggest rainbow 14lb 2oz, the 7th biggest ever taken in England. The biggest brown was an impressive 10lb 2oz. Average for the most recent season for which figures are available 11lb 15oz
Permits: day & evening permits (advance booking advisable) telephone (080 54) 371/360

STOUT FISHERY
Billingsmoor, near Cullompton, Devon
2 acre lake of rainbow and brown trout
Permits: season and day permits available by appointment only with Mr E J Berry, Billingsmoor Farm, Cullompton , Bickleigh (088 45) 248

TOTTIFORD RESERVOIR
Near Bovey Tracey
Permits: day & evening permits available from self-service unit on site

TRENCHFORD RESERVOIR
Moretonhampstead
Operated as experimental brook trout fishery. The most recent season produced a total catch of 3,924 rainbow & 1,300 brown trout

VENFORD RESERVOIR
33 acres brown trout, SWWA, natural trout fishery
Ashburton
Natural trout fishing
Permits: not required

WEST BLACKSTONE FARM
Rackenford, near Tiverton
Secluded 2 acre lake, brown and rainbow trout
Permits: advance booking only, Contact C L Thomas (0884 88) 251

WISTLANDPOUND RESERVOIR
Barnstaple
Stocked trout fishing
(fly only)
Permits: day & evening permits available from self-service unit on site

Sea Fishing

APPLEDORE
Shore fishing quite successful, main catches bass & flatties. Fishing from Quay may bring you bass, flounders & dabs.Shark fishing is popular here

BIGBURY-ON-SEA
Excellent bass caught from shore & boat. Apart from bass the most common species caught are flatties

BRIXHAM
Brixham's breakwater is ideal for conger, especially on winter nights when there's frost.
Boat charter: Tremlet Fisherman, Skipper, Albert King, (080 45) 6380

CLOVELLY
All year round fishing with a good variety of species available. Bull, huss, conger, cod, whiting and dogfish are among the species you can expect. Bass & mackerel are prevalent in the summer as are ray in the winter

DARTMOUTH
Daytime fishing is best for bass & pouting. Dusk and after dark are best for flounders, dabs & occasional plaice. During the summer large numbers of mackerel gather here and the best time to catch them is early morning or late evening. Winter is best for flounders.**Boat Charter:**
'Penny Louise', Skipper: Lawrie Dawson (08043) 28381
'Pisces', Skipper: B Dash (08043) 3069

EXMOUTH
Pier opposite Dawlish Warren provides excellent pollack, wrasse, bass, pouting & flatties. Autumn is the best time for bass, garlish & mackerel. Flounder are common in winter and plaice are caught from time to time

HARTLAND
Excellent sea fishing with many species available including whiting, mullet and pouting. Bass up to 13lbs have been caught. Conger are also reasonably good size

ILFRACOMBE
The pier provides good catches of mackerel, garfish, bass and flatties. Beach fishing produces good catches of bass, mackerel and mullet. The best boat fishing takes place not far from the Quay where you can expect good hauls of tope, skate and cod
Boat Charter:
'Exel', Skipper: Dave Clemence (0271) 63460
'Princess', Skipper: J Barbeary (0271) 64957

LYNMOUTH

Reasonable shore & boat fishing. Usual species including some good mullet can be had when boat fishing in some of the rougher waters. Good shark fishing available

NEWTON FERRERS

Good shore & boat fishing, species caught from the shore include pollack, bass & flounder. Boat fishing produces good catches of mackerel, flatties, mullet & conger. Shark season is from June-Oct

PAIGNTON

Beach fishing good especially during summer & autumn. Species include bass, mullet & mackerel. Boat fishing is good for mackerels in its season

PLYMOUTH

Boat fishing offers deep water wrecks and reef fishing within 40 miles radius of Plymouth. Conger, ling, pollack, coalfish, turbot and electric ray are common catches. Plymouth harbour is good for congers of up to 60lb, also ray. Trinity Pier is excellent for flounders, bass and grey mullet

Boat Charters:

'Buster', Skipper: J Folland (0752) 668322
'The Gay Girls', Skipper: Bob Williamson (0752) 4575
'June Lipet', Skipper: Jim Campbell (0822) 832652
'Marco', Skipper: Colin Johns (0752) 339220
'Satrat', Skipper: Harry Steptoe (0752) 708476
'Terry Launce' (0752) 261739
'Solan Goose', Furzeland Fishing & Charters (0752) 59673 (day or weekly charters)
'Sunlight', Skipper: Ray Parsons (0752) 21722

SALCOMBE

Good boat fishing location, main catches are plaice, turbot, dabs & flounder. The gilt-head bream is also a common visitor to the area

SIDMOUTH

Excellent beach & boat fishing in Sidmouth Bay area. Mackerel are best during spring & summer, as are pollack. Bass to 13lbs, skate to over 100lbs, good sized tope & bull huss are common catches. Other common species are plaice, turbot, whiting, dabs & flounders

START POINT

Skerries bank produces excellent catches turbot, plaice, dabs & rays for boat anglers. The best catch from the beach is wrasse and a good number of black bream in summer, especially near the shore line. Good catches of dabs, rays & plaice are also possible from the shore if the angler casts into the sandy area between the rocks

TEIGNMOUTH

Good for plaice, flounders & bass. The biggest catches coming between Oct and March. The rocks between Teignmouth and Dawlish, excellent for big catches of bass

TORBAY

Best shore fishing mark is Hopes Nose, via the Marine Drive. One of many good catches in these waters is wrasse. In the rocks to the right of the main area there are excellent conger to be had. Black bream & mullet are two more good sized catches often caught here

TORQUAY

Plenty of wreck fishing available along Skerries Bank where there are excellent catches of conger, pollack, bass, flatties and turbot. Babbacombe

Pier is excellent for mackerel in its season. Many good beach marks including Hopes Nose for bass & plaice, Abbey Sands & Astey's Cove

Coarse Angling Clubs

Abbreviations:
A. Angling
A.A. Angling Association
C. Club
F. Fishing
P. Preservation
S. Society

BARNSTAPLE & DISTRICT A.C.
Secretary: M J Andrew
Braunton (0271) 8144743 Wrafton Road, Braunton
Formed: 1931
Members: 300
Membership: unrestricted coarse & game, restricted game
Facilities: coarse, ponds up to 2 acres in size with small stretch of river Jaw.

BIDEFORD & DISTRICT A.C.
Secretary: V B Eveleigh
Bideford (02372) 2470, Club: Bideford (02372) 77996
21 Capern Rd, Bideford
Formed: 1964
Members: 300 male, 45 female, 60 juniors, 100 associates
Membership: unrestricted
Facilities: club lake at Langtree, near Torrington; game fishing available, HQ open to members of Angling Clubs producing proof of AC membership

EXETER & DISTRICT A.A.
Secretary: D L Beaven
Exeter (0392) 75925
46 Hatherleigh Road, Exeter
Formed: 1970
Members: 3500
Membership: unrestricted
Facilities: approx 12 miles of river fishing on rivers Exe, Clyst, Culm & Creedy, also the Exeter Ship Canal.

Direct control over approx 5 miles both banks with ponds at Kingsteignton, Tiverton & Mamhead

S.W.E.B. (TORBAY DISTRICT) A.C.
Secretary: T Holton
Torquay (0803) 26200
Electric House, Union Street, Torquay
Formed: 1973
Members: 70
Membership: restricted
Facilities: none, but have knowledge & information about complete area

TIVERTON & DISTRICT A.C.
Secretary: M Trump
Tiverton (08842) 57761
5 Lodge Road, Tiverton
Formed: 1975
Members: 200
Membership: unrestricted
Facilities: 3 ponds at Butterleigh near Tiverton, with tench, roach, carp and rudd; 2 stretches of river Exe; the first is the Exe walk in Tiverton, ½m in Tiverton, a half mile down stream of road bridge in town; dace, grayling, roach & trout; the second is three quaters of a mile of the river Exe in Exeter, stretching north of Station Rd; dace, roach & grayling

Game Angling Clubs

BARNSTAPLE & DISTRICT A.A.
See Coarse Clubs

KENNICK FLYFISHERS A.
Secretary: P Mugridge
Ivybridge (05488) 30522
29 Champernowne, Modbury
Formed: 1975
Members: 140
Membership: unrestricted

PLYMOUTH & DISTRICT FRESHWATER A.A.
Secretary: J Evans
Spring Cottage, Hemerdon, Plymouth
Formed: 1947
Members: 100
Membership: restricted
Facilities: 2 day tickets issued for small section of river Plym. Brown trout, sea trout and a few salmon tickets issued by D K Sports, Exeter Street, Plymouth

S.W.E.B. (TORBAY DISTRICT) A.C.
See Coarse Angling Clubs

TIVERTON FLY F.C.
Secretary: J M Ford
Tiverton (08842) 254770
c/o Country Sports
9 Williams Street, Tiverton
Members: 100
Membership: restricted to people living in the area; junior membership available
Facilities: approx three & a half miles of river Exe at Tiverton

UPPER TEIGN F.A.
Secretary: A J Price
Chagford (06473) 3253
Formed: 1870
Members: 25
Membership: restricted
Facilities: approx 14 miles of river Teign from Chagford downstream to Dunsford. Brown trout fishing is available to non-members by the season, week or day. 2 day tickets per day available to non-members for salmon & sea trout

Aquariums

AQUALAND
Map 4 Ab/p124
Torquay (0803) 24439
Beacon Quay, Harbourside, Torquay

Open: April-Oct, daily 10.00-22.00; Nov-March, daily 10.00-16.00
Charge: 65p (ch 45p, disabled free); group reductions by arrangement
Largest aquarium in the West Country specialising in tropical marine fish, exhibition of local marine life, tropical fish, otters and turtles
Dogs on leads
🅿 🚻 ♿

MARINE AQUARIUM
Map 4 Ab
Brixham (080 45) 2204
12 The Quay, Brixham
Open: Easter-end Sep, daily 10.00-21.00
Charge: 40p (ch 20p)
Largest tank in Britain containing only fish caught within 40 miles of the town, despite this there is a wealth of jellyfish, crustacea, squid, octopus, rays and other fish, also display of model trawlers
♿

SEASHORE AQUARIUM
Map 4 Ab
Paignton (0803) 522913
The Harbour, Paignton
Open: Easter-end Sep, daily 10.00-dusk
Charge: 40p (ch 25p), subject to alteration
🅿 🚻 ♿

PLYMOUTH AQUARIUM
Map 3 Ab
Plymouth (0752) 21761
Marine Biological Association, The Hoe, Plymouth
Open: all year, Mon-Sat 10.00-18.00 (closed 25 & 26 Dec, Good Fri)
Charge: 50p (ch 25p)
Group reductions by arrangement
One of the finest aquariums in Europe
No dogs
🅿 ♿

Archaeo-logical Sites

BAYARD'S COVE CASTLE
Map 4 Ab
Dartmouth Harbour, Dartmouth
Open: anytime
Free
Low circular stronghold built in the 16th century to protect inner harbour, now in ruins
DofE

BLACKBURY CASTLE
Map 4 Ba
2m NW Seaton off B3174
Open: anytime
Free
Oval shaped earth hillfort dating from Iron Age with complicated entrance on south side; ideal picnic spot
🅿

CHALLACOMBE STONE AVENUE
Map 3 Ba
4½m SW Moretonhampstead off B3212
Long row of upright stones thought to have been ceremonial route during the Bronze Age period

GRIMSPOUND
Map 3 Ba/p77
4m S Moretonhampstead, 2m E of B3212
Foundations of 24 dry stone huts and outer wall (once 9ft wide), thought to date from 1,000 BC

HAMEL DOWN
Map 3 Bb
5m S Moretonhampstead, 2m E of B3212
Well preserved groups of Bronze Age burial chambers

HEMBURY FORT
Map 2 Bc/p23
3m NW Honiton on A373
Excellent example of Iron Age hillfort described by experts as the 'grandest monument to military skills of Britons in Devon', oval defences enclose 8 acres within double ditches and banks, supplemented by wooden palisades

KENTS CAVERN
Map 4 Ab/p121
Torquay (0803) 24059
The Caves, Wellswood, 1¼m NE of B3199
Open: April-mid June, daily 10.00-18.00; mid June-mid Sep, 10.00-21.00 (Sat 10.00-18.00); mid Sep-Oct, 10.00-18.00; Nov-March 10.00-17.00
Charge: £1 (ch14 50p), group reductions by arrangement (subject to alteration)
Guided tours every 20 mins
Caves of natural beauty and prehistoric interest, excavations have revealed skulls, bones and teeth of man and animals
🅿 ⌷

LYDFORD CASTLE
Map 3 Aa
Lydford, 5m SW Okehampton off A386
Open: anytime
Free
Site first fortified by Alfred during the 9th century against the Danes; remains of Norman keep visible
DofE 🅿

MARISCO CASTLE
Lundy Island
Remains of 13th century castle with walls 9ft thick
See also Country Parks

MERRIVALE HUT CIRCLES
Map 3 Bb
Tavistock
Open: any reasonable time
Free
DofE 🅿

OLD BARROW
Map 2 Aa
3½m M E Lynmouth on A39
Early roman fort build 48 AD to keep
watch on the Silures tribe in South
Wales

SPINSTERS ROCK
Map 1 Bc/p27
2½m W Drewsteignton, 6m E
Okehampton on A382
Remains of 4,000-year-old Bronze
Age communal burial place, consisting
of three upright granite stones sup-
porting a massive capstone

UNDERGROUND PASSAGES
Map 4 Aa/p46
Exeter (0392) 56724
Princesshay, Exeter
Open: all year, Tue-Sat 14.00-16.30;
groups at other times by arrangement
Charge: 40p (ch 20p)
Unique medieval aquaducts which
supplied water to the city until mid-
19th century

Art Galleries

BEAFORD CENTRE
Map 1 Bb
Beaford (080 53) 201½02
Beaford, 4m SE Great Torrington on
B3320
Open: all year, daily
Free
Exhibitions of archive photographs
and work of local artists, craftsmen
and photographers
🅿

BURTON ART GALLERY
Map 1 Ab/p16
Bideford (023 72) 6711
Victoria Park, Kingsley Rd, Bideford
Open: all year, w:days 10.00-13.00
& 14.00-17.00; Sat 9.45-12.45
Free
Work of late H Coop, collections of
19th century oil paintings, 19th and
20th century water colours, model
ships, silver, pewter N Devon slip
ware
No dogs
🅿 ♿

CITY MUSEUM & ART GALLERY
See Museums: City Museum

HEMERDON HOUSE
See Historic Homes: Hemerdon
House

MARKET PLACE GALLERY
Map 2 Bc
Colyton (0297) 52918
Colyton
Open: Feb-Dec, Mon-Sat 10.00-
13.00 & 14.00-17.00 (early closing
Wed)
Free
Small gallery showing contemporary
figurative oil paintings and water
colours, also thematic exhibitions
Dogs by permission
🅿 ♿ ♿

MEARSDON MANOR GALLERY
Map 3 Ba/p79
Moretonhampstead (064 74) 483
Cross St, Moretonhampstead
Open: all year, daily 9.00-18.00
Free
13th century building containing
wealth of paintings and objets d'art
including Chinese jade and cloissone,
teak carvings, wildlife paintings; bird
sanctuary in garden; all painting and
items for sale
🅿 ♿

OTTERTON MILL GALLERY
See Mills: Otterton Mill

ROYAL ALBERT MEMORIAL MUSEUM
See Museums: Royal Albert Memorial Museum

SALTRAM
See Historic Homes: Saltram

TORRE ABBEY MANSION
See Museums: Torre Abbey Mansion

SPACEX GALLERY
Map 4 Aa
Exeter (0392) 31786
45 Preston St, Exeter
Open: Tue-Sat, 10.00-17.00
Free
Programme devoted to latest developments in contemporary fine art, prints and pictures
&

Bird Reserves

ROYAL SOCIETY FOR THE PROTECTION OF BIRDS
The Lodge, Sandy, Beds SG19 2DL
The RSPB is a charity and part of its work involves managing 85 bird reserves in Great Britain. The aim of these reserves is the conservation of birds and their habitat. The RSPB organises many activities connected with birdwatching and bird conservation. There is a special organisation for young people: Young Ornithologist Club (YOC)
   If you would like to know more about the RSPB and YOC, if you would like to make a donation or become a member contact the address above.

The following list of reserves in Devon are free to members of the RSPB but there is sometimes a charge for the general public. When visiting reserves remember that they are there for the birds so do nothing which would in any way disturb them or harm their environment. Always keep to marked paths. Reserves are closed on Nov 2-5 and Dec 25-16.

AYLESBEARE COMMON
Map 2 Ac
6m E Exeter on A3052
Open: all times (keep to public footpath, no permit required)
Free
Heathland and common with variety of bird life, nightjar and curlew
RSPB P

CHAPEL WOOD
Map 1 Aa
1½m N Croyde off B3231
Open: all year, daily
Permits available in advance from C G Manning, Sherracombe, Raleigh Park, Barnstaple
Free
Valley with common woodland birds, including nuthatch, redstart and spotted flycatcher
P

Boat Trips

DART PLEASURE CRAFT LTD
Dartmouth (080 43) 3144
5 Lower St, Dartmouth
Open: April-Oct, daily
Trip: Dartmouth-Totnes, 1¼ hours
Charge: £1.70 (ch 90p) single, group reductions 30«
Trip: circular trip of harbour & river Dart

Charge: single £1.30 (ch 70p) 1 hour, return £2.50 (ch £1.30) 1½ hours
Lavatories
  ♿ 🚻 ☕

GRAND WESTERN HORSEBOAT CO
Tiverton (0884) 253345
The Wharf, Canal Hill, Tiverton
Open: April-end Sep (timetable available from Tourist Information Offices, telephone for details)
Trip: 2½ hour return trip on horse-drawn passenger boat up the Grand Western Canal
Charge: £2.50 (ch £1.65)
Also available for private charter; capacity 82, weather protection
Lavatories
See also Country Parks: Grand Western Canal
☕

MILLBROOK STEAMBOAT COMPANY
Plymouth (0752) 822202
Cremyll, Plymouth
Open: April-end Oct, daily; departures every 20 mins from Phoenix Wharf
Trip: 1 hour return trip across Plymouth Sound up the river Dart
Charge: £1.20 (ch 60p), group reductions by arrangement

PLYMOUTH BOAT CRUISES LTD
Plymouth (0752) 822797
Phoenix Wharf, Plymouth
Open: April-Dec, daily; departure 10.45 & every ½ hour according to demand
Trip: 1 hour trip around H M Dockyard & warships
Charge: £1.20 (ch 60p)
Alos trips to Looe & Cawlyford, consult local evening newspaper for departure details

Caravan & Camping Sites

CARAVANS
Any reference in this section to caravans is to touring caravans, not to permanent vans. Some of the sites will have permanent caravans for hire (perhaps being very large holiday camp caravan parks) while others are open only to touring caravans, dormobiles & tents. If you have a preference for a particular type of caravan park always telephone ahead to check.

TENTS
Tents are admitted to the following camping and caravan sites where indicated.

CHARGES
Charges given are for one day ight. Unless otherwise indicated charges for caravans & tents include a car; charges for caravans, tents & dormobiles include two people. There many be a range of charges for tents depending on size.

LOCATIONS
The sites listed are a selection of the smaller touring and camping sites in Devon. For details of larger sites contact your local tourist information centre. Sites are listed under the nearest town

Axminster

ANDREWS HAYES CARAVAN PARK
Map 2 Bc
Wilmington (0404 83) 225

3m W Axminster on A35
Pitches: 60 caravans, 25 tents
Charge: £4 per pitch
Children's playground, swimming pool
🐾

Barnstaple

LOBB FIELDS CARAVAN & CAMPING PARK
Map 1 Bb
Braunton, 3m NE Barnstaple on
B3231
Pitches: 180 (total) caravans & tents
Charge: caravans £4.50 (low season
£2.50); tents £3.50 (low season £2)
Children's play area, access to facilities
at Croyde Bay, electrical hookup
Dogs on leads
🐾

MIDLAND CARAVAN PARK
Map 1 Bb
Barnstaple (0271) 43691
1m W Barnstaple on A361
Pitches: 35 caravans, 100 tents
Charge: Caravans £5 (low season
£2); tents £4 (low season £2)
Children's playground
Dogs on leads
🐾 ⛺ ✕ ⛾

Bideford

STEART FARM
Map 1 Ab
Clovelly (023 73) 239
Horns Cross, 1m S Clovelly, 9m W
Bideford on A39
Pitches: 60 (total) caravans, tents &
dormobiles
Charge: £2 per pitch
Children's playground
🐾

Brixham

HILL HEAD CAMP
Map 4 Ab
Paignton (0803) 842336
Brixham, 1m from town centre on
B3205
Pitches: 380 (total) tents
Charge: £2 per person (£1 low
season)
Children's playground, 2 swimming
pools, evening entertainment
🐾 ⛺ ✕ ⛾

Crediton

SPRINGFIELD CARAVAN PARK
Map 3 Ba
Cheriton Bishop (0647 24) 242
Cheriton Bishop, 5m W Exeter on
A30
Pitches: 100 (total) caravans, tents &
dormobiles
Charge: caravans £3, tents £2.50
Children's play area
🐾

Dartmouth

UNION INN CARAVAN SITE
Map 3 Bc
Kingsbridge (0548) 580241
Kingsbridge, 4m SW Kingsbridge off
A381
Pitches: 10 (total) caravans &
dormobiles
Charge: £3.40 per pitch
Children's play area, games room,
dogs on leads
🐾 ⛺ ⛾

Caravans

Exeter

PATHFINDER TOURING CARAVAN PARK
Map 3 Ba
Cheriton Bishop (064 76) 239
Tedburn St Mary, 5m W Exeter off A30
Pitches: 2 (total) caravans
Charge: £3.50 per pitch
Children's playground, games room, dogs on leads (no large dogs)
🛁 ⌂ ✕ ⚲

BIDGOOD ARMS CARAVAN SITE
Map 3 Ba
Whimple (0404) 822262
Rockbeare, 4m E Exeter on A30
Pitches: 20 caravans, 10 tents
Charge: caravan £2.60, tent £2.10
Children's playground, games room
Dogs on leads
🛁 ⚲ ⌂ ✕

CLIFFORD BRIDGE
Map 3 Ba
Cheriton Bishop (064 72) 226
Dunsford 7m SW Exeter on B3212, 2m W Dunsford
Pitches: 20 (total) caravans, tents & dormobiles
Charge: caravan £3-£4, tents £2 plus 50p per person
Children's play area, swimming pool, dog exercise area
🛁 ✕ ⚲ ⌂

Great Torrington

SMYTHAM CARAVAN & CAMP SITE
Map 1 Bb
Torrington (080 52) 2110
Little Torrington, 1m SW Great Torrington on A386
Pitches: 20 caravans, 30 tents
Charge: £2.50 per pitch
Swimming pool
Dogs on leads
🛁

Honiton

FOREST GLADE HOLIDAY PARK
Map 4 Ba
Broadhembury (0404 84) 381
7m NW Honiton, 3m off A373
Pitches: 75 tents
Charge: £5.70 per pitch
Children's adventure playground, swimming pool
Dogs on leads
🛁 ♿ ⌂

FISHPONDS HOUSE CAMPSITE
Map 2 Bc
Luppitt (0404 89) 698
Dunkeswell, 3m N Honiton on Honiton to Dunkeswell Rd
Pitches: 15 tents
Charge: £4 per pitch
Children's playground, swimming pool, grass tennis court

Ilfracombe

SANDAWAY HOLIDAY PARK
Map 1 Ba
Combe Martin (0271 88) 3555
¼m W Combe Martin A399
Pitches: 15 caravans, 40 tents
Charge: weekly rate, caravans £21, tents £18
Children's playground, swimming pool, private beach
🛁 ⌂ ✕ ⚲

Lynton

CHANNEL VIEW CARAVAN PARK
Map 1 Ba
Lynton (059 85) 3349
Manor Farm, 2m W Lynton town centre on A39
Pitches: 80 (total) caravans, tents & dormobiles
Charge: £5 per pitch
No dogs
🛁 ⌂ ⚲ ✕

SIX ACRE CARAVAN PARK
Map 1 Ba
Lynton (059 85) 3224
Six Acre Farm, 2m SW Lynton off A39
Pitches: 105 (total) caravans, tents & dormobiles
Charge: £3 per pitch
Dogs on leads
🛉

SUNNY LYN CARAVAN SITE
Map 1 Ba
Lynton (059 85) 3384
¾m S Lynmouth on B3234
Pitches: 7 caravans or dormobiles, 30 tents
Charge: £4.70 caravan, £4.60 tent, dogs 35p
Trout fishing, games room, TV lounge
🛉 ⇆ ✕ ♀

Lyme Regis

HOOK FARM CAMPING SITE
Map 4 Ba
Lyme Regis (029 74) 2801
Uplyme, 1¼m NW Lyme Regis off A3070
Pitches: 100 tents
Charge: £3.25 per pitch
🛉

Newton Abbot

ASHBURTON CARAVAN PARK
Map 3 Bb
Moretonhampstead (064 74) 543
3m SE Newton Abbot, 1½m N Ashburton off A38
Charge: £4.20 per pitch
Children's playground
🛉

LEMONFORD HOLIDAY PARK
Map 3 Bb
Newton Abbot (0626 82) 242
Lemonford Farm, 3m E Newton

Abbot on A383
Pitches: 20 tents, 17 caravans
Charge: caravan £3.20, tent £2.40
🛉

RIVER DART COUNTRY PARK LTD
Map 3 Bb
Ashburton (0364) 52511
4m E Newton Abbot, 1½m off A38 on Two Bridges Rd
Pitches: 120 (total) tents
Charge: £7.50 per pitch (low season), £9.20 (high season)
Swimming pool, children's play area, tennis court, riding, fishing
Dogs on leads
🛉 ⇆ ✕ ♀

Okehampton

BRIDESTOWE CARAVAN PARK
Map 3 Ba
Bridestowe (0837 86) 261
½m SE Bridestowe, 2m SW Okehampton
Pitches: 45 (total) caravans, tents & dormobiles
Charge: £3.50 per pitch
Games room
Dogs on leads
🛉 ⇆

CULVERHAYES CAMPSITE
Map 3 Ba
North Tawton (083 782) 431
Sampford Courtenay, 2m NE Okehampton on A3072
Pitches: 75 (total) caravans, tents & dormobiles
Charge: £4 per pitch (high season), £3.50 (low season)
Children's playground, swimming pool
🛉

GRIGGS PREWLEY CARAVAN SITE
Map 3 Ba
Bridestowe (0837 86) 349
2m SW Okehampton on A386

Caravans

Pitches: 52 (total) caravans, tents & dormobiles
Charge: caravans £3.60 (high season), £3.30 (low season), tents £2.50, £2.30
Children's playground, swimming pool, off-licence
Dogs on leads
🐾

MARTIN FARM CARAVAN & CAMPING SITE
Map 3 Ba
Whiddon Down (0647 23) 202
Pitches: 40 (total) caravans, tents & dormobiles
Charge: £3-£4 per pitch
🐾

MOORCROFT CARAVAN PARK
Map 3 Ba
North Tawton (0837 82) 293
Belstone Corner, 3m NE Okehampton on B3215
Pitches: 40 (total) caravans, tents & dormobiles
Charge: caravan £3.50, tent £2.50
Children's playground, swimming pool, games room
🐾 ⌨ ♀ ✕

OKEHAMPTON MOTEL CARAVAN HARBOUR
Map 3 Ba
Okehampton (0837) 2879
1m E Okehampton on A30
Pitches: 25 (total) caravans, tents & dormobiles
Charge: £4.50 per pitch
Children's playground, swimming pool, disco
🐾 ⌨ ✕ ♀

Paignton

HOLLY GRUIT CAMP
Map 4 Ab
Paignton (0803) 5507 63
Pitches: 70 (total) tents
Charge: on application
Children's playground, games room
Dogs on leads
🐾 ⌨ ♀

UPTON MANOR FARM CAMPING SITE
Map 4 Ab
Brixham (080 45) 2384
Brixham, 1m S of town on B3205
Pitches: 75 (total) tents or dormobiles
Charge: £4 per pitch
No dogs
🐾

Seaton

SHRUBBERY CARAVAN PARK
Map 2 Bc
Lyme Regis (029 74) 2227
3m E Seaton on A3052
Pitches: 77 caravans or dormobiles, 10 tents
Charge: £4.60 per pitch (high season), £3.45 (low season)
🐾

South Molton

MOLLAND CARAVAN PARK
Map 1 Bb
Bishops Nympton (076 97) 297
1¼m E South Molton on A361
Pitches: 65 (total) caravans, tents & dormobiles
Charge: £3.50 per pitch
Sauna, swimming pool, dogs under control
✕ ♀

ZEACOMBE CARAVAN & CAMPING PARK
Map 1 Bb
Anstey Mills (039 84) 279
Blackerton Cross, 3½m E South Molton
Pitches: 40 (total) caravans, tents & dormobiles
Charge: £2.50 per pitch (high season), £2 (low season)
🏕

Sidmouth

KINGS DOWN TAIL CARAVAN & CAMPING SITE
Map 2 Bc
Branscombe (029 780) 313
3m NE Sidmouth on A3052
Pitches: 100 (total) caravans, tents & dormobiles
Charge: £3.15 per pitch (high season), £2.75 (low season)
Children's play area, games room
Dogs on leads
🏕

SALCOMBE REGIS CARAVAN & CAMPING SITE
Map 2 Bc
Sidmouth (039 55) 4303
1m NE Sidmouth off A3052
Pitches: 110 (total), 40 caravans, 60 tents
Charge: caravan £4.50, tent £3.50
Adventure playground, dogs on leads
🏕

South Brent

GREAT PALSTONE CARAVAN PARK
Map 3 Bb
South Brent (036 47) 2227
2m W Totnes, 1m S South Brent off A38
Pitches: 50 (total) caravans, tents & dormobiles

Charge: £3.60 (high season), £2.80 (low season)
Children's playground, no groups of young people
Dogs on leads
🏕

Tavistock

HIGHER LONGFORD FARM CARAVAN SITE
Map 3 Ab
Tavistock (0822) 3360
1½m E Tavistock on B3357
Pitches: 52 (total) caravans, tents & dormobiles
Charge: £4 per pitch
Children's playground, games room
Dogs on leads
🏕 ⊐ 🗙 ♀

WOODOVIS CARAVAN PARK
Map 3 Ab
Tavistock (0822) 832968
2m W Tavistock off A390, 1½m N Gulworthy cross roads
Pitches: 60 (total) caravans, tents, dormobiles
Charge: £3.80 per pitch
Children's playground
🏕

Tiverton

OLD ORCHARD CARAVAN PARK
Map 2 Ab
Bampton (0398) 31563
The Garden, Cove, 2m N Tiverton on A396
Pitches: 15 (total) caravans, tents & dormobiles
Charge: caravan £2, tent £1.50-£2.50
Dogs on leads
🏕 ⊐

YEATHERIDGE FARM CARAVAN PARK
Map 2 Ab
Tiverton (0884) 860330
4½m W Tiverton off B3042
Pitches: 50 (total) caravans, tents, dormobiles
Charge: £2.50 («VAT) per pitch
Children's play area, swimming pool, fishing lake
Dogs on leads
🐾

Totnes

BUCKFAST CARAVAN PARK
Map 3 Bb
Buckfastleigh (036 44) 2479
3m NW Totnes off A38
Pitches: 90 (total) caravans
Charge: £3.50 per pitch (low season), £4.50 (high season)
Children's play area
Dogs on leads
🐾

EDESWELL CARAVAN SITE
Map 3 Bb
South Brent (036 47) 2177
2m W Totnes on a385
Pitches: 20 (total) caravans, tents & dormobiles
Charges: £2.30 (low season), £3.45 (high season)
Badminton court, children's adventure playground
🐾 ♟ ✕ ☕

Castles

BAYARD'S COVE CASTLE
Dartmouth
Open: anytime
Free
DofE
🅿

BERRY POMEROY CASTLE
Map 3 Bb/p14
Totnes (0803) 863397
2m NE Totnes
Open: Easter-Oct, daily 10.00-17.00; Nov-March, w/days 9.30-15.30
Free
Dogs under control
🅿 🐾 ♿ ☕🍴
See Historic Homes: Bickleigh Castle

BLACKBURY CASTLE
See Archaeological Sites: Blackbury Castle

CASTLE DROGO
Map 1 Bc
Chagford (064 73) 3306
Drewsteignton, 4m NE Chagford off A382
Open: April-end Oct, daily 11.00-18.00 (last admission 17.30)
Charge: £2, £1 (garden & grounds only); group reductions by arrangement with administrator, Chagford (064 73) 3306
No dogs
NT 🅿 ♿ ☕✕

COMPTON CASTLE
See Historic Homes: Compton Castle

DARTMOUTH CASTLE
Map 4 Ab/p38
Dartmouth
Open: standard DofE, also April-end Sep, Sun 9.30-dusk
Charge: 60p (ch16 & OAPs 30p)
🅿

LYDFORD CASTLE
See Archaeological Sites: Lydford
Castle

MARISCO CASTLE
See Archaeological Sites: Marisco
Castle

OKEHAMPTON CASTLE
Map 4 Aa/p86
Okehampton, S town off A30
Open: standard DofE, also April-Sep,
Suns 9.30-dusk
Charge: 40p (ch16 & OAPs 20p)
P

POWDERHAM CASTLE
Map 4 Aa/p9
Starcross (0626) 890?43
2m S Exeter off A379
Open: Easter BH & late May-early
Sep, Sun-Thur 14.00-18.00
Charge: £1.75 (OAPs £1.50, ch
90p); Connoisseur's day £2, (£1.75
& £1.15), group reductions (20«) by
arrangement
Connoisseur's Day Thursday
Dogs on leads

ROUGEMONT CASTLE RUINS
Map 4 Aa/p46
Exeter
Norman gateway & tower, Roman,
Saxon & Norman walling are all that
remain; castle yard now contains
Exeter Crown Court

TIVERTON CASTLE
Map 2 Ab
Tiverton (0884) 253200
Tiverton, N town centre on A396
Open: Easter w/k & May-late Sep,
Sun-Thur 14.30-17.30
Charge: £1.20 (OAPs 90p, ch 70p);
group reductions, guided tours, sup-
pers & lunches by arrangement
P L

TOTNES CASTLE
Map 3 Bb/p125
Totnes
Open: standard DofE, also April-Sep,
Sun 9.30-dusk
Charge: 40p (ch16 & OAPs 20p)
DofE P

WATERMOUTH CASTLE
See Unusual Outings: Watermouth
Castle

Church Buildings

BUCKFAST ABBEY
Map 3 Bb/p24
Buckfastleigh (036 44) 3301
Buckfast, 1m N Buckfastleigh on A38
Open: all year, Mon-Sat 8.00-21.00;
Sun 7.00-21.00
Free
Guided tours
P & L

BUCKLAND ABBEY
See Historic Homes: Buckland
Abbey

THE CHURCH HOUSE
Map 3 Bb/p130
Widecombe-in-the-moor, 5m NW
Ashburton, 5m SW Bovey Tracey
Open: Spring BH-early Sep, Tue &
Thur 14.00-17.00
Free
National Trust Information Centre
forms part of Church House, formerly
village school and sixteenth-century
brewhouse
NT L &

EXETER CATHEDRAL
Map 4 Aa/p44
Exeter (0392) 74779
Open: all year, daily 7.00-18.30
Charge: 50p (donations gratefully received)
Facilities: guided tours by arrangement only
No dogs

LOUGHWOOD MEETING HOUSE
Map 2 Bc
1m S Dalwood, 4½m E Honiton off A35
Free (donations gratefully received)

PRYSTEN HOUSE
See Museums: Prysten House

ST ANNE'S CHURCH
See Museums: St Anne's Chapel

ST NICHOLAS' PRIORY
Map 4 Aa/p48
Exeter (0392) 56724
The Mint, off Fore St, Exeter
Open: all year, Tue-Sat 10.00-13.00 & 14.00-17.00 (other times by arrangement)
Charge: 40p (ch 20p)

TORRE ABBEY
The King's Drive, Torquay, ½m from town centre on A379
Ruins of monastic abbey and early eighteenth-century church
See also Museums: Torre Abbey Mansion

Country Parks

Unless otherwise stated parks are open all year, daily and are free. There is sometimes a small charge for car parks

ARLINGTON COURT
Shetland ponies and Jacobs sheep graze in this park; nature trail with leaflet, lake, wildfowl and heronry
See Historic Homes: Arlington Court

ASHCOMBE ADVENTURE PARK & FRUIT FARM
Map 4 Ab
Dawlish (0626) 866766
3m NW Dawlish off B3192
Open: early June-late Sep, daily 10.00-20.00
Free
200 acres of park and woodland, nature trail, fishing, fruit picking, exhibition on bee keeping
🅿 ♿ ▭ ♿ ⛱

BECKY FALLS ESTATE
Map 3 Ba/p35
Manaton (0647 22) 259
3½m NW Bovey Tracey on B3344
Open: Easter-Nov, daily 10.00-18.00
Free
Beautiful waterfall in 50 acres of natural woodland, riverside walks
Lavatories, dogs on leads
🅿 ♿ ♿ ▭

BERRY HEAD
Map 4 Ab/p20
Brixham, 1m NE town off B3205
100 acres, high limestone headland with lighthouse, Napoleonic fortifications and linked to long distance footpath; also nature reserve, nature trails
Torbay District Council
🅿 ▭

DARTMEET
Map 3 Bb
Poundsgate (036 43) 213
6m NW Ashburton on A384
One of Devon's most popular beauty
spots at foot of deep-sided valley;
excellent for walking, picnicking and
good views from top of nearby Yar
Tor
Dogs on leads
Lavatories
P ⌷ ✕

FARWAY COUNTRY PARK
Map 2 Bc
Farway (0404 87) 227
3m S Honiton, 1½m S Farway
signposted from B3174
Open: Good Fri-late Sep, daily (except
Sat) 10.00-18.00
Charge: £1.20 (ch & OAPs 60p),
group reductions by arrangement
189 acres including nature trails,
pony trekking, donkey rides, pets
corner
Dogs on leads
P ⌷ ⌷ ⊞ �

GRAND WESTERN CANAL COUN-TRY PARK
Map 2 Ab/p119
Canal Basin, Tiverton
11¼ mile canal from Tiverton to
Somerset border, excellent for walk-
ing, coarse fishing, boating and nature
study, horse drawn boat trips **See
Boat Trips**
Lavatories
P ⅗

LUNDY
Map 1 Aa/p69
Bristol Channel, 11m N Hartland
Point
Open: all year, daily
Charge: £1 (passengers on 'Polar
Bear' or island helicopter free)
Sea passage from Ilfracombe all year
by island vessel 'Polar Bear' or
helicopter from Hartland Point (advis-
able to book in advance)

Island leased to Landmark Trust,
Shottesbrooke, Maidenhead, Berks
(telephone Littlewick Green 3431)No
dogs, no cars
NT ⌷ ⌷

LYDFORD GORGE
Map 3 Aa/p74
Lydford (0822 82) 320
Lydford village, 6m SW Okehampton
off A386
Open: April-end Oct, daily 10.30-
18.00; Nov-end March, daily; water-
fall entrance only
Charge: £1, group reductions on
application to administrator
1½m long gorge containing Devil's
Cauldron, emerges in wooded valley
leading to 90ft White Lady waterfall
Lavatories
NT **P** ⌷ ⌷

MOUNT EDGCUMBE HOUSE & COUNTRY PARK
Map 3 Ab/p93
Plymouth (0752) 822236
Cremyll, 1½m SW Plymouth, access
via Cremyll pedestrian ferry from
Admiral's Hard
Open: all year (park) May-late
Sep, Mon & Tue 14.00-18.00
(house), groups at other times by
arrangement
Charge: house 65p (ch 30p), park
free
Tudor mansion standing in magnifi-
cent parkland with superb views of
Plymouth Sound; formal gardens,
coastal walks, woodland
Dogs on leads
⌷ ⌷ ⅗

NORTHAM BURROWS COUNTRY PARK
Map 1 Ab
2m NW Bideford off B3286
Charge: 50p (car park)
654 acres of coastal salt marsh, sand
dunes and unique pebble ridge adjoining fine sandy beach, suitable for surfing and fishing, nature walks
P

PARKE
Map 3 Ba
Bovey Tracey, ½m NW Bovey Tracey
off B3344
Open: all year, daily
Free
200 acres of parkland, woodland
walks
National Trust and Dartmoor National
Park Interpretation Centre
See also Farms
NT ⬛ 🎚 ☕🎋

STOVER COUNTRY PARK
Map 4 Ab
2m NE Newton Abbot at junction of
A382 & A38
Charge: 20p (car park)
Walking, fishing, nature study, delight-
ful woodland

RIVER DART COUNTRY PARK
Map 3 Bb/p9
Ashburton (0364) 52511
Holne Park, 1m S Ashburton on A38
Open: April-end Sep, daily 10.00-
17.30
Charge: £1.60 (ch £1.10), group
reductions by arrangement
80 acres park, leisure activities,
children's play area, kontiki boating
lake, river and nature walks, tree
houses, pony rides, fly fishing, family
campsite
Lavatories
⬛ 🎚 ☕🎋 ⛲

TAMAR LAKES
Map 1 Ab
12m SW Bideford off A39
51 acre lake and 81 acre reservoir;
waterfowl, bird watching (permit
required), recreation area, sailing,
boardsailing, canoeing, fishing
Lavatories
⬛ 🎋 ☕

WATERSMEET
Map 1 Ba/p50 Map
Famous beauty spot in deep tree lined
gorge; riverside and woodland walks,
fine views, information centre
See also Watersmeet House
NT

Crafts

Furniture

CHRISTOPHER FAULKNER
Totnes (0803) 862861
Ashbridge Barn, Dartington
Open: by arrangement only
Maker of fine furniture, working
entirely on commissions and cus-
tomer's requests

ENDGRAIN
Colaton Raleigh (0395) 68031
Otterton Mill, Otterton
Open: Mon-Sat 9.00-17.30,
telephone in advance
Modern furniture made and designed
to order in English and imported tim-
bers, selection of domestic woodware

General

BICKLEIGH MILL CRAFT CENTRE
Various crafts mainly produced on site
including pottery, engraved glass,
silver, pewterware, copper, brass,
leatherwork, turnery, cloth centre
See also Mills: Bickleigh Mill Craft
Centre & Farm

CIDER PRESS CENTRE
Totnes (0803) 864171
Shinners Bridge, Dartington
Open: all year, Mon-Sat 9.30-17.30;
also Sun, early June-mid Sep
Craft centre with exhibitions and
shops arranged as a village selling
goods ranging from food to furniture
Owned by the Dartington Hall Trust

COUNTRY CRAFTS
Budleigh Salterton (039 54) 2371
5 High St, Budleigh Salterton
Open: all year, Mon-Sat 9.30-17.00
Local crafts, specialises in a wide
range of tapestries also artists'
material

DARTMOOR CRAFT CENTRE
Buckfastleigh (036 44) 2660
46 Fore St, Buckfastleigh
Open: all year, daily 9.30-18.00
Specialises in English craft work, mac-
rame, original batiks, silver jewellery,
toys, sheepskins; also an art gallery;
restaurant selling home-made
products

GULL STUDIO
Moretonhampstead (064 74) 671
Cross St, Moretonhampstead
Open: all year, daily 9.30-19.00
(10.00-18.00 during winter)
Sterling silver jewellery, table ware, all
handmade in studio, also traditional
and modern oil paintings and
woodcarvings

LOTUS GALLERY
Stoke Gabriel (0804 28) 303
Stoke Gabriel
Open: w/days, 9.00-13.00 & 14.00-
17.30
Wide range of crafts from the West
Country, including weaving, jewellery,
rugs and turnery

OTTERTON MILL
Restored corn mill with workshops
making pottery, furniture and weaving
See Mills: Otterton Mill

QUINCE HONEY FARM
Honey in jars, pottery, comb honey,
candles, cosmetics and polish made
from pure beeswax
See Farms: Quince Honey Farm

Ironwork

ERME WOOD FORGE
Ivybridge (075 54) 2343
Woodlands, Ivybridge
Open: w/days 9.00-17.00
Ornamental entrance gates, balus-
trades, firebaskets, dogs; work done
to customers' designs

Jewellery

CROYDE GEMROCK & SHELL
MUSEUM
Jewellery made of gem stones and
shells
See Museums: Croyde Gemrock &
Shell Museum

EDWIN SPENCER
Seaton (0297) 22482
36 Fore St, Seaton
Open: all year, Mon-Sat 9.00-17.00
Jewellery in rare exotic woods,
laminated to give contrasting grain
and colour effects

Pottery

BEAFORD POTTERY
Beaford (080 53) 306
Old Parsonage, Beaford
Open: Mon-Sat 9.00-17.30
(telephone in advance)
Hand thrown domestic stoneware,
mugs, jugs, coffee sets, teapots and
dishes

Crafts

THE BIG JUG CRAFT STUDIO
Chudleigh (0626) 852191
31 Fore St, Chudleigh
Open: Mon-Sat 9.00-17.30
Hand thrown stoneware pottery by
Ian Steele, weaving by Barbara Steele
all on the premises; also selection of
jewellery and wooden toys

BRANSCOMBE POTTERY
Branscombe (0297 80) 248
Higher House, Branscombe
Open: All year, Mon-Sun 9.00-17.30
Table and ovenware, plates, bowls,
vases

C.H. BRANNAM LTD
Barnstaple (0271) 43035
Litchdon St, Barnstaple
Open: all year, w/days (closed last
week in July & first week in Aug)
Tours by arrangement
One of the oldest and best known
potteries in the West Country; red
earthenware, glazed ware and
flowerpots

KEITH SMITH
Colaton Raleigh (0395) 68031
Otterton Mill, Otterton
Open: All year, w/days 9.00-17.00
(telephone in advance)
Domestic stoneware

MALTHOUSE POTTERY
North Molton (059 84) 324
North Molton
Open: May-end Sep, w/days 10.00-
17.00
Small pottery workshop producing
domestic earthenware in local clays

MICHAEL EMMET STONEWARE
Broadhembury (040 484) 254
Higher Slade Farm, Sheldon
Open: all year, daily (telephone in
advance)
Hand thrown stoneware and porcelain

NEWPORT POTTERY
Barnstaple (0271) 72103
72 Newport Rd, Barnstaple
Open: Mon-Sat 10.00-20.00
Decorative and functional craft pottery,
specialises in commemorative pieces

SANDYBROWN
16 Station Rd, South Molton
Open: all year, Mon-Sat 10.00-17.00
Stoneware, platters, jars, teapots,
cups, saucers; selected to show at the
Chelsea Craft Fair 1983

SHEBBEAR POTTERY
Shebbear (0409 28) 271
2m N village signposted A388
Open: all year, daily (telephone in
advance)
Tableware, oven dishes, storage jars,
hand thrown crockery in red earthenware, terracotta flowerpots

SOUTH TAWTON POTTERY
Sticklepath (0837 84) 609
Exeter
Open: all year, w/days 10.00-17.00
Hand thrown pottery; courses also
available

STUDIO CERAMICS
East St, Braunton
Open: all year, Tue-Fri 10.00-17.00
Slip-cast decorated goldware, ceramic
lamp bases

Weaving

BOVEY HANDLOOM WEAVERS
Bovey Tracey (0626) 833424
1 Station Rd, Bovey Tracey
Open: Easter-Oct, Mon-Sat 9.30-
17.30 (early closing Wed)
Pure wool tweeds, ties, scarves and
rugs all woven on the premises

NIKI PETCH
Colaton Raleigh (0395) 68031
Otterton Mill, Otterton
Open: all year, w/days 9.00-17.30

Hand-made rugs, wall hangings to commission, also rough silk and hand knitted sweaters

Woodturner

WOODTURNERS CRAFT CENTRE
Modbury (0548) 830405
New Rd, Modbury
Open: all year, w/days 9.00-18.00, Sat 11.00-18.00
Family business producing quality hand-made wooden ware from egg cups to furniture in homegrown hardwoods and imported teak; commissions to customers' own designs

Cricket

In terms of national cricket Devon is classified as a minor county. Devon won the County Championship in 1978 and has nurtured a number of first class players. Ken Caldwell went on to play for Worcestershire and Roger Tolchard, who began playing for Devon when he was 15, is now captain of Leicestershire. Devon is also well represented in the minor county representative team.
Home games are played at various grounds all over the country, including Exeter, Torquay and Tavistock. Details of fixtures are advertised in the local press and on the local radio during the season. One of the most important aspects of the Devon County Cricket Club is the encouragement and support it gives to youth cricket, embracing every age group from under 11s to under 19s. The Youth

Committee ensures that no young player of ability is overlooked. The success of this policy has been demonstrated by the under 16s who won the 1982 County Championship. It is also worth noting that the 1983 Devon team consisted of four players under 21 years of age who were selected directly through the Youth Committee. For further information contact:
Secretary: Rev K J Warren
Lapford (036 35) 321
49 Highfield, Lapford, Crediton

DEVON CRICKET LEAGUE
Secretary: B Page-Dove
Torquay (0803) 22008
The Carlton Hotel, Torquay
League games are organised on an at home basis and played every Saturday from the first Saturday in May to the last Saturday in August. The league consists of five divisions. For details of fixtures and further information contact the secretary of the league. Although Devon Cricket League is the largest organised body for club cricket in Devon, there are also the North Devon and East Devon Leagues.

DEVON CRICKET ASSOCIATION
Secretary: W F Stutchbury
Torquay (0803) 36549
228 Litchfield Avenue, Torquay
This is the ruling body for cricket in Devon. It is mainly involved in youth cricket, organising over 20 coaching courses for all age groups from 11-17 years. Membership is not only restricted to teams within Devon but also includes teams from all over the world. The Association runs a fixture bureau for visiting teams. All members receive a monthly newsletter produced and published by Mr Stutchbury.

Events

Village Cricket

One of the prettiest pitches in Devon must be in the Valley of the Rocks near Lynton, nestling amidst sloping hillsides. Formed in 1876, the Lynton and Lynmouth Cricket Club play here every Sunday afternoon during the season.

Events

Annual events are listed under the month in which they normally occur but for exact dates and further details of events contact local Tourist Information Centres.

April

TORQUAY
Devon Art Society Picture Exhibition
Gastronomic Exhibition

May

BARNSTAPLE
Folk Festival

EXETER
Devon County Show
Exeter Air Day

KINGSTEIGNTON
Street Market & Floral Dance
Ram Roasting Fayre

TORRINGTON
May Fair

June

BIDEFORD
Foot Race

BISHOPSTEIGNTON
Carnival

BRIXHAM
Trawler Race

DARTMOUTH
Carnival

KINGSBRIDGE
Glove Hanging Ceremony

LYNTON
Annual Festival

PLYMOUTH
Devonport Field Gun Public Runs,
Drake Fair

TORQUAY
Babbacombe & St Mary's Church
Annual Charity Carnival Fayre, Babbacombe Regatta

July

BARNSTAPLE
Folk Festival

BERRY POMEROY
Totnes & District Agricultural Show

BOVEY TRACEY
Carnival Fete

DARTMOUTH
Town Week

DAWLISH
Regatta

HONITON
Annual Fair
Hot Penny Ceremony

MINEHEAD
National Morris Ring
Minehead & Exmoor Festival

NEWTON ABBOT
Country Sports Show

PAIGNTON
Annual Torbay run for vintage motor-cyles & cars

SALCOMBE
Regatta

TAVISTOCK
Carnival

TEIGNMOUTH
Regatta

THORVERTON
Country Fayre & Horse Show

TIVERTON
Carnival

TOPSHAM
Towny Fayre

YEALMPTON
Agricultural Show
Real Ale Festival

August

BEER
Regatta

BOVEY TRACEY
Carnival Procession
Annual Flower Show

BRIXHAM
Flower Show

BUDLEIGH SALTERTON
Cricket Week

CHAPELTON BARTON
Traction Engine Rally

COCKWOOD HARBOUR
The Revels

COMBE MARTIN
Annual Carnival

DARTMOOR
Folk Festival

DAWLISH
Carnival Week

EXMOUTH
West Country Craft Show

HONITON
Lace Exhibition

September

BARNSTAPLE
Annual Fair

BIDEFORD
Regatta & Carnival

KINGSBRIDGE
Agricultural & Horticultural Show

SANDFORD
Carnival

TAVISTOCK
Festival

TIVERTON
River Exe Struggle & Fair

TORQUAY
West Country Embroiderers' Annual Exhibition

WIDECOMBE
Annual Fair

Farms

October

BAMPTON
Pony Fair

CREDITON
Carnival

EXETER
Carnival

HONITON
Marathon & Carnival

OKEHAMPTON
Carnival

TAVISTOCK
Goose Fair

November

OTTERY ST MARY
Guy Fawkes Night

Farms

These are highly productive, working farms which offer visitors an opportunity to see how farm work is carried out. In addition to the farms mentioned here many farms offer open days during the summer, so it is worthwhile checking with tourist information offices.

When visiting a farm wear protective footwear and keep to marked paths.

ASHCOMBE FRUIT FARM
Map 4 Ab
Dawlish (0626) 866766
3m NW Dawlish off B3192
Open: June-Sep, daily 10.00-20.00
20 acres of fruit and vegetables to pick yourself; leisure activities for children
See also Country Parks
🅿 🐾 🚻 ♿ 🍴

ASHLEY COUNTRY COLLECTION
Map 1 Bc
Ashreigney (076 93) 226
Ashley House, 1m NW Wembworthy, 10m SW Crediton on Crediton to Barnstaple Rd
Open: Easter-early Oct, Sat, Mon & Wed 10.00-18.00; Aug, daily (except Thurs) 10.00-18.00
Charge: £1 (ch 45p, OAPs 80p); group reductions by arrangement
Unique collection of 48 breeds of British sheep, fleece exhibition, wheelwrights, coopers, blacksmiths, country craftsmen's tools, 18th century cider pres showing traditional cider production
🅿 ♿ 🍴 🐾

BICKLEIGH MILL FARM
Demonstrates farming the old fashioned way
See Mills: Bickleigh Mill, Craft Centre & Farm

DEVON SHIRE HORSE FARM
Map 3 Bb/p132
Plymouth (0752) 880268
Lower Dunstone Farm, Yealmpton
Open: all year, daily 10.00-17.30; parades at 11.30, 14.30 & 16.15
Charge: £1.50 (ch 75p, OAPs £1.25), group reductions by arrangement
Farm walk, nature trail, craftsmen's workshop, garden, produce centre, children's assault course, pets area
🅿 🐾 🚻 🍴 ♿

EXMOOR FARM ANIMALS
Map 1 Ba
Parracombe (059 83) 227
Mannacott Farm, 2m N Parracombe,
3½m SW Lynton off the A39
Open: Spring BH week, summer
school holidays, Sun-Thurs 12.00-
17.00; early June, Wed & Sun
12.00-17.00
Charge: 50p (ch15 30p), subject to
alteration
50 breeds of cattle and sheep, shear-
ing demonstrations during season,
children's pets corner
Dogs on leads

QUINCE HONEY FARM
Map 1 Bb/p110
South Molton (076 95) 2401
North Rd, South Molton 7m SE
Barnstaple on A367
Open: all year, daily 8.00-18.00 (win-
ter 9.00-17.00)
Charge: £1 (ch free), group reduc-
tions by arrangement
Observations hide; comb and liquid
honey, beeswax candles, cosmetics
and polish
🅿 ⛟🍴 🍺

RARE BREEDS FARM
Map 3 Ba
Parke, Bovey Tracey ½m NW Bovey
Tracey N of B3344
Open: April-end Oct, daily 10.00-
18.00 (last admission 17.30)
Charge: £1.20 (ch 75p), group
reductions by arrangement telephone
Bovey Tracey (0626) 833909
Rare and traditional breeds of dairy
cows, cattle, sheep, pigs and poultry,
designed to preserved genetically pure
stock; pets corner, play area
No dogs
See also Country Parks: Parke
NT 🅿 🍺 ⛟ ♿ 🍴

Gardens

Devon has many glorious gardens
which are open to the public. Many of
them are owned by the National Trust
or are attached to historic homes or
castles. Others are privately owned.

NATIONAL GARDENS SCHEME
01-730 0359
59 Lower Belgrave St, London
SW1W OLR
This charitable trust receives its funds
from many gardens throughout
England and Wales. Most of them are
small, private gardens which open
only a few times a year. Some larger
gardens also contribute their takings
on particular days. Money raised helps
many causes, but particularly district
nurses in need, either because of old
age or illness or because of the stress
and pressure of their work.

  Those gardens which support the
scheme are indicated by the initials
NGS.

  It is not possible to list here all the
gardens in Devon which support the
scheme since many of them are open
only once a year. Included here is a
selection of those open more often.
The NGS publishes a booklet describ-
ing all the gardens in Devon which
support the scheme, as well as a
booklet giving a complete list of all
NGS gardens in England and Wales.
To obtain copies of these booklets
and for further information contact the
address above.

BABBACOMBE MODEL VILLAGE
5 acres of conifers around lake, waterfall and streams
See Unusual: Babbacombe Model
Village

Gardens

BICKHAM HOUSE GARDENS
Map 3 Ab
Yelverton (0822) 852478
4m N Plymouth off A386
Open: April & May, Sun, Easter Mon, Spring BH Mon, selected Suns in July 14.00-18.00 (other times by arrangement for groups)
Charge: 50p
No dogs, home-made teas
🅿 ☕

BICTON PARK
Map 4 Aa/p25
Budleigh Salterton (039 54) 3881
Colaton Raleigh (0395) 68465
2m N Budleigh Salterton on A376
Open: early April-late Oct, daily 10.00-18.00
Charge: £1.95 (ch & OAPs £1.75), includes admission to countryside museum, group reductions by arrangement
50 acres of garden including Italian and American gardens, rare Montezuma pine, tropical and cacti houses
Woodland railway, countryside museum, adventure playground, vintage bus rides
🅿 ♿ ☕🍴

BLACKPOOL GARDEN
Map 4 Ac
Stoke Fleming (0804 27) 261
Blackpool Sands, 2m SW Dartmouth off A379
Open: by arrangement
Charge: 25p (ch 10p)
Steep hillside shrub garden, fine views of the sea, unsuitable for elderly or infirm
Dogs on leads
🅿

BOWDEN HOUSE
Map 4 Ac
Stoke Fleming (0804 27) 234
1½m S Portsmouth, ½m W Stoke Fleming off A379

Open: end April & May, Suns & BH Mons, other times for groups by arrangement
Charge: 50p (ch 25p)
Shrub garden with over 300 varieties of roses, water and heather gardens; superb daffodil displays in spring
No dogs
☕

BUZZACOTT MANOR HOUSE & GARDEN CENTRE
Map 1 Ba/p30
Combe Martin (0271 88) 2359
Combe Martin
Open: Easter-end Sep, daily 10.00-18.00
Charge: 50p (ch 20p, OAPs 30p)
Nature trails, adventure playground fishing, grass sleds
Dogs on leads
🅿 ♿ ☕

CASTLE DROGO
Medium sized garden, shrubs, woodland, walk overlooking fringe gorge
See Castles: Castle Drogo

CASTLE HILL
Map 1 Bc/p95
Filleigh (059 86) 366
Open: by arrangement only
Charge: 30p
Delightful ornamental garden, shrub, woodland garden and arboretum
See also Historic Homes: Castle Hill

CHAMBERCOMBE MANOR
See Historic Homes: Chambercombe Manor

COLETON FISHACRE GARDEN
Map 4 Ac
Open: all year, Sun, Wed & Fri 11.00-18.00; groups by arrangement with Mrs Taylor: Kingswear (0804 25) 617
Charge: £1 (ch 50p)
18 acre garden in stream-fed valley, splendid scenery, garden planted with rare and exotic shrubs created by Lady Dorothy D'Oyly Carte
NT ♿

Gardens

DARTINGTON HALL & GARDENS
Map 3 Bb/p33
1½m NW Totnes off A385
Open: all year, daily; groups by arrangement only, write: Mary Clare Dix, 4 The Mount, Totnes
Free 50p donation gratefully accepted
Visitors may walk round the court-yard, gardens & enter the great hall when not in use; please respect privacy of those who live and work here
Dogs on leads, plants for sale
🅿 🚾

FORTESCUE GARDEN TRUST
Map 3 Ab
Yelverton (082 285) 2493
Buckland Monachorum, 5m N Plymouth, 1½m W of A386 at Yelverton
Open: early April-late Sep, Mon-Fri 14.00-18.00, other times by arrange-ment (not w/ends)
Charge: £1 (ch 25p), group reduc-tions by arrangement
8 acres including 2 acre walled garden
No dogs, plants for sale
🅿 🚾

KILLERTON HOUSE & GARDEN
Map 4 Aa
Exeter (0392) 881345
Broadclyst, Exeter, 5m NE Exeter off B3185
Open: all year, daily 9.00-dusk
Charge: £1.30
See also Museums & Historic Homes: Killerton House
15 acres of rare trees & shrubs, splendid views and walks
NT

KNIGHTSHAYES COURT
Map 2 Ab/p119
Tiverton (0884) 254665
2m N Tiverton off A396
Open: April-end Oct 13.30-18.00 (house); 11.00-18.00 (garden), last admission 17.30

Charge: £2 (house), £1.50 (garden); group reductions by arrangement with administrator
House set in large woodland garden overlooking river Exe, containing shrub garden, specimen trees, formal terraces
Plants for sale
🚾 ♿ 🚻 🍽 ✕

LEEFORD GARDENS
Map 4 Aa
Budleigh Salterton (039 54) 3747
Leeford, 1m NW Budleigh Salterton on B3179
Open: selected Mons in April & Suns in May (telephone for details)
Charge: 60p (ch 30p, OAPs 50p), group reductions by arrangement
40 acres parkland
Cream teas, dogs on leads
🅿 ♿ 🚻

MARWOOD HILL GARDENS
Map 1 Bb
Marwood Hill (0271) 42528
Marwood, 4m N Barnstaple off B3230
Open: all year, daily dawn-dusk (closed 25 Dec), groups by arrangement
Charge: 50p (ch 10p)
8-10 acres of rare trees with shrubs, rose garden, alpine plants, 2 small lakes & bog garden, greenhouses
Cream teas, plants for sale, dogs on leads
🅿 ♿

OLDWAY
Large variety of sub-tropical plants, rock gardens, 2 lakes, waterfall, italian garden and woodland
See Historic Homes: Oldway

OVERBECKS
See Museums: Overbecks Museum & Garden

ROSEMOOR GARDEN TRUST
Map 1 Bb
Torrington (080 52) 2256
Great Torrington, 1m SE town on B3220

179

Open: early April-end Oct, daily dawn-dusk
Charge: 70p (ch 30p, OAPs 50p), group reductions by arrangement
Woodland, shrub roses, ornamental trees, peat and scree garden
🅿 🐾 ⌨🍴

SALTRAM

300 acres landscaped and shrub garden, 18th century octagonal summerhouse, orangery, small classical garden 'Fanny's Bower'
See Historic Homes: Saltram

SANDERS
Map 4 Ac
Stoke Fleming (0804 27) 341
1½m SE Dartmouth on A379
Open: anytime by arrangement only with Mr Julian Gascoigne, Stoke Fleming
Donations gratefully accepted
Outstanding sea views, flowering shrubs, fuchsia collection, woodland garden
No dogs

TAPELEY PARK HOUSE & GARDEN
Map 1 Ab/p7
Instow (0271) 860528
Instow, 1½m S Instow on A39
Open: Easter-late Oct, Tue-Sun & BH Mons 10.00-18.00 (gardens & dairy only); tours of house if numbers justify
Charge: gardens 80p (ch14 40p), disabled free; house & garden £1.50 (ch14 80p)
House set in beautiful Italian garden with rare plants, walled kitchen garden, wooded garden and lily pond
Dogs on leads, plants for sale, craft shop
🅿 🐾 ♿ ⌨🍴

TORRE ABBEY MANSION
Map 4 Ab
Torquay (0803) 23593
King's Drive, Torquay
Italian and water garden, palm house, fine views
See also Historic Homes & Museums

WOODSIDE GARDEN
Map 1 Bb
Barnstaple (0271) 43095
Higher Raleigh Rd, Barnstaple
Open: May-Aug, selected Suns (telephone for details), other times by arrangement
Charge: 50p (ch 25p)
2 acres outstanding ornamental grasses, monocots, hedges, variegated shrubs, plantsman and enthusiast's garden
Dogs on leads
🅿

Golf Clubs

AXE CLIFF GOLF CLUB
Map 4 Ba
Axmouth, Haven Ball ½m S Axmouth off B3172
18 holes/undulating clifftops/4998 ydsPar 67/SSS 64
Visitors: Mon-Sat & Sunafter 13.30 (telephone in advance)
Charge: w/days £5.00 day; w/ends &BHs £5.50 day
🅿 ⌨🍴🏌🍷

BIGBURY GOLF CLUB
Map 3 Bc
Bigbury (0548 81) 557
Bigbury-on-sea, 4m W Kingsbridge off B3392
18 holes/clifftop downland/6007 ydsPar 69/SSS 69/pro

Visitors: w/days (telephone in advance); must have recognised handicap certificate
Charge: w/days £6.00 day or round
🅿 🦽 🖵✕ 🍽 ♀

CHURSTON GOLF CLUB
Map 4 Ab
Churston (0803) 842894
3m S Paignton off A379
18 holes/clifftop downland/6243 ydsPar 71/SSS 70/pro
Visitors: w/days (except Tue),telephone in advance; must have recognised handicap certificate
Charge: £7.00 day or round
🅿 🦽 🖵✕ ♀

EAST DEVON GOLF CLUB
Map 4 Aa
Budleigh Salterton (039 54) 3370
North View Road, Budleigh Salterton
5m E Exmouth off A376
18 holes/downland & heather/6214 yds
Par 69/SSS 70/pro
Visitors: must have recognised handicap certificate (telephone in advance)
Charge: w/days £7.50 day, w/ends £8.50
🅿 🦽 🖵✕ ♀

ELFORDLEIGH GOLF CLUB
Map 3 Bb
Plymouth (0752) 336428
Elfordleigh Hotel, Plymouth 2m NE Plymouth off A374
9/saucer shaped parkland/5600 yds
Par 67/SSS 67/pro
Visitors: welcome anytime
Charge: w/days £4, w/ends £5

🅿 🦽 🖵✕ ♀

HOLSWORTHY GOLF CLUB
Map 1 Ac
Holsworthy (0409) 253177
Holsworthy, 1½m E Holsworthy off the A3072

18 holes/parkland/2671 yds
Par 70/SSS 68
Visitors: telephone in advance
Charge: £5.00 day
🅿 🖵 ♀

HONITON GOLF CLUB
Map 2 Bc
Honiton (0404) 2943
Marlpits Hill, 2m S Honiton off A35
18 holes/parkland/5239 yds
Par 67/SSS 66/pro
Visitors: must have recognised handicap certificate
Charge: w/days £5.00, Sun & BHs £7.00
🅿 🦽✕ ♀ 🖵

ILFRACOMBE GOLF CLUB
Map 1 Ba
Ilfracombe (0271) 62176
Hele Bay, 1½m E Ilfracombe off A399
18 holes/clifftop downland/5857 yds
Par 69/SSS 68/pro
Visitors: telephone in advance
Charge: £6.00 w/days, £7 Suns & BHs
🅿 🦽 🖵✕ ♀ ♀

MANOR HOUSE HOTEL
Map 3 Ba
Moretonhampstead 2m S town off B3212
18 holes/parkland/6016 yds
Par 69/SSS 69/pro
Visitors: telephone in advance
Charge: w/days £6.25 round, w/ends & BHs £9 day, £9.50 round
🅿 🦽✕ ♀ 🖵

NEWTON ABBOT (STOVER) GOLF CLUB
Map 4 Ab
Newton Abbot (0626) 2460
2m NW Newton Abbot on A382
18 holes/parkland/pro
Visitors: must have recognised handicap certificate (telephone in advance)
Charge: w/days £7.00 day, w/ends & BHs £8.00
🅿 🦽✕ ♀ 🖵

Golf Clubs

OKEHAMPTON GOLF CLUB
Map 1 Bc
Okehampton (0837) 2113
Tors Road, Okehampton ½m S off
A30
18 holes/parkland/5272 yds
Par 68/SSS 67/pro
Visitors: telephone in advance
Charge: w/days £5 round, Sat £6,
Sun £7
🅿 🍴 ✕ 🍸 ♀

ROYAL NORTH DEVON GOLF
CLUB
Map 1 Ab
Bideford (023 72) 3817
Westward Ho! 1m N Bideford off
B3238
18 holes/links/6644 yds
Par 72/SSS 72/pro
Visitors: anytime (telephone in
advance)
Charge: £6 day
🅿 🍴 🛏 ✕ 🍸

SAUNTON GOLF CLUB
Map 1 Ab
Braunton (0271) 812436
5m NW Barnstaple off B3231
18(18) holes/championship
parkland/6703(6322)
Par 71 (70)/SSS 73(71)/pro
Visitors: telephone in advance
Charge: championship course w/
days £8, w/ends & BHs £9; west
course £5 w/days £6 w/ends
🅿 🍴 ✕ 🍸 🛏

SIDMOUTH GOLF CLUB
Map 4 Ba
Sidmouth (039 55) 3023
½m NW Sidmouth off B3176
18 holes/links/5188 yds
Visitors: telephone in advance
Charge: w/days £5 day, w/ends &
BHs £6
🅿 🍴 ✕ 🍸 🛏

STADDON HEIGHTS GOLF CLUB
Map 3 Ab
Plymouth (0752) 42475
2m S Plymouth off A379
18 holes/seaside course/5861yds
Par 68/SSS 68/pro

Visitors: must have recognised handicap certificate
Charge: summer w/days £6, w/ends
£7; winter w/ays £5, w/ends £6 day
🅿 🍴 🛏 ✕

TAVISTOCK GOLF CLUB
Map 3 Ab
Tavistock (0822) 2344
Down Rd, Tavistock, 1m E town cen-
tre off B3357
18 holes/moorland/6250 yds
Par 70/SSS 70/pro
Visitors: telephone in advance
Charge: £6 day
🅿 🍴 🛏 ✕ 🍸

TEIGNMOUTH GOLF CLUB
Map 4 Ab
Teignmouth (062 67) 4194
1m NW Teignmouth on B3192
18 holes/heathland/6200 yds
Par 71/SSS 69/pro
Visitors: anytime, must have
recognised handicap certificate
charge: £7.50 day
🅿 🍴 🛏 ✕ 🍸

THURLESTONE GOLF CLUB
Map 3 Bc
Thurlestone (0548 57) 405
Kingsbridge, 4m SW town off A381
18 holes/seaside course/6337 yds
Par 71/SSS 69/pro
Visitors: must have recognised han-
dicap certificate, telephone in advance;
no societies
Charge: w/days £7 day, w/ends £8
🅿 🍴 🛏 ✕ 🍸

TIVERTON GOLF CLUB
Map 2 Ab
Tiverton (0884) 252187
Post Hill, 2m NE Tiverton on A373
18 holes/parkland/6227 yds
Par 71/SSS 70/pro
Visitors: must have recognised han-
dicap certificate, telephone in advance
Charge: w/days £6 day, w/ends &
BHs £7.50 (reductions for students &
juniors)
🅿 🍴 🛏 ✕ 🍸

TORQUAY GOLF CLUB
Map 4 Ab
Torquay (0803) 37471
30 Petitor Rd, St Marychurch, 2m N
Torquay town centre on A379
18 holes/parkland/6251 yds
Par 70/SSS 70/pro
Visitors: must have recognised handicap certificate
Charge: w/days £6.25, w/ends &
BHs £7.50 day
🅿 🛏 🍽 ♀

TORRINGTON GOLF CLUB
Map 1 Bb
Bideford (023 72) 2792
Furzbeam Hill, Torrington, 1m N
Great Torrington on A386
9 holes/SSS 63
Visitors: Mon-Sat after 13.30,
telephone in advance
Charge: w/days £4 day, £5 w/ends
& BHs
🅿 ♀

WARREN GOLF CLUB
Map 4 Ab
Dawlish (0626) 862255
Dawlish 9m S Exeter, 1½m NE
Dawlish off A379
18 holes/flat links/5652 yds
Par 69/SSS 69/pro
Visitors: must have recognised handicap certificate, telephone in advance
Charge: £5.50 w/days, £7 w/ends
& BHs
🅿 🍽 🛏 ♀ 🛋

WRANGATON & SOUTH DEVON GOLF CLUB
Map 3 Bb
South Brent (036 47) 3229
Wrangton, S South Brent off A38
9 holes/moorland/5790 yds
Par 68/SSS 68
ro
Visitors: anytime, telephone in
advance
Charge: available on application
🅿 🛋 ♀

YELVERTON GOLF CLUB
Map 3 Ab
Yelverton (0822 85) 2824
Golf Links Road, Yelverton, 5m S
Tavistock on A386
18 holes/moorland/6300 yds
Par 70/SSS 70/pro
Visitors: must have recognised handicap certificate, telephone in advance
Charge: available on application
🅿 🛏 🛋 🍽 ♀

Historic Homes

A LA RONDE
Map 4 Aa/p51
Exmouth (0395) 265514
Summer Lane, Exmouth 1½m from
town centre off A376
Open: Easter-end Oct, Mon-Sat
10.00-18.00 (Sun 14.00-19.00);
groups in evening by arrangement
Charge: £1 (ch & OAPs 50p); group
reductions by arrangement
Guided tours, Devonshire cream teas
🛏 🅿 🛋 🛃

ARLINGTON COURT
Map 1 Bb/p7
Arlington, 7m NE Barnstaple on A39
Open: house, carriages, stables, shop
& restaurant, April-end Oct, Sun-Fri,
BH Sat & Good Fri 11.00-18.00 (last
admission 17.30)
Garden & park, April-end Oct, daily
11.00-18.00; Nov-end March, daily
11.00-dusk
Charge: £2 (house & carriage collection); £1.30 (gardens & stables);
group reductions by arrangement with
administrator, telephone Shirwell (027
182) 296
Dogs on leads, carriage rides
NT 🛏 🅿 🛋 🛃 🍽

Historic Homes

BICKLEIGH CASTLE
Map 2 Ac
Bickleigh (088 45) 363
Bickleigh, 4m S Tiverton off A396
Open: Easter week; May, Wed, Suns
& BHs; June-mid Oct, Sun-Fri 14.00-
17.00; groups (20£) by arrangement
Charge: £1.50 (ch 75p, OAPs
90p) 🅿 ♿ 🚻

BRADLEY MANOR
Map 4 Ab/p81
½m SW Newton Abbot on A381
Open: early April-end Sep, Wed
14.00-17.00 (last admission 16.45);
also first two Thurs in May & last two
Thurs in Sep 14.00-17.00; groups
(15£) by arrangement in writing
Charge: £1
No lavatories, no coaches, no indoor
photography
NT

BUCKLAND ABBEY
See Museums: Buckland Abbey
13th century monastery converted
into a house by Sir Richard Greville in
1576, bought by Sir Francis Drake in
1581, now a naval and Devon folk
museum

BUZZACOTT MANOR HOUSE
See Gardens: Buzzacott Manor
House & Garden

CADHAY
Map 2 Bc/p88
Ottery St Mary (040 481) 2432
1m NW Ottery St Mary on B3176
Open: spring & summer BHs, mid
July-late Aug, Tue, Wed & Thur
14.00-17.30; groups at other times
by arrangement
Charge: £1 (ch 50p), group reduc-
tions by arrangement
No dogs
🅿 ♿

CASTLE HILL
Map 1 Bb
Filleigh (059 86) 227
Filleigh, 3½m W South Molton off
A361

Open: April-end Sep, groups by
arrangement only
Charge: £1.50
18th century Palladian house with
fine furniture, porcelain, pictures and
tapestries
See also Gardens: Castle Hill

COMPTON CASTLE
Map 4 Ab/p77
(080 47) 2112
2m NW Torquay off A380
Open: April-end Oct, Mon, Wed &
Thur 10.00-12.00 (last admission
11.45) & 14.00-17.00 (last admission 16.30); other times by
arrangement
Charge: £1.10, group reductions by
arrangement with secretary, telephone
(080 47) 2112
🚻 ♿ 🚻

CHAMBERCOMBE MANOR
Map 1 Ba/p61
Ilfracombe (0271) 62624
1m E Ilfracombe off A399
Open: Easter Sun-end Sep, w/days
10.30-17.00, Sun 14.00-17.00
(closed Sats)
Charge: £1 (ch 50p); group (15«)
reductions by arrangement
No dogs
🅿 🚻 ♿

DARTINGTON HALL
See Gardens: Dartington Hall &
Gardens

ELIZABETHAN HOUSE
See Museums: Elizabethan House

FLETE HOUSE
Map 3 Bc/p133
Holberton (0755 30) 308
Ermington, Ivybridge, 3m E
Yealmpton s off A379
Open: early May-late Sep, Wed &
Thur 14.00-16.00
Charge: 50p (ch 25p)
Guided tours by arrangement
♿

FURSDON HOUSE
Map 4 Aa
Exeter (0392) 860860
½m SE Cadbury, 3½m S Tiverton off
A3072
Open: Easter-end Sep; Thur, Sun &
BHs 14.00-17.00, other times by
arrangement
Charge: £1.60 (ch16 75p), group
reductions by arrangement
Guided tours 14.00-16.00
🛇 🅿 🎋

HEMERDON HOUSE
Map 3 Bb
Plymouth (0752) 330964/23816
2m NE Plymouth on Plympton to Cor-
nwood Rd, 1m N A38
Open: early-late May, mid Aug-late
Aug, daily 14.00-17.30; groups (10)
by arrangement
Charge: £1
Guided tours only
🅿 ♿

KILLERTON HOUSE
Map 2 Ac/p21
Exeter (0392) 881345
Broadclyst, 5m NE Exeter on B3185
 Open: April-end Oct, daily 11.00-
18.00 (last admission 17.30)
Garden, all year, daily during light
hours
Charge: £2, £1.50 (garden only);
groups by arrangement with
administrator
Dogs in park only
🛇 🅿 ♿ ✕ �̣

KIRKHAM HOUSE
Map 4 Ab
Mill Lane, Paignton
Open: April-Sep, standard DofE
Charge: 30p (ch16 & OAPs 15p)
Restored Devon stone house, interest-
ing example of 14th century
architecture

KNIGHTSHAYES COURT
See Gardens: Knightshayes Court

THE MANSION HOUSE
Map 4 Ab
Dartmouth (080 43) 2272
Batterbee's Ltd, Dartmouth
Open: all year, Mon-Sat 9.00-17.00
(also Sun during July & Aug, 10.00-
16.00
Free
Official residence of former mayors of
Dartmouth, built 1739; attractively
renovated with Italian style plaster-
work and staircase

MEARSDON MANOR
See Art Galleries: Mearsdon Manor
Now privately owned, this is possibly
the oldest house in Devon and houses
an art collection

OLDWAY
Map 4 Ab/p88
Torquay (0803) 26244
Paignton (0803) 550711
Open: early May-late Sep, Mon-Sat
9.00-13.00 & 14.00-17.15, Suns
14.00-17.00; Oct-April, w/days
9.00-13.00 & 14.00-17.15
Free
Dogs on leads
🅿 �̣

POWDERHAM CASTLE
See Castles: Powderham Castle

SALTRAM
Map 3 Ab/p9
Plymouth (0752) 336546
2m W Plympton, 3½m E Plymouth
between A38 & A379
Open: house, kitchen & art gallery
April-end Oct, Tue-Sun & BH Mons
12.30-18.00; garden, April-end Oct,
daily 11.00-18.00, Nov-March, daily
during daylight hours
Charge: £2.30 (house), 70p (garden
only); group reductions by arrangement with administrator
Dogs in ground only
🛇 🅿 ♿ �̣✕

TAPELEY PARK
See Gardens: Tapeley Park House
and Gardens
William and Mary mansion overlooking the Atlantic; home of the Christie
family of Glyndebourne; conducted
tour of house according to numbers

TORRE ABBEY
Map 4 Ab
Torquay (0803) 23593
The King's Drive, Torquay
Open: April-end Oct, daily 10.00-
17.00
Charge: 30p (ch & OAPs free)
Guided tours
🅿 �#

TUDOR
See Museums: Devonshire Collection of Period Costumes
Restored residence now housing
extensive costume collection

UGBROOKE
Map 4 Ab/p84
Chudleigh (0626) 852179
3m NE Newton Abbot off A380
Open: spring BH-late Sep, daily
12.30-17.30 (grounds), 14.00-
17.30 (house)
Charge: £1.50 (ch 80p), £1
(grounds only); group reductions by
arrangement
Adventure playground, boating lake,
trout fishing & pets corner
🐾 🅿 �# ♿

YOULSTON PARK
Map 1 Bb
Shirwell (0271 82) 200
Shirwell, 3m NE Barnstaple off A39
Open: by arrangement for Historic
Association members only
Charge: on application
Georgian house featuring medieval
beamed roof, 18th century stucco
ceilings, a fine staircase, chinese
decorations and a collection of
Victoriana

Horseracing

DEVON & EXETER NATIONAL HUNT RACECOURSE
Map 4 Aa
Exeter (0392) 832599
Great Haldon, 5m SW Exeter on A38
Meetings: 15 per year
Charge: daily membership £5, tatter-
salls £3, grandstand £1.50
🅿 🚊#

NEWTON ABBOT RACECOURSE
Map 4 Ab/p84
Newton Abbot (0626) 3235
½m N Newton Abbot on A380
Meetings: 20 per year
Charge: £1.50 entry to course,
£4.20 tattersall
National Hunt racing
🅿 🚊#

Industrial Archaeology

BLACK TOR BLOWING HOUSES
Map 3 Bb
Black Tor Falls, river Meavy, 2½m NE
Yelverton off B3212
Access from the Yelverton/
Princetown Rd across Walkhampton
Common near Black Tor
The remains of two blowing houses
on each bank of the river; outstanding
feature is the doorway with its lintel
still in position

Industrial Archaeology

FINCH FOUNDRY
The foundry, powered by water wheels, produced tools used by Devon miners and farmers between 1814 and 1960; it was also the site of the village blacksmith
See Museums: Finch Foundry Museum

HAYTOR GRANITE TRAMWAY
Map 3 Bb/p82
3m SW Bovey Tracey off B3344
Much of the trackway which ran from Holwell Quarry to Teigngrace Wharf can still be traced; made of granite blocks about 1 foot square with a rebate 7½ inches wide and 3 inches deep cut on either side, designed to carry heavy goods

HAYTOR QUARRY
Map 3 Bb
Haytor granite was used to build London Bridge in 1825 and the library of the British Museum; the quarry flourished during the mid-nineteenth century; today the quarries are flooded, deserted and provide a tranquil retreat

MORWELLHAM QUAY
Restored copper port, once the greatest in Queen Victoria's Empire
See Museums: Morwellham Quay

THE POWDER MILLS
Map 3 Bb
Beside Cherry Brook, 2m N Two Bridges, NW off B3212
Mills visible from road but privately owned and not open to the public Founded by George Frean in 1844 the mills produced gunpowder or black or rock powder; the mills were served by a leat fed by the East Dart;

the walls of the wheel house remain and the small mortar or eprouvette used for testing is visible from the road

RIVER WALKHAM BLOWING HOUSES
On east bank of the river Walkham from Merrivale Bridge on A384
The first blowing house is a fairly large furnace well preserved beneath which is a float; also a mould stone next to the furnace with a sample mould cut in its rim. The second is half a mile upstream where the remains of a wheel pit and mould stone can be seen

SILVERBROON MINE
½m S Ilsington village, close to stream which flows between the woods
Said to be 200-years-old; once produced dead ore

WARREN HOUSE INN
6m SW Moretonhampstead, ½m N Postbridge on B3212
The existing inn is still a thriving pub which replaced an older house on the opposite side of the road; a footpath leads down to the headstream of the Vitifer tin mine where the artificial ravines made by the workers before the days of shaft mining can be seen.

WHEAL BETSY
Map 3 Aa/p89
N Mary Tavy, E of A386
Visible from the road
Shell of a fine old engine house with stack, the last of its kind on the moor, surrounded by old working, spoil tips, dry channels, tracks and shafts once produced arsenic, silver, lead and copper
NT

187

Lighthouses

TRINITY HOUSE LIGHTHOUSE SERVICE
01-480 6601
Tower Hill, London EC3
The lighthouses and lightships are important coastal land and navigation marks on the British coastline are controlled from Trinity House, London

BULL POINT LIGHTHOUSE
Map 1 Aa
Woolacombe (0271) 870535
Open: all year, Mon-Sat 13.00-hour before dusk (closed during fog telephone in advance)
Free
Constructed in 1879, destroyed by cliff subsidence in 1972, rebuilt 1974

LYNMOUTH FORELAND LIGHTHOUSE
Map 1 Ba
Brendon (059 87) 226
2m NE Lynmouth
Open: all year, Mon-Sat 13.00-hour before dusk (closed during fog, telephone in advance)
Free
Built in 1900, well worth a visit, magnificent views from the cliffs

SMEATON'S TOWER
See Other Historic Buildings:
Smeaton's Tower

START POINT LIGHTHOUSE
Map 4 Ac
Kingsbridge (0548) 580225
Open: all year, Mon-Sat 13.00-hour before dusk (closed during fog, telephone in advance)

Situated on one of the most exposed peninsulas on the English coast; built in 1836 and designed by James Walker it has features of the 'gothic' movement; accessible by narrow road cut from the rock face

HARTLAND POINT LIGHTHOUSE
Map 1 Ab/p55
Hartland (023 74) 328
Open: all year, Mon-Sat, 13.00-1 hour before dusk. Closed during fog & at other times. Advisable to phone in advance

Local Industry

AXMINSTER CARPETS LTD
Map 2 Bc/p9
Axminster (0297) 32244
Woodmead Rd, Axminster
Open: all year, w/days 9.30-12.00 & 14.30-16.30
Free
Visitors welcome to visit the factory where Axminster carpets are still made

DARTINGTON GLASS
Map 1 Bb
Torrington (080 52) 3797
School Lane, Great Torrington
Tours: all year, w/days 9.30-10.30 & 12.00-15.30 (closed 16 Dec-9 Jan); groups (10«) by arrangement only
Free
Skilled glass blowers moulding fine lead crystal tableware
P ‌

ENGLISH LACE SCHOOL
Map 2 Ab/p52 & 119
Tiverton (0884) 253918
St Peter's St, Tiverton
Open: April-end Sep, w/days 10.00-16.30; open days, Easter BH, spring BH & summer BH, 10.00-16.30
Charge: 50p lace display, 85p open days
Courses: telephone for details
No dogs
🐾

J & F J BAKER & CO LTD
Map 4 Ba/p30
Colyton (0297) 52282
Hamlyns Mill, King St, Colyton
Open: all year, w/days 10.00-16.00
Free
Visitors welcome to visit the only oak-bark tannery in England, where skins are processed to produce high quality leather
No dogs or small children
🅿 🐾

Mills

BICCLESCOMBE MILL
Map 1 Aa
Ilfracombe (0271) 65477
Bicclescombe Park, Ilfracombe
Open: early April-early Oct, daily 10.30-18.30
Charge: 5p (ch 2p)
Recently restored 18th century corn mill situated in pleasant park
🅿 ⬚

BICKLEIGH MILL, CRAFT CENTRE & FARM
Map 2 Ac/p15
Bickleigh (088 45) 419
Bickleigh, 4m S Tiverton on A396

Open: Jan-March, daily 14.00-17.00; April-Dec, daily 10.00-18.00
Charge: not available at time of publication
Retail craft and workshops, 19th century farm, agricultural museum, fish farm
Dogs on leads
🅿 🐾 ⬚ ✕ ♀ ⅋

COLDHARBOUR MILL
Map 2 Bc/p31
Craddock (0884) 40960
Uffculme, 6m E Tiverton on B3181
Open: Easter-end Sep, Mon-Sat 9.00-17.00; early Oct-Easter, w/days 9.00-17.00
Charge: £1 (ch 50p, OAPs 75p)
Group and family reductions
18th century working mill/museum in rural setting, also produces knitting and woven cloth
No dogs
🅿 ⬚ 🐾 ⅋

OTTERTON MILL
Map 4 Aa
Colaton Raleigh (0395) 68521
2m N Budleigh Salterton off A376
Open: Easter-end Oct, daily 11.00-17.30; Oct-March, daily 14.00-17.30
Charge: 60p (ch 30p), group reductions by arrangement
Restored corn mill in working order producing wholemeal flour by water power; exhibition gallery and workshops making pottery furniture, woven cloth, woodcraft, lace
Guided tours
🅿 🐾 ⬚ ✕ ⅋

PLAISTOW MILL
Map 1 Bb
Shirwell (027 182) 224
Muddiford, 2m N Barnstaple, ½m S village on B3230
Open: all year, daily
Free:
Restored mill and water wheel under restoration; small collection of farm animals
🅿 ⅋

Museums

THE OLD CORN MILL
Map 1 Ba
Ilfracombe (0271) 63162
1m E Ilfracombe town centre off
A399
Open: Easter-end Oct, w/days
10.00-17.00 (Sun 14.00-17.00)
Charge: 60p (ch 30p)
Complete watermill dating from 16th
century with 18ft overshot water
wheel and mill machinery, now pro-
duces wholemeal flour
No dogs
🅿 🏃

WEMBURY MILL
Map 3 Ac
Wembury beach, 2m SE Plymouth
near Yealm estuary
Open: April-end Oct, daily 11.00-
18.00 (including shop); Nov-Dec
selected times
Beach cafe and shop housed in for-
mer mill house
No dogs
🅿 🏃 🖙

Museums

AGRICULTURAL & COUNTRY
CRAFT MUSEUM
See Farms: Bickleigh Mill Farm

ALLHALLOWS MUSEUM
Map 4 Ba/p59
Farway (040 487) 307
High St, Honiton
Open: Easter Sat & Mon, mid May-
late Sep, Mon-Fri 10.00-17.00 (early
April-mid May by arrangement)
Charge: 25p (ch 5p)
Superb displays of Honiton lace with
craft demonstrations during summer
🅿 🏃

ALSCOTT FARM AGRICULTURAL
MUSEUM
Map 1 Ab/p105
Shebbear (040 928) 206
Shebbear, 12m S Bideford, 5m SW
Torrington off A386
Open: Easter-end Sep, daily noon-
dusk; Oct-Easter by arrangement only
Charge: 60p (ch 20p, OAPs 40p),
prices subject to alteration, group
reductions by arrangement
Collection of vintage farm tractors and
equipment, unique scale model of
Edwardian travelling fair
🏃

ARLINGTON COURT
Large collection of horse drawn
vehicles
See Historic Homes: Arlington Court

ASHBURTON MUSEUM
Map 3 Bb/p8
Ashburton (0364) 52298
1 West St, Ashburton, 3m SW New-
ton Abbot on A38
Open: mid May-late Sep, Tue, Thur,
Fri & Sat 14.30-17.00
Free
Local and American indian antiques,
geology specimens
No dogs
🅿 🏃

ASHLEY COUNTRY COLLECTION
See Farms: Ashley Country Collection

BICKLEIGH CASTLE MUSEUM
See Historic Homes: Bickleigh
Castle

BRAUNTON & DISTRICT MUSEUM
Map 1 Ab
Church St, Braunton, 2½m NW
Barnstaple on A361
Open: mid May-end Sept, Tues-Sat
10.00-12.00 & 14.00-16.00, other
times by arrangement
Charge: 10p (ch 5p)
Guided tours by arrangement
🅿 🏃

BRITISH FISHERIES MUSEUM
Map 4 Ab
Brixham (080 45) 2861
The Old Market House, The Quay,
Brixham, 2m S Paignton on A3022
Open: Spring BH-end Sept, daily
10.00-1900; Oct-Mar, Tues-Sat
9.00-13.00 & 14.00-17.00
Charge: 25p (ch & OAPs **Free**)
🅿 🐾 ♿

BRIXHAM MUSEUM
Map 4 Ab/p20
Brixham (080 45) 3250
Bulton Cross, Brixham
Open: end April-mid Oct, Mon-Sat
10.00-17.00, Sun 11.00-13.00 &
14.00-17.30
Charge: 40p (ch 10p, OAPs 20p)
Reductions for groups by
arrangement
🅿 🐾

BRUNEL ATMOSPHERIC RAILWAY MUSEUM
Map 4 Aa
Starcross (0626) 890000
Starcross, 2m S Exeter town centre
off A379
Open: Easter-end Oct, Mon-Fri
10.00-13.00 & 14.15-17.15, Sun
14.15-17.15; Nov-Easter by arrange-
ment only
Charge: £1 (ch 50p)
Reductions for groups by
arrangement
♿ 🐾

BUCKLAND ABBEY
Map 3 Ab/p134
Plymouth (0752) 6800 ext 4378
6m S Tavistock, 1¼m SW Yelverton
off A386
Open: Easter-end Sept, Mon-Sat (incl
BHs) 11.00-18.00, Sun 14.00-
18.00 (last admission 17.30); Oct-
Wed before Easter, Wed, Sat, Sun
14.00-17.00 (last admission 16.30)
Charge: £1.20 (subject to alteration)
Reductions for groups by written

arrangement with Director, City
Museum & Art Gallery, Drakes Circus,
Plymouth
Dogs in grounds only
🅿 🐾 🖵

CITY MUSEUM & ART GALLERY
Map 3 Ab
Plymouth (0752) 668000 ext 4378
Drakes Circus, Plymouth
Open: all year, Mon-Sat, 10.00-
18.00
Free
Guided tours by arrangement
♿

COBBATON COMBAT VEHICLES MUSEUM
Map 1 Bb/p110
Chittlehamholt (076 94) 414
Cobbaton, 5m W South Molton, 2m
NW Chittlehampton off B3227
Open: March-May & Oct, Sun-Thurs
10.00-18.00; June-Sept, daily
10.00-18.00
Charge: £1 (ch 50p)
Reductions for groups
Children's play area & assault course
🅿 🐾 ♿ 🍴

COOKWORTHY MUSEUM SOCIETY
Map 3 Bc/p65
Kingsbridge (0548) 3235
The Old Grammer School, Fore St,
Kingsbridge, 5m S Totnes on A381
Open: Easter-mid Oct, Mon-Sat
10.00-17.00
Charge: 50p (ch & OAPs 30p)
Reductions for school groups by
arrangement
♿

COUNTRY LIFE MUSEUM
Map 4 Ab/p52
Exmouth (039 52) 74533
Sandy Bay, 1m SE Exmouth off A376
Open: early May-early Oct, daily
10.30-17.00
Charge: £1.20 (ch 50p, OAPs 80p)
Reductions for groups by
arrangement
🅿 🖵 ♿

COUNTRYSIDE MUSEUM
Bicton Park, East Budleigh
Comprehensive range of old agricultural vehicles, including tractors, wagons & a gipsy caravan; Hall of Transport has early steam & electric cars as well as petrol models.
See Gardens: Bicton Park

DARTMOUTH MUSEUM
Map 4 Ab/p40
Dartmouth (080 43) 2923
The Butterwalk, Dartmouth
Open: Easter-late Oct, Mon-Sat 11.00-17.00; Nov-March, Mon-Sat 14.15-16.00, other times by arrangement
Charge: 30p (ch 10p), subject to alteration)
Dogs on leads

DAWLISH MUSEUM
Map 4 Ab/p41
Dawlish (0626) 863318
The Knowle, Dawlish
Open: early May-end Sept, Mon-Sat 10.00-12.30 & 14.00-17.00, Sun 14.00-17.00
Charge: 35p (ch 10p)

DEVON MUSEUM OF MECHANICAL MUSIC
Map 1 Ac
Milton Damerel (0409 26) 378, Shebbear (040 928) 483
Mill Leat, Thornbury 5m NE Holsworthy off A388
Open: Easter-end Sep, daily 10.30-12.30 & 14.00-17.00, evening groups by arrangement
Charge: £1 (ch 65p, OAPs 85p, disabled 50p), reductions for groups (25«) by arrangement

DEVONSHIRE COLLECTION OF PERIOD COSTUME
Map 3 Bb
Totnes (0803) 862423
10a High St, Totnes
Open: spring BH-early Oct, w/days11.00-17.00, Sun 14.00-17.00
Charge: 40p (ch 10p), subject to alteration
Guided tours for groups (26«) by arrangement

DEVONSHIRE REGIMENT MUSEUM
Map 4 Aa
Exeter (0392) 76581 ext 208
Wyvern Barracks, Barracks Road, Exeter off B3182
Open: all year, w/days 9.00-16.15
Free

ELIZABETHAN HOUSE
Map 3 Bb/p126
Totnes (0803) 863821
70 Fore St, Totnes
Open: March-Oct, Mon-Sat, 10.30-13.00 & 14.00-17.30
Other times by arrangement
Charge: 25p (ch 10p)

FAIRLYNCH ARTS CENTRE & MUSEUM
Map 4 Aa/p25
Budleigh Salterton (039 54) 2666
27 Fore St, Budleigh Salterton, 1½m E Exmouth on A376
Open: Easter-end Sep, w/days 14.30-17.30; July-Aug, Mon-Sat 10.30-13.00 & 14.30-17.00, Sun 12.30-17.30; 26 Dec-mid Jan, w/days 14.30-16.30
Charge: 30p (ch & OAPs 10p)
Reductions for groups by arrangement

FINCH FOUNDRY MUSEUM
Map 3 Ba/p86
Sticklepath (083 784) 286
Sticklepath, 1m E Okehampton off A30
Open: all year, daily 11.00-17.00 or dusk if earlier
Charge: £1 (ch 50p)
Reductions for groups by arrangement

GEM ROCK & SHELL MUSEUM
Map 1 Ab/p31
Croyde (0271) 890407
Croyde, 4m NW Barnstaple on
B3231
Open: Easter-end Sept, daily
10.00-17.30 (July & Aug 10.00-
22.00); Oct-March by arrangement
only
Charge: 10p (ch 5p)
🅿 🏊 ♿

HARTLAND QUAY MUSEUM
Map 1 Ab/p57
Hartland (023 74) 594
Hartland Quay, 1½m W Hartland
Open: Easter week & spring BH-end
Sep, daily 10.00-17.00
Charge: 30p (ch 15p)
Guided tours by arrangement
🅿 ⊡⇥

HOLSWORTHY MUSEUM
Map 1 Ac
Holsworthy (0409) 253718
Manor Car Park, Holsworthy, 10m
SW Bideford at junction A388 &
A3072
Open: early May-end Sep, Tue, Wed
& Thurs 10.00-16.00
Charge: 25p (ch free)
Reductions for groups by
arrangement
🅿 ♿

ILFRACOMBE MUSEUM
Map 1 Aa/p61
Ilfracombe (0271) 63541
Runnymeade Gardens, Wilder Road,
Ilfracombe
Open: Oct-Easter, daily 10.00-13.00;
Easter-Sep, daily 10.00- 17.30
Charge: 30p (ch 10p)
Reductions for OAPs at certain times
in the year
No dogs
🏊 ♿

KILLERTON HOUSE
Map 4 Aa
Exeter (0392) 881345

Broadclyst, 5m NE Exeter off B3185
Open: April-end Oct, daily 11.00-
18.00
Charge: £1.80
Reductions for groups by
arrangement
No dogs
See also Gardens: Killerton House &
Garden
NT 🏊 ♿ ⊡✕

LYN & EXMOOR MUSEUM
Map 1 Ba/p50
St Vincents College, Market St,
Lynton
Open: Easter-end Sep, w/days
10.00-12.30 & 14.00-17.00, Sun
14.00-17.00
Charge: 20p (ch 10p)

LYNTON SMITHY
Map 1 Ba/p50
Castle Hill, Lynton
Open: April-Sep, daily 9.30-18.00
Charge: 10p (Honesty Box)
🅿

MARITIME & LOCAL HISTORY
MUSEUM
Map 3 Bc/p102
Salcombe (054 884) 2736
Cook's Boat Store, Customs House
Quay, Salcombe
Open: Spring BH-end Sep, daily
10.30-12.30 & 14.30-16.30
Charge: 20p (ch14 free)
Dogs on leads
🅿 🏊

MARITIME MUSEUM
Map 4 Aa/p47
Exeter (0392) 58075
Town Quay & Canal Basin, approach
via Alphington Street & Haven Road,
Exeter
Open: June-Sep, daily 10.00-18.00;
Oct-May, daily 10.00-17.00
(closed 25 & 26 Dec)
Evening visits for groups by
arrangement

Charge: £2 (ch £1, OAPs £1.60)
Reductions for groups by
arrangement
🅿 🛗 ⛱

MORWELLHAM QUAY OPEN AIR MUSEUM
Map 3 Ab/p80
Tavistock (0822) 832766
Morwellham Quay, 2m SW Tavistock
off A390
Open: all year, daily 10.00-18.00 or
dusk if earlier (closed 25 Dec)
Charge: £2.50 (ch £1.20, OAPs £2
Reductions for groups by
arrangement
Trail guides issued free to each car
🅿 🛗 ⛱ ✕

MOTOR CYCLE COLLECTION
Map 1 Ba/p30
Combe Martin (027 188) 2346
Cross St, Combe Martin, 2m E
Ilfracombe on A399
Open: end May-mid Sep, daily
10.00-18.00
Charge: 50p (ch & OAPs 30p)
Reductions for groups by
arrangement
🅿 ♿

NATIONAL COASTGUARD MUSEUM
See Museums: Brixham Museum

NATURAL HISTORY SOCIETY MUSEUM
Map 4 Ab
Torquay (0803) 23975
529 Babbacombe Rd, Torquay
Open: late March-late Oct, Mon-Sat
10.00-16.45; late Nov-late Feb, w/
days 10.00-16.45. (closed Good Fri,
25 Dec, 1 Jan)
Charge: 50p (ch 25p)
Guided tours by arrangement
🅿

NORTH DEVON MARITIME MUSEUM
Map 1 Ab/p6
Bideford (023 72) 6042

Odun House, Odun Rd, Appledore,
1m N Bideford on A386
Open: Easter-end Sep, daily 14.30-
17.30, also Tues & Fri 11.00-13.00
Charge: 50p (ch 10p) groups and
guided tours by arrangement only
🅿 ♿

OKEHAMPTON & DISTRICT MUSEUM OF DARTMOOR LIFE
Map 1 Bc/p86
Okehampton (0837) 3020
3 West St, Okehampton
Open: April-Oct, Mon-Sat 10.30-
16.30
Charge: 60p (ch 30p, OAPs 40p),
group reductions by arrangement
Tourist Information Office
🛗 ♿

OVERBECKS MUSEUM & GARDEN
Map 3 Bc/p102
Sharpitor, 1½m SW Salcombe,
signposted from Marlborough &
Salcombe
Open: museum April-end Oct, daily
11.00-13.00 & 14.00-18.00 (last
admissions 12.45 & 17.30); garden
all year, daily
Charge: museum & garden £1.10,
garden only 80p
Parking refunded when buying ticket
No dogs in museum
🅿 🛗 ⛱

PAPERWEIGHT CENTRE
Map 3 Ab
Yelverton (0822) 854250
Buckland Terrace, Leg O' Mutton cor-
ner, Yelverton, 2m SE Tavistock on
A386
Open: week before Easter-end Oct,
Mon-Sat 10.00-17.00
Free
🅿 ⛴ ♿

PAULISE DE BUSH COLLECTION OF COSTUMES
See: Killerton House

PLYMOUTH HISTORY MUSEUM
See Other Historic Buildings:
Merchant's House

PRYSTEN HOUSE
Map 3 Ab/p93
Plymouth (0752) 661414
Finewell St, off Royal Parade,
Plymouth
Open: all year, Mon-Sat 10.00-16.00
(closed on Church Festival days)
Charge: 40p (ch & OAPs 20p)
Reductions for groups by
arrangement

ROUGEMOUNT HOUSE MUSEUM
Map 4 Aa
Exeter (0392) 56724
Castle St, Exeter
Open: all year, Tue-Sat 10.00-13.00
& 14.00-17.15
Charge: 40p (ch 20p) subject to
alteration
Guided tours for school groups by
arrangement

ROYAL ALBERT MEMORIAL MUSEUM
Map 4 Aa/p48
Exeter (0392) 56724
Queen St, Exeter
Open: all year, Tue-Sat 10.00-17.00
Charge: 60p (ch16 free)
&

ST ANNE'S CHAPEL MUSEUM
Map 1 Bb/p12
Barnstaple (0271) 72511 ext 272
St Peter's churchyard, Barnstaple
Open: May-Sep, Mon-Sat 10.00-
13.00 & 14.00-17.00 (Weds 10.00-
13.00)
Other times by arrangement
Charge: 15p (ch free)

SIDMOUTH MUSEUM
Map 2 Bc
Sidmouth (039 55) 2946/6139
Hope Cottage, Church St, Sidmouth
Open: Easter-late Oct, Mon-Sat
10.30-12.30 & 14.30-16.30, Sun
14.30-16.30
Other times by arrangement
Charge: 25p (ch16 10p, OAPs 25p)

SOUTH MOLTON MUSEUM
Map 1 Bb/p110
South Molton (076 95) 2501
The Guildhall, South Molton
Open: Feb-Nov, Mon, Tue, Thurs &
Fri 10.30-12.30 & 14.00-16.00;
Wed & Sat 10.00-12.00
Free
P &

TEIGNMOUTH MUSEUM
Map 4 Ab
Teignmouth (062 67) 4084
29 French St, Teignmouth
Open: early May-late Oct, Tue-Fri
10.00-12.30 & 14.30-17.00 also
Thurs 19.00-21.00 & Sun 14.30-
17.00
Other times by arrangement
Charge: 30p (ch 10p)
Guided tours by arrangement
P &

TIVERTON MUSEUM
Map 2 Ab/p117
Tiverton (0884) 256295
St Andrew's St, Tiverton
Open: all year, Mon-Sat 10.30-16.30
(closed BHs & Dec 25-Jan 1)
Free
Guided tours
P &

TOPSHAM MUSEUM
Map 4 Aa/p120
Topsham (039 287) 3244
25 The Strand, Topsham, 2m SE
Exeter on B3181
Open: all year, Mon, Wed & Sat
14.00-17.00
Free

**TORBAY TRAINS ROBES ROSES &
AIRCRAFT MUSEUM**
Map 4 Ab/p77
Paignton (0803) 553540
Higher Blagdon, 2m W Paignton off
A385
Open: Easter-late Oct, daily, 10.00-
18.00
Charge: £1.80 (ch 90p, OAPs
£1.20), prices subject to change
Reductions for groups 20« by
arrangement
No dogs
🅿 ♿ ⛲🍴

TORRE ABBEY MANSION
Map 4 Ab/p123
Torquay (0803) 23593
The Kings Drive, Torquay, ½ from
town centre on A379
Open: early April-end Oct, daily
10.00-17.00
Charge: 30p (ch & OAPs free)
🅿 ⛲🍴

TORRINGTON MUSEUM
Map 1 Bb/p52
Town Hall, Great Torrington, 4m SW
Bideford on A386
Open: early May-late Sept, w/days
10.00-12.45 & 14.15-16.45
Free

TOTNES GUILDHALL
See Other Historic Buildings: Totnes Guildhall

TOTNES MOTOR MUSEUM
Map 3 Bb/p127
Totnes (0803) 862777
The Quay, Totnes
Open: all year, daily 10.00-17.30
(Oct-Easter 17.00) closed 25, 26, 27
Dec
Charge: £1 (ch 50p, OAPs 85p)
♿

VINTAGE TOY & TRAIN MUSEUM
Map 2 Bc
1st floor, Field's Department Store,
Sidmouth

Open: early April-end Oct, Mon-Sat
9.00-17.00 (Thurs 13.00)
Charge: 60p (ch 30p)
No dogs
🅿 ⛲

National Parks

A National Park is a large area of
country with a wild and sparsely pop-
ulated core where special care is
taken to conserve beauty and points
of interest. In Devon Exmoor and
Dartmoor are classified as National
Parks and should not be confused
with the properties of the National
Trust or National Nature Reserves. A
national park is not a nationalised park
but land belonging to an individual,
including organisations, public bodies
and farmers. As a visitor your rights
are few, however by custom and
tradition, the walker and rider will
experience little or no restrictions
across the open moor if they observe
the few simple rules of the country
code. The National Parks were created
under the 1949 National Parks and
access to the Countryside Acts and
their main statutory duties are to preserve and enhance the landscape and
to promote the enjoyment of National
Parks by the public. The Coun-
trysideCommission was formed in
1968 and is generally responsible for
the conservation of the countryside in
England and Wales. The Commission
published a **Country Code** whose 12
points should be observed by all
visitors to the countryside: guard
against all risks of fire, fasten all
gates, keep dogs under control, keep

to paths across farmland, avoid damaging fences, hedges and walls, leave no litter, safeguard water supplies, protect wildlife, plants and trees, go carefully on country roads, respect the life of the countryside, make no unnecessary noise.

Information about all National Parks in England and Wales can be obtained by writing to the Countryside Commission.

COUNTRYSIDE COMMISSION

John Dower House, Crescent Place, Cheltenham, Gloucester GL50 3RA

Dartmoor

Dartmoor extends over 365 square miles encompassing high open moorland in the centre and fringe farmland on the edge. Scattered over the moor is a hoard of prehistoric relics including the remains of Bronze Age man's huts, enclosures, burial chambers and ritualistic stone rows. See also **Archaeological Sites.** The visitor will be able to make his own discoveries with the help of an Ordnance Survey map. There are medieval churches, bridges and castles, notably **Castle Drogo** (see Castles).

The moor has been the site for many industries and mining enterprises whose remains are still visible, including **The Betsy Engine House, Finch Foundry** at Sticklepath, **Black Tor Blowing Houses, The Powder Mills, Hay Tor Granite Tramway** and the tin workings east of Warren House Inn. **See Industrial Archaeology.**

Common land forms 95,000 acres of the National Park. The Duchy of Cornwall owns 70,000 acres of it and the remainder of the open land is owned by the lords of the manor who may be organisations, local councils or individuals. Designation as a National Park in no way affects the ownership. Only on very few commons do people have a legal right. A commoner is the occupier of land, in a parish or manor, possessing common rights. These rights have been vigorously preserved and Dartmoor and commoners have the right to graze their cattle, ponies, sheep, dig peat for fuel, take heather for thatching, stone and sand to repair their houses and land.

Walking is the best way to enjoy Dartmoor with over 500 miles of footpaths, bridle paths, forest and nature trails and the open moorlands offer additional walking opportunities. When undertaking a long walk be certain you are well prepared with maps, compass, proper footwear and clothing. Keep to the rights of way. The method of waymarking is currently being changed from orange dots to yellow for footpaths and blue for bridleways. There are also guided walks organised by the National Park, details of which can be obtained from one of the information offices listed below.

There are **firing ranges** on Dartmoor so walkers must take great care. The Ministry of Defence uses 33,000 acres for training, most of which is on the northern side of Dartmoor. Access is possible at weekends and during August but be sure to check firing times first either in one of the local newspapers every Friday, at a local police station, post office or National Park Centre. There is also a recorded firing information service available if you telephone the following numbers: Torquay (0803) 24592; Plymouth (0752) 701924; Exeter (0392) 70164; Okehampton (0837) 2939. There are three ranges within the training area, the boundaries of which are marked on the ground by a series of red and white posts, also by noticeboards on the main approaches. When red warning flags or red lights are displayed entry is forbidden.

National Parks

Details of activities on Dartmoor are available from the information centres listed below, also in other sections of the Leisure A-Z, **see also** Angling, Riding, Walking, Caravans & Camping

Information Centres

BUCKFAST
Within the Abbey complex
Open: Easter-Oct, daily

NEW BRIDGE
Mobile caravan in car park on two Bridges Rd from Ashburton
Open: Easter-Oct, daily 11.00-17.00

OKEHAMPTON
Okehampton (0837) 3020
West St
Open: Easter-Oct, Mon-Sat 10.30-16.30

PARKE
Located on Haytor Rd from Bovey Tracey
Open: Easter-Oct, daily 11.00-18.00
The National Park Headquarters is housed in the National Trust Estate (not open to the public)

POSTBRIDGE
Postbridge (0822) 88272
Located in car park on B3212
Open: Easter-Oct, daily 11.00-17.00

PRINCETOWN
Princetown (0822 89) 414
Town Hall
Open: Easter-Oct, Sun-Fri 11.00-17.00

STEPS BRIDGE
Caravan sited on Dartmoor side of the bridge over the river Teign, on B3212 near Dunsford
Open: Easter-Oct, daily 11.00-17.00

TAVISTOCK
Tavistock (0822) 2398
Guildhall Building, Bedford Square
Open: Easter-Oct, daily 11.00-17.00

Exmoor

Exmoor National Park lies within both Somerset and Devon covering 265 square miles. It is administered by the Exmoor National Park Committee of the Somerset County Council. They are responsible for controlling development, with attention to both local life and industry, also to preserve the landscape and wildlife of Exmoor.

It is a landscape of superb contrasts with a magnificent coastline of hog's back cliffs, wild heather moorland and deep wooded coombes. Like Dartmoor most of the land is privately owned and the main activity is farming. Traditionally however the public enjoys considerable freedom, but this is dependent upon visitors respecting the life of the countryside and the rights of those who make a living from it.

Early man has left his mark on the moor in the form of Bronze Age barrows, such as Setta Barrow, and earthworks namely, Cow Castle and Mounsey. Many of the churches and buildings are of medieval origin. The area was a Royal Forest and wilderness until the 1800s when the land was utilised for farming. For the walking, angling and horseriding enthusiasts, Exmoor Park Authority produces a number of leaflets outlining a variety of waymarked trails and riding establishments. **See also** Angling, Riding, Walking, Caravan & Camping sections of Leisure A-Z

Information Centres

EXMOOR NATIONAL PARK CENTRE
Dulverton (0398) 23665
Exmoor House, Dulverton, Somerset
Open: all year

BRENDON
Brendon (059 87) 321
County Gale, on A39 between Porlock
& Lynmouth
Open: Easter-end Sep

COMBE MARTIN
Combe Martin (0271 88) 3319
Cross St
Open: Easter-end Sep

DUNSTER
Dunster (0643 82) 835
Dunster Steep Car Park, Dunster,
Somerset
Open: Easter-end Oct

LYNMOUTH
Lynton (059 85) 2509
Open: Easter-end Oct

Nature Reserves

These protected areas allow plants,
trees and wildlife to thrive in their
natural habitat. Most of the Devon
countryside has been taken up either
for farming or for urban development
so nature reserves are particularly
important for the study of ecology and
for conservation of indigenous plants
and wildlife. Too many human visitors
would destroy the environment and
disturb the wildlife so access to many
reserves is restricted.

The reserves listed below are
accessible to the public but in many
of them this is only because they are
crossed by public footpaths. Do not
leave the footpaths or in any way disturb the environment.

Organisations

**NATURE CONSERVANCY
COUNCIL**
South West Regional Office
Roughmoor, Bishop's Hull, Taunton,
Somerset TA1 5AA
The Society is a voluntary organisation
founded in 1912 seeking to promote
the conservation, study and apprecia-
tion of nature and the protection of
flora and fauna by creating and
establishing nature reserves representing typical natural and semi-
natural habitats. It acts as the national
association of the local Nature Conservation Trusts which are established on
a county or regional basis throughout
the UK, providing a co-ordinating centre for these independent Trusts,
administering funds and providing
practical advice on conservation to
public and private bodies. Together
with the Trusts is owns or manages
1,200 nature reserves and has a
membership of over 128,000

**BOVEY VALLEY WOODLANDS
NATURE**
Map 3 Bb
2m NW Bovey Tracey
Access restricted to public footpaths
Oak woodlands with variety of
woodland birds including wood pec-
kers, wood warblers, pied flycatchers,
also small heronry
NCC

**BRAUNTON BARROWS NATURE
RESERVE**
Map 1 Ab/p6
Braunton (0271) 812552
4m NW Barnstaple off B3231
Open: no access when red flags
flying
1,500 acres, famous for geology and
botany with wild flowers, various
birds; natural history groups should
contact the warden: Braunton (0271)
812552
NCC 🅿

CAIRN TOP
Map 1 Ba
Ilfracombe ½m S town centre
19 acres steep wooded hill sides rich in flora and fauna; nature trail, leaflet available
DTNC

COOKWORTHY MOOR
Map 1 Ac
Beaworthy, 2½m SE Holsworthy off B3218
Open: by permit only (bona fide naturalists)
5 acre pond in forest, observation hide
FC

DENDLES WOOD
Map 3 Bb
1½m N Cornwood, 7m SW Buckfastleigh off A38
Open: by written permission, apply to chief warden, 20 Belgrave Square, London SW1X 8PY
Oak and beech wood, with woodland birds including buzzard, great spotted woodpecker, nuthatch, also red and fallow deer
NCC

DOWNLAND CLIFFS & LANDSLIPS NATURE RESERVE
Map 3 Ba/p10
1m SE Axmouth off B3172
5 mile coastal strip covering 800 acres, where a massive landsip occured in 1839; variety of wildlife including badgers, lizards and over 400 species of wild flowers, 7m nature trail

DUNSFORD & MEADHAYDOWN WOOD
Map 4 Ba/p43
5m W Exeter on B3212
140 acres of mixed deciduous woodland
Reserve booklet available
DTNC

LUNDY ISLAND
See Country Parks: Lundy Island

SLAPTON LEY NATURE RESERVE
Map 4 Ac/p108
Slapton, 5m SW Dartmouth on A379
Two lakes edged with reeds attracting winter wildfowl and rare birds; bird observatory, nature walk, information centre
Permits from Slapton Field Centre: Kingsbridge (0548) 580466

WARLEIGH POINT WOOD
Map 3 Ab
5m NW Plymouth town centre off B3373
32 acres mixed deciduous woodland conserving wildlife; freshwater stream, pond and tidal mud flats offer wide scope for teaching ecology and conservation management; nature centre for use by school parties, naturalist guide
Plymouth City Museum
DTNC

WISTMANS WOOD FOREST NATURE RESERVE
Map 3 Bb/p36 & 128
7m NE Tavistock on B3357, 1m N Two Bridges, access via public footpath
Oak trees amidst granite boulders, famous for twisted dwarf trees covered in mosses and lichen
Permit required for collecting speciments
Do not light fires and keep outside experimental plots
NCC

YARNER WOOD NATIONAL NATURE RESERVE
Map 3 Bb/p17
Bovey Tracey (0626) 832330
2m NW Bovey Tracey off B3344
Access restricted to self guided nature trails, permits required for rest of reserve
Woodland, mainly oak with birch, conifers; butterflies, nightjar, woodpecker, roe, fallow and red deer
3m woodland walk, 1½m educational trail
NCC ▪P

Other Historic Buildings

AGINCOURT HOUSE
Map 4 Ab/p38
Dartmouth (080 43) 2472
Open: all year, Mon-Sat 10.00-17.30
(Sun 14.30-17.00)
Free
Once a merchant's house, one of the oldest in Dartmouth built in 1380; twice restored, it now houses an antique shop and small museum
🛥

BLACKFRIARS DISTILLERY
Map 3 A b/p92
Plymouth (0752) 665292
60 Southside Street,(Coates & Co Ltd)
Open: guided tours; May-Sept, w/k days 10.30-13.00 & 14.00-16.30 (subject to availability, advisable to telephone in advance)
No groups
Free
One of oldest buildings in Plymouth, Pilgrim Fathers reputed to have held their final meeting here before sailing to America, 1620. Now part of Coates & Co Plymouth Gin Distillery and protected as a national monument

CUSTOMS HOUSE
Map 4 Aa/p47
Exeter (0392) 74021
The Quay, Exeter
Open: all year, w/days 10.00-12.00 by arrangement with H M Customs & Excise
Free
Brick building dating from 1681, illustrates first use of brickwork in Exeter. Some fine plasterwork ceilings, architectural value only

ELIZABETHAN HOUSE
Map 3 Ab
32 New St, Plymouth
Open: Easter-Sept, Mon-Sat 10.00-13.00 & 14.15-18.00; Sun 15.00-17.00
Charge: 20p (ch 10p)
Composite ticket including admission to Merchant's House & Smeaton's Tower also available

EXETER GUILDHALL
Map 4 Aa
Exeter (0392) 72979
High St, Exeter
Open: all year, Mon-Sat 10.00-17.30 (subject to civic functions)
Free
Medieval guildhall, one of the oldest in Britain; dates back to 1160; civic regalia, silver & paintings on display
♿

PLYMOUTH GUILDHALL
Map 3 Ab
Royal Parade, Plymouth
Open: all year, w/days 10.00-16.00 (at the discretion of the porters)
FreeVictorian building, bombed during Second World War but since renovated has 14 windows of executed sculpt work, illustrating historical events in Plymouth, 1355-1953; also 12 labours of Hercules in sculptured panels on ceilings & east wall and Gobelin tapestry depicting the Miraculous Draught of Fishes

SOUTH MOLTON GUILDHALL
See Museums: South Molton Museum

MERCHANTS HOUSE
Map 3 Ab/p92
33 St Andrews St, Plymouth
Open: all year, Mon-Sat 10.00-18.00
Charge: 20p (ch 10p)
Composite ticket including admission to Elizabethan House & Smeaton's Tower also available
Large, restored tudor town house with 16th & 17th century period features, former house of William Parker, mayor of Plymouth; now museum of Plymouth history

Picnic Sites

ROYAL CITADEL
Map 3 Ab/p91
Plymouth (0752) 660582
Plymouth
Open: May-Sep, daily 14.00-17.00
Regular tours for individuals every
hour (14.00, 15.00, 16.00 & 17.00)
Groups (max 25) at other times by
arrangement
Free (groups £4 per guide)
DofE

SMEATONS TOWER
Map 3 Ab/p91
Plymouth (0752) 261125
The Hoe, Plymouth
Open: last Sat in April-first Sat in Oct,
daily 10.30-1 hour before dusk
Charge: 20p
reductions for groups 20« by
arrangement
Composite ticket including admission
for Merchant's House & Elizabethan
House also available

TOTNES GUILDHALL
Map 3 Bb
Totnes (0803) 862147
Ramparts Walk, Totnes
Open: Easter-end Sept, w/days 9.30-
13.00 & 14.00-17.00, other times
by arrangement
Charge: 20p (ch 10p)
Reduced rates for school groups by
arrangement
P

TUCKERS HALL
Map 4 Aa
Exeter (0392) 36244
Fore St, Exeter
Open: June-Sep, Tue, Thurs &Fri
10.30-12.30
Free

WATERSMEET HOUSE
Map 1 Ba
Watersmeet, 1½ E Lynmouth off A39
Open: April-end Oct, daily 11.00-
18.00
Free
Fishing lodge built 1832 in very
attractive location. Now run by

National Trust as information centre
See also Country Parks:
Watersmeet
NT 🐾 ☐

Picnic Sites

The following sites have been
specially created for picnics and
usually have picnic tables. They have
car parks, are open at all times and
are free unless otherwise stated.

**ABBEYFORD WOODS PICNIC
PLACE**
Map 1 Bc
1m N Okehampton, ½m W B3217
Set in attractive mixed woodland,
managed on a selection system with
natural regeneration of young saplings
in small cleared areas; varied species
including oak, beech, pine and larch;
2½m forest walk starts here
See Woodlands: Abbeyford Woods
FC **P**

BELLEVER FOREST PICNIC PLACE
Map 3 Bb
1m S Postbridge off B3212
Grassy bank on river Dart, mature
spruce forest; 3m and 1½m forest
walks start here, leaflet available
See Woodlands: Bellever Forest
FC **P**

**FERNWORTHY RESERVOIR PIC-
NIC PLACE**
Map 3 Ba
3¾m SW Chagford off B3212,
signposted at entrance of reservoir
One acre near forest and reservoir,
picnic tables; forest trail
Lavatories
See Woodlands: Fernworthy Forest
P ♿

FLASHDOWN WOODS PICNIC PLACE
Map 1 Bb
Flashdown Woods, ½m SW Egges-ford Station
On grassy rise near site of larch and beech trees planted by FC in 1919 and 1969 to commemorate Commission's Jubilee
FC

HALDON PICNIC PLACE
Map 4 Aa
8m S Exeter off A38
Set in natural Scots pine and birch wood; extensive views across the Exe estuary

HONITON CLYST
Map 4 Aa
2m NE Exeter off A30
One acre adjacent to Exeter Airport
P

MAMHEAD PICNIC PLACE
Map 4 Ab
2m NE Ashcombe, 1m S B3381
Small picnic area with magnificent views from obelisk over the Exe estuary to Blackdown Hills
FC

MELBURY WOODS PICNIC PLACE
Map 1 Ab
2½m SE Woolfardisworthy, 5m S Clovelly on Clovelly to Stibb Cross Rd
Roadside picnic place beside beech avenue; forest trail
See Woodlands: Melbury Wood
FC

MORWELLHAM QUAY PICNIC PLACE
Map 3 Ab
Tamar Valley, 4m SW Tavistock, 1m S A390
Picnic site in village
Lavatories
P

PLYM PICNIC PLACE
Map 3 Bb
3m NW Plympton on unclassified Plympton Shaugh Prior Road
Open: April-Sep
Mature mixed coniferous woodland, roadside picnic place
1½m Plym forest trail starts here
See Woodlands: Plym Bridge
FC P

ROYAL STONE PICNIC PLACE
Map 1 Bc
1m S Eggesford on A377
Under tall Douglas fir beside grassy area surrounding stone unveiled by the Queen in 1956 commemorating one million acres of plantations by FC Information Centre; 1m Home Valley Walk, guide available also Hilltown Trail start here
FC P

STOKE WOODS PICNIC PLACE
Map 2 Ac
3m N Exeter on A396
Pleasant setting above river Exe good views; 1½m Stoke Woods forest walk, leaflet available
See also Woodlands: Stoke Wood

Railways

LYNTON
Map 1 Ba
Lynton, between cliff railway rd and Lynton esplanade at Lynmouth
Open: March-Dec, daily
Charge: 12p single
Built 1980, the 900ft journey links Lynton and Lynmouth via 30 degree slope, originally the steepest of its kind. The system is water-powered with secure braking system

Railways

DART VALLEY RAILWAY
Map 3 Bb/p23
Buckfastleigh (0364) 42338
Buckfastleigh Station off A38
Open: Easter, end May-mid Sep, daily
10.00-17.00 (last train 15.30)
Charge: £2.50 (ch £1.60, OAPs £2)
Restored steam locomotive between
Buckfastleigh and Totnes via the Dart
Valley; 55 mins round trip including
stops at Staverton Bridge and the
Railway Museum at Buckfastleigh
🅿 ⛽ 🚉 ♿

GORSE BLOSSOM MINIATURE RAILWAY PARK
Map 3 Bb
Bickington (361) 062682
Liverton, 2½m NW Newton Abbot,
access via former A38
Open: July-Sep, daily 10.00-17.00
Charge: £1 (ch & OAPs 70p), group
reductions by arrangement
Steam operated miniature railway
through acres of beautiful woodland
🚉 ⛽ 🅿 🍴

THE GREAT EXMOUTH 00 MODEL RAILWAY
Map 4 Aa
Exeter (0395) 278383
Seafront, Exeter
Open: early April-early Nov, daily from
10.30
Charge: £1 (ch 50p, OAPs & stu-
dents 80p)
This vast model complex includes the
world's largest 00 gauge railway,
created over the last 14 years by
Gerry Nicholson. It is set in panoramic
landscapes, busy towns and working
docks
No dogs: 🅿

KINGSBRIDGE MINIATURE RAILWAY
Map 3 Bc
Bickington (062 682) 361 The Quay,
Kingsbridge
Open: Easter & mid May-mid Sep,
daily 11.00-17.00

Charge: 40p
7¼ inch gauge miniature railway carrying passengers, half mile return trip;
for details contact Mr Kichenside
🅿 🚉 ♿

SEATON ELECTRIC TRAMWAY
Map 2 Bc
Seaton (0297) 21702
Riverside Depot, Harbour Rd, Seaton
Open: all year, daily 10.00-18.00
(limited service during winter)
Charge: £1.50 (ch £1.20, OAPs
£1.20), group (10«) reductions by
arrangement
Unique 3m service of narrow gauge
electric tram cars operating between
Seaton & Carlyton along river Exe

TORBAY & DARTMOUTH RAILWAY
Map 4 Ab
Paignton (0803) 555872 or
Buckfastleigh (0364) 42338
Queen's Park Station, Paignton
Open: April-May & Oct, daily 10.30-
16.15
Charge: £2.50 (ch £1.30, OAPs £2)
Steam trains running along former
Great Western line from Paignton to
Kingswear connecting with ferry
across to Dartmouth, taking in spec-
tacular Torbay coastline, Goodrington
Sands & Churston; model railway
exhibition at Paignton Station
♿

WOODLAND RAILWAY
Map 4 Aa/p25
Bicton Park, East Budleigh, ½m N
East Budleigh on A376
Open: early April-late Oct, daily
10.00-18.00
Charge: 70p (ch 50p)
Narrow gauge with steam locomotives
running through the attractive gardens
of Bicton Park
See also Bicton Park (Gardens)

Riding Stables

This list includes stables offering riding instruction and hacking (country rides). Most lessons are in classes of groups but private tuition is often available. Hacking is not usually allowed unaccompanied unless the ability of the rider is known. Stables which provide livery or stud services are not included. Exact locations of stables are not given since it is always advisable to telephone in advance.

ABIGAIL EQUESTRIAN CENTRE
Chudleigh (0626) 852167
Woodway St, Chudleigh
Open: daily (except Fri)
Lesson: £3.50 hour, £6 private hour
Hack: £3 hour
10 mounts

BARTON RIDING STABLES
Torquay (0803) 35233
Barton Cross, Torquay
Open: daily
Lesson: £3.50 hour
Hack: £3 hour
Children welcome, jumping

BOLD TRY RIDING STABLES
Chumleigh (0769) 80485
Leigh Rd, Chumleigh
Open: daily
Lesson/Hack: £3.50 hour
20 mounts, children's lessons, hunting, pony club

CALIFORNIA RIDING SCHOOL
Gara Bridge (054 882) 346
California Cross, Modbury
Open: daily
Lesson: £3.75 45 mins

Hack: £3.75 hour
10 mounts, children and beginners welcome

CHESTON FARM RIDING CENTRE
South Brent (036 47) 3266
Wrangaton South Brent
Open: daily
Lesson/Hack: £3.50 hour
20 mounts, children's lessons, jumping

CHOLWELL FARM & RIDING STABLES
Mary Tavy (082 281) 526
Mary Tavy, Tavistock
Open: daily
Lessons: £2.50 hour
Hack: £2 hour
30 mounts

COMYN FARM RIDING STABLES
Ilfracombe (0271) 65371
Ilfracombe
Open: daily
Lesson: £4 hour, £5 private hour
Hack: £3 hour
20 mounts, children's lessons, hunting

CROSSWAYS RIDING SCHOOL
Yelverton (082 285) 3025
Axtown Lane, Yelverton
Open: daily
Lesson: £4 hour, £5 private hour
Hack: £3.50 (ch £3) hour
12 mounts, children's lessons, jumping

DARTMOOR RIDING CENTRE
Sticklepath (083 784) 412
Belstone, Nr Okehampton
Open: daily
Lessons: by arrangement
Hack: £2.50 hour
35 mounts, riding holidays

DOONE VALLEY RIDING STABLES
Brendon (059 87) 234
Parsonage Farm, Malsmead, Brendon
Open: Spring BH-end Oct, daily
Hack: £3 hour
20 mounts

Riding Stables

ELLIOTS HILL RIDING CENTRE
Ashburton (0364) 53058
Buckland-in-the-Moor
Open: April-Sep, daily
Hack: £3 hour, £6 half day, £12 all day (including lunch)
10 mounts, hacking on the moors

EXETER & DISTRICT RIDING SCHOOL
Topsham (039 287) 3472
The Shieling, Ebford, Nr Exeter
Open: daily (except Thur)
Lesson/Hack: £5 hour, £10 private hour
20-25 mounts, disabled riders welcome, children's lessons

FAIRTOWN RIDING SCHOOL
Yelverton (082 285) 3494
Buckland Monachorum
Open: daily
Lesson: £2.50 half hour
Hack: £3.40 hour
10 mounts, disabled riding holidays

FROGWELL RIDING CENTRE
Tiverton (0884) 252794
Frogwell Farm, Tiverton
Open: daily (except Mon)
Lesson: £3 hour, £7 private hour
Hack: £4 hour
10 mounts, qualified instructors, showjumping, eventing

GREAT SHERBERTON PONY STUD
Poundsgate (036 43) 276
Princetown
Open: Spring BH-end Oct, daily
Lesson: £3 hour, £10 day
Hack: £3 hour
20 mounts, disabled riders welcome, free campsite for riding customers

HEAZLE RIDING CENTRE
Hemyock (0823) 680280
Heazle Farm, Clayhidon, Cullompton
Open: daily (except Fri)
Lesson/Hack: £3 hour (£3.50 after 18.00 hours), £6 private hour
35 mounts, BHSI cross-country school

KINGSLAND RIDING STABLES
Clovelly (023 73) 378
Woolsery, Bideford
Open: all year, Mon-Sun
Lesson/Hack: £3.50 hour
20 mounts, children welcome, hunting

LAKESIDE RIDING STABLES
Ilfracombe (0271) 65066
Bickenbridge Farm, Nr Mullacott, Ilfracombe
Open: all year, Mon-Sat
Lesson/Hack: £3 hour, £5 private hour
20 mounts, children's lessons

LOWER DOWNSTOWN STABLES
South Brent (036 47) 3340
Open: daily
Lesson/Hack: £3.50 hour
14 mounts, specialises in children

MAIDENCOMBE PARK RIDING CENTRE
Torquay (0803) 34913
Teignmouth Rd, Torquay
Open: daily
Lesson: £3 45 mins, £3 private half hour
Hack: £3.50 hour, £7 2 hours, £9 half day

MANOR HOUSE RIDING SCHOOL
Honiton (0404) 2026
Springfield House, Honiton
Open: daily
Lesson: £25.50 for 10 one hour lessons, £18.20 for 10 half hour lessons
4 mounts, children, cross-country

MOORLAND RIDING STABLES
Mary Tavy (082 281) 293
Will Farm, Peter Tavy, Tavistock
Open: daily
Lesson: £2 hour
Hack: £1.60 hour
50 mounts, children's lessons

OLD BAILEY RIDING CENTRE
Shaldon (062 687) 3281
Stokeinteignhead
Open: daily
Lesson: £4 hour
Hack: £3.50 hour
8 mounts, beach and pub rides

PENHILL RIDING STABLES
Barnstaple (0271) 73868
Penhill, Barnstaple
Open: daily (except Mon)
Lesson: £2 hour
10 mounts, children welcome,
jumping

PINHOE RIDING CENTRE
Exeter (0392) 68683
Church Hill, Pinhoe
Open: daily
Lesson:/Hack: £3 hour
14 mounts, liveries, jumping tuition

**SHILSTONE ROCKS RIDING &
TREKKING CENTRE**
Widecombe (036 42) 281
Chittleford Farm, Widecombe-in-the
Moor
Open: March-Oct, daily
Hack: £6 2 hours
40 mounts
Beginners welcome

SKAIGH STABLES FARM
Sticklepath (083 784) 429
Belstone, Sticklepath
Open: Spring BH-mid Sep, daily
Lesson: £3 hour
Hack: £3 hour, £10 day
Hacking on Dartmoor, residential rid-
ing holidays

**SOUTH TREW RIDING & HOLIDAY
CENTRE**
Black Torrington (040 923) 277
Highhampton, Beaworthy
Open: June-end Sep, daily
Lesson: £1.50 half hour, £2.50 hour
14 mounts, caters mainly for children

ROLLSBRIDGE RIDING CENTRE
Exeter (0392) 211363
Pocombe Bridge, Ide

Open: daily
Hack: £2.50 hour
Beginners and groups welcome

TABRE RIDING
Winkleigh (083 783) 616
Wagon Wheels Stables, Winkleigh
Open: daily
Lesson/Hack: £3.50 hour, private
£3.50
8 mounts, children's lessons

THE GLEN RIDING STABLES
Bickington (062 682) 393
The Glen, Caton Cross, Ashburton
Open: daily
Lesson: £3.50 hour
Hack: £3 hour
8 mounts, jumping

TIDICOMBE RIDING STABLES
Shirwell (027 182) 300
Tidicombe Farm, Arlington, Nr
Barnstaple
Open: daily
Lesson/Hack: £3 hour
15 mounts, trekking, riding holidays,
cross-country

TIN PARK RIDING STABLES
Cornwood (075 537) 262
Tin Park Farm, Cornwood, Ivybridge
Open: daily
Hack: £2 hour
25 mounts

VENTON FARM
Bideford (023 72) 4244
Golf Links Rd, Westward Ho!
Open: Easter-Oct, daily
Hack: £2 hour
25 mounts. children welcome

**WARCOMBE FARM RIDING
CENTRE**
Woolacombe (0271) 870501
Warcombe Farm, Mortehoe,
Woolacombe
Open: daily
Lesson/Hack: £3 hour
35-40 mounts, children, cross-
country course

WEMBURY BAY RIDING SCHOOL
Plymouth (0752) 862676
Church Wood Estate, Wembury
Open: daily
Lesson: £3.50 hour, £5 private
Hack: £3.30 hour
27 mounts, children and disabled
riders welcome

WOOLACOMBE RIDING STABLES LTD
Woolacombe (0271) 870332
South Street, Woolacombe
Open: daily
Hack: £3 hour
5 mounts, children must be able to
ride

Sports Centres

These centres offer a wide range of
activities. Full timetables and charges
are available from each centre. Membership fees given are for a year.
Charges given are a selection. Where
necessary, changing rooms and
showers are provided. Opening times
given are for the centres, not for any
specific activities. Many of the
activities will be organised by clubs.
Full details from each centre. Centres
often provide detailed brochures.

DYRONS SPORTS CENTRE
Map 4 Ab
Newton Abbot (0626) 60426
Wain Lane, Newton Abbot
Open: all year, w/days 12.30-22.30,
w/ends 9.30-21.30
Facilities: badminton, 5-a-side foot-
ball, squash, karate, multi-gymn, tram-
poline, keep-fit

Charges: squash £1.60 (peak) 35
min, £1.20 (off peak); badminton £2
court; keep-fit 75p session, 5-a-side
football £6.50 per pitch
Membership: £5 (under 18 £2.50),
day membership 15p (ch 10p)
🅿 ☕

HAWKESHYDE MOTEL & LEISURE CENTRE
Map 4 Ba
Seaton (0297) 20932
Harepath Hill, Seaton. 1m W Colyford
on A3052
Open: all year, daily 9.00-23.00
(closed 23 Dec-3 Jan)
Facilities: squash, badminton, table
tennis, multi-gymn, sauna, outdoor
pool, cricket nets, olympic gymnastics
Charges: squash £1.20 43 min;
badminton £2.40 hour; sauna £1.30
hour
Membership: £32 year, day membership 75p
🅿 ✗ 🍸

HONITON SPORTS CENTRE
Map 2 Bc
Honiton (0404) 2325
School Lane, Honiton
Open: all year, w/days 18.00-22.00,
Sat 9.30-21.00, Sun 10.00-22.00
Facilities: squash, badminton, 5-a-
side football, cricket nets, weight
training
Charges: main hall £8 hour; badmin-
ton £2 hour; weight training 75p
hour; outdoor floodlit area £4 hour
(£3.20 daylight)
🅿 ♿

KITTO CENTRE (YMCA)
Map 3 Ab
Plymouth (0752) 702492
Honicknowle Lane, Plymouth
Open: all year, Mon-Sat 9.00-20.00
Facilities: squash, badminton, multi-
gymn, aerobics, 5-a-side football
Charge: squash £1.20 40 min; bad-
minton £1.20 hour; keep-fit 25p (non
member 75p) session; gymnastics
15p (35p); spectators 10p; 5-a-side
football £3 hour (floodlit)
🅿 ☕ ♿

MAYFLOWER SPORTS CENTRE
Map 3 Ab
Plymouth (0752) 54112
Central Park, Plymouth
Open: all year, daily 9.00-23.00
(closed BHs & 24 Dec)
Facilities: squash, badminton, basketball, gymnastics, keep-fit, volleyball, fitness training
Charge: admission charge non members 35p (ch 20p); badminton £2.20 (members), £3.40 (non members) hour; squash 45p (off peak), non members 55p (off peak 45p); tennis, basketball & netball court £7.20 (non members £8.35) hour; fitness training 95p (non members £1.30)
Membership: £10 (ch10 & OAPs £3.70)

NORTH DEVON LEISURE CENTRE
Map 1 Bb/p12
Barnstaple (0271) 73361
Seven Brethern Bank, Barnstaple
Open: all year, Mon-Sat 10.00-22.30, Sun 9.00-17.00
Facilities: swimming, badminton, indoor bowling, table tennis, squash, snooker
Charge: squash £1.75 40 min; badminton £1.80 hour; basketball £4.50 hour
🅿 ♿ ⛻ ⛾

TORBAY LEISURE CENTRE
Paignton (0803) 521990
Under construction, should be open early 1984

Swimming Pools

Barnstaple

NORTH DEVON LEISURE CENTRE
Map 1 Bb
Seven Brethren Bank, Barnstaple
Main pool 33m x 12.3m; also 25m x14m
See also: Sports Centres

Brixham

SELF HELP POOL
Map 4 Ab
Brixham (080 45) 7151
Higher Ranscombe Rd, Brixham
Open: all year, daily
Main pool 25m x 8.5m x 1.3m
Room for 150 spectators

Dawlish

DAWLISH SWIMMING POOL
Map 4 Ab
Dawlish (0626) 864394
Playing Fields, Exeter Rd, Dawlish
Open: all year, daily 10.00-18.00
Main pool 25m x 12m
Spectators' gallery

Exeter

EXETER POOL
Map 2 Ac
Exeter (0392) 54489
Heavitree Rd, Exeter
Main pool 33.5m x 10.7m
Room for 500 spectators

Swimming Pools

Honiton

HONITON POOL
Map 2 Bc
Honiton (0404) 3430/41577
Main pool 25m x 10.5m

Ilfracombe

ILFRACOMBE SWIMMING POOL
Map 1 Aa
Ilfracombe (0271) 64480
Hillsborough Rd, Ilfracombe
Open: summer, daily 10.00; winter,
Wed-Sun 13.00 (closed Mon & Tue)
Main pool 33.3m x 12.5m
Room for 80 spectators

Ottery St Mary

SALSTON HOTEL
Map 4 Ba
Ottery St Mary
Open: all year, daily 6.00-20.00
Pool 40ft x 20ft
Room for spectators

Paignton

TORBAY POOL
Map 4 Ab
Paignton (0803) 521990
Open: all year, Mon-Sun 9.00
Main pool 33.3m x 12.5m
Room for 100 spectators

Plymouth

**BALLARD CENTRE SWIMMING
POOL**
Map 3 Ab
Plymouth (0752) 664644
The Crescent, Plymouth
Main pool 22.9m x 7.6m

CENTRAL PARK SWIMMING POOL
Map 3 Ab
Plymouth (0752) 264894
Main pool 33.3m x 12.8m; diving
pool and learner's pool
Room for spectators

Tiverton

TIVERTON SWIMMING POOL
Map 2 Ab
Tiverton (0884) 254221
Bolham Rd, Tiverton
Open: winter, Tue-Sun 12.30; sum
mer, daily 10.00
Main pool 25m x 12.8m, diving
board
Room for 200 spectators

Torquay

SWIM TORQUAY
Map 4 Ab
Torquay (0803) 33400
Plainmoor (off St Mary Church Rd)
Open: all year, daily 10.00-18.00
Main pool 25m x 8m
Room for 40 spectators

Torrington

TORRINGTON SWIMMING POOL
Map 1 Bb
Torrington (080 52) 2597
School Lane, Torrington
25m x 10m

Totnes

TOTNES SWIMMING POOL
Map 3 Bb
Totnes (0803) 863848
Station Rd, Totnes
Open: all year, daily 10.00-22.00
Main pool 25m x 10m
Room for 100 spectators

Tourist Information Offices

Tourist Information Offices can be helpful whether you are a visitor to Devon or a resident. They have a wealth of information on local attractions, places to stay and eat, events, activities, history and much more. For example if you have trouble in contacting any of the places listed in this directory contact the local information office for help. If you want to find out what you can do in your area contact your local information office and always make a point of contacting the information office at any place you are intending to visit.

AXMINSTER
Axminster (0297) 34386
Market Car Park, Coombe Lane
Open: April-Sep

BARNSTAPLE
Barnstaple (0271) 72742
20 Holland St
Open: all year

BIDEFORD
Bideford (023 72) 77676
The Quay
Open: May-Sep

BOVEY TRACEY
Bovey Tracey (0626) 832047
Open: summer only

BRIXHAM
Brixham (080 45) 281
Old Market House, The Quay
Open: March-Oct:

BUDLEIGH SALTERTON
Budleigh Salterton (039 54) 5275
Rolle Mews Car Park, Fore St
Open: Easter & May-Sep

CHAGFORD
Chagford (064 73) 3226
The Old Forge Cafe
Open: April-Oct

COMBE MARTIN
Combe Martin (0271 88) 2117
Cross St
Open: summer

CREDITON
Crediton (036 32) 3755
Mid-Devon District Council Offices
Market St
Open: all year

CROYDE
Croyde (0271) 890479
Publicity Officer, Langdale House
Open: all year

CULLOMPTON
Cullompton (0844) 33126
Mrs Horgan, 31 Bockland Close
Open: all year

DARTMOOR TOURIST ASSOCIATION
8 Fitzford Cottages, Tavistock
Personal callers only

DARTMOUTH
The Quay
Open: June-Aug

DAWLISH
Dawlish (0626) 863589
The Lawn
Open: all year

EXETER
Exeter (0392) 72434
Civic Centre, Dix's Field
Open: all year

EXMOUTH
Exmouth (039 52) 3744
Manor Gardens, Alexandra Terrace
Open: Easter-Oct

Tourist Offices

HONITON
Honiton (0404) 3716
Angel Hotel Car Park, High St
Open: March-Oct

ILFRACOMBE
Ilfracombe (0271) 63001
The Promenade
Open: all year

KINGSBRIDGE
Kingsbridge (0548) 3195
The Quay
Open: April-Oct

LYNTON
Lynton (059 85) 2225
Lee Rd
Open: all year

NEWTON ABBOT
Newton Abbot (0626) 67494
8 Sherborne Rd
Open: all year

OKEHAMPTON
Okehampton (0837) 3020
3 West St
Open: Easter-Oct

OTTERY ST MARY
Ottery St Mary (040 481) 2252
Council Offices, Silver St
Open: all year

PAIGNTON
Paignton (0803) 558383
Festival Hall, Esplanade
Open: all year

PLYMOUTH
Plymouth (0752) 264849
Civic Centre, Royal Parade
Open: all year

SALCOMBE
Salcombe (054 884) 2736
Market St
Open: all year

SEATON
Seaton (0297) 21660
The Esplanade
Open: May-Sep

SIDMOUTH
Sidmouth (039 55) 6441
Esplanade
Open: April-Oct

SOUTH MOLTON
South Molton (076 95) 2378
1 East St
Open: July-Aug

TAVISTOCK
Tavistock (0822) 2398
Bedford Square

TEIGNMOUTH
Teignmouth (062 67) 6271
The Den, Sea Front
Open: all year

TIVERTON
Tiverton (0884) 256295
Museum, St Andrew St
Open: all year

TORQUAY
Torquay (0803) 27428
Vaughan Parade
Open: all year

TORRINGTON
Town Hall
Open: May-Sep

TOTNES
Totnes (0803) 863168
The Plains
Open: May-Sep

WOOLACOMBE
Woolacombe (0271) 870553
Hall '70, Beach Rd
Open: May-Sep

Unusual Outings

BABBACOMBE MODEL VILLAGE
Map 4 Ab/p124
Torquay (0803) 38669
Torquay, 2m NE town centre on
B3199
Open: Easter-Oct, daily 9.00-22.00;
Nov-Easter, daily 9.00-17.00
Charge: £1.30 (ch 70p), group
reductions 20« by arrangement
Model village and railways set in 4
acres of beautiful miniature
landscaped gardens
P 🏧 ⊋u

BEER MODELRAMA & PLEASURE GARDEN
Map 4 Ba/p14
Seaton (0297) 21542
Underleys, Beer ½m SW Seaton off
B3174
Open: Oct-Easter, w/days 10.00-
17.00, Sat 10.00-13.00; telephone
for details of summer opening times,
not available at time of printing
Charge: £1.25 (ch 75p) composite
ticket
On hillside overlooking Beer the complex comprises extensive gardens
with miniature railway, putting green,
croquet lawn, children's corner;
exhibition hall with 12 model railways,
station buffet serving snacks, the preserved Golden Arrow Pullman car
serving lunches, souvenir shop
P 🏧 ⊋✕

DONKEY SANCTUARY
Map 4 Ba/p107
½m NW Salcombe Regis off A3052
Open: all year, daily 9.00-17.00
Free
Registered charity caring for donkeys
in beautiful setting close to the coast

EXMOOR BRASS RUBBING CENTRE
Map 1 Ba/p49
Lynton (059 85) 2529
Queen St, Lynton
Open: April-Sep, w/days 10.00-
17.00; Aug, Sat 10.00-17.00, Sun
14.00-17.00; groups during winter
by arrangement
Charge: 20p (ch 10p), reductions for
school and youth groups
Equipment provided and friendly
guidance, details of diploma courses
at the Academy of Monumental Brass
Rubbing on request
Dogs on leads
P 🏧 ♿

GNOME RESERVE
Map 1 Ab/p105
Bradworthy (040 924) 435
West Putford, 8m SW Bideford, 5m
W of A388
Open: Easter-end Oct, Sun-Fri 10.00-
13.00 & 14.00-18.00, also summer
evenings 19.00-21.00
Charge: 30p (ch 20p)
Over 1,000 gnomes and pixies in
woodland setting, pixie nature trail,
also indoor exhibition
P 🏧

GOLDEN HIND REPLICA
Map 4 Ab/p20
Brixham (080 45) 6223
Brixham Harbour
Open: Easter-end Oct, daily 10.00-
16.00
Charge: 60p (ch & OAPs 30p)
Copy of Sir Francis Drake's famous
ship, built to the original dimensions
and containing Elizabethan relics,
armour, costumes and guns

KITLEY CAVES
Map 3 Bc/p132
Plymouth (0752) 880202
Yealmpton (075 531) 202
Kitley Estate, Yealmpton 2m SE
Plymouth off A379
Open: Easter BH w/end, early June-
end Sep, daily 10.00-17.30
Charge: £1 (ch 50p), group reduc-
tions by arrangement
Floodlit caves, lime kilns and museum
on banks of river Yealm; originally dis-
covered by quarrymen the caves have
been excavated
🅿 🛒 ⛶

LUNDY ISLAND
See Country Parks: Lundy Island

NEWCOMEN ENGINE HOUSE
Map 4 Ab
Dartmouth (080 43) 2923
Royal Avenue Gardens, Dartmouth
Open: Easter-end Oct, Mon-Sat
11.00-13.00 & 14.15-17.00; Sun
14.00-17.00, other times by
arrangement
Charge: 30p (ch 10p)
Glass fronted building commemorates
300th anniversary of Newcomen's
birth, housing his atmospheric pressure steam pumping engine
🅿 ♿

ROYAL NAVY DOCKYARDS
Davenport, ½m SW Plymouth town
centre off A388
Open: all year, Tue, Wed & Thur
10.00-14.00; groups 30« write to
Port Admiral's Dept, H M Naval Base,
Davenport (no casual callers)
Free (donations gratefully accepted)
Historical tour of dockyard by Mr
Peter Rodolfo explaining the develop-
ment of the docks from its origins in
1691
🅿 ♿

WATERMOUTH CASTLE
Map 1 Ba
Ilfracombe (0271) 63879
2m NE Ilfracombe off A399
Open: Easter-spring BH & Oct, Sun-
Thur 14.30-16.00; June & Sep, Sun-
Fri 11.00-16.00; July & Aug, Sun-Fri
10.00-16.00
Charge: £1.50 (ch £1)
Opening times and charges subject to
alteration
Neo-gothic castle built 1825 includ-
ing mechanical music demonstratons,
rural byegones, animated fairytale
scenes, model railway
🅿 🛒 ⛶ ♿

Walking

The diversity of the Devon landscape
and the mild climate combine to make
Devon excellent walking country.
Walks vary from quiet peaceful footpaths linking villages and places of
particular beauty to more strenuous
tracks crossing the uninhabited open
moorland of Dartmoor. The long distance footpath, the South West Peninsula Coast Path follows the dramatic
and diverse coastline of the whole
southern peninsula.

There are many walking groups in
the county and a great deal has been
achieved through their efforts in keeping the paths open and reclaiming
rights of way. For the enthusiast there
are many long walks to be taken but
those interested in a casual stroll are
also well catered for. To begin this
section, here are some suggestions
for shorter walks along marked trails
and walks set out in leaflets. Details
can be found in other sections of the
Leisure A-Z

MARKED TRAILS
Many organisations have marked
walks and produce leaflets to accom-

pany walks which explain the landscape and describe the plant life and wildlife encountered. These walks are often through Forestry Commission woodland, country parks, farms, nature reserves, locations offering good views and areas of outstanding beauty. Many start from picnic sites or car parks.

See: Woodlands, Country Parks, Picnic Sites, Nature Reserves, Farms

Dartmoor National Park Authority organise a programme of guided walks of varying length. Details are available from the Exmoor National Park Authority Office, Parke, Haytor Rd, Bovey Tracey TQ13 9JQ

The Western National Omnibus Co Ltd, National House, Queen St, Exeter also produce a number of free leaflets of various rambles in the Exeter, South Devon and Torbay districts, available on written application (please include SAE)

The Exmoor National Park Authority produces a number of leaflets which cover suggested walks in the North Devon area. These are available from the Exmoor National Park Centre, Exmoor House, Dulverton, Somerset.

Organisations

RAMBLERS' ASSOCIATION

Southern Area

1-5 Wandsworth Rd, London SW8 2IJ

The Ramblers' Association campaigns for public access to all rural areas. Its members keep paths clear and fight any development which hinders access to public footpaths. They also waymark paths to make them easier to follow and work to protect the countryside.

The RA also organises excursions and group walks, including trips to differenct areas of the country. There are hundreds of RA groups throughout Britain, keeping a close watch on footpaths and ensuring they are well maintained, as well as enjoying walking together. Even those who prefer to walk alone may consider joining the RA, since it is responsible for enabling lone walkers to have unhindered access to the countryside.

If you come across a public footpath which is closed, is not accessible or is in any way impassable you should contact the Devon Area RA (see below) and report this.

The RA also publishes many leaflets on all aspects of its work as well as a Bed & Breakfast Guide for walkers and a regular journal (free to members).

Membership: £6; couple £7.50; couple retired £3.75; cñf 18, students, unemployed & OAPs £3; life membership £210, members get free copy Bed & Breakfast Guide (each year), free journal 'Rucksack' (3 each year), local area news, access to Ordnance Survey 1:50,000 map library; special offers & reductions on publications from shops

RAMBLERS' ASSOCIATION

Hon Secretary: Mr F S Candy
Stockland (040 488) 208
Friar's Keep, Stockland, near Honiton EX14 9EF
Footpath Secretary: Mr R S Bagshaw
Newton Abbot (064 77) 278
Brockthwaite, Lustleigh

SOUTH WEST WAY ASSOCIATION

Secretary: Mrs M Macleod
Newton Abbot (080 47) 3061
1 Orchard Drive, Kingskerswell, Newton Abbot
Formed in 1973 the SWWA promotes the interests of the users of the South West Peninsula Coast Path. It is an independent body but works in close co-operation with the Rambler's Association and its main aim is to secure completion of the path. It produces an annual guide which is updated each spring and contains booklists and information and accommodation, camping, transport, maps

and a brief description of the whole path.

Membership: £4; couple £5; local authorities & associations £6.50; life membership available, members receive yearly copy of the annual guide, two newsletters per year and a free copy of
each footpath description

Long Distance Pathways

THE SOUTH WEST PENINSULA COAST PATH
Route: 560m from Minehead in North Devon to Poole Harbour in Dorset, encircling the whole South West peninsula of England. It is the longest pathway in the country, mostly easy walking and habitation is never far away. The coast path falls into four sections, two of which lie in Devon, namely the North Devon Coast Path and the South Devon Coast Path

SOMERSET & NORTH DEVON COAST PATH
Route: 132 kilometres from Minehead Quay to Marsland Mouth on the Devon/Cornwall border. The path follows the coastline as closely as possible, covering a variety of terrain from pebble beaches to high, wide viewed cliffs. Places of particular interest are Selworthy Beacon, Foreland Point Lighthouse, the Valley of the Rocks, Watermouth Castle, Saunton Sands Nature Reserves and Clovelly

SOUTH DEVON COAST PATH
Route: 98m from Plymouth to Lyme Regis following the coastline in south and east Devon of outstanding natural beauty. Walkers should have little difficulty in following the path and it is well within the capabilities of most

people, with the exception of landslip at the Dorset end which is best left to the experienced walker as it is very rough terrain and once committed it is impossible to turn off the trail. Places of particular interest include Burgh Island, Bolt Tail and Bolt Head, Slapton Ley Nature Reserve, Dartmouth Castle, Berry Head Country Park, Landslips Nature Reserve.

TWO MOORS WAY
Route: 102m from Ivybridge, South Devon to Lynmouth on the North Devon coast, passing through the heart of Dartmoor to Drewsteignton, on through mid-Devon to West Anstey and Exmoor National Park. The terrain is varied with stretches of open moor, deep wooded river valleys, green lanes and some unavoidable lengths of roads.
Suggested access: Dartmeet, Drewsteignton, Morchard Bishop. Members of the Two Moors Way Committee regularly survey parts of the Way most liable to become overgrown and organise clearing parties. They also produce an official guide which includes an accommodation list. The guide is available from the secretary of the Ramblers' Association or from The Two Moors' Way Association, Coppins, The Poplars, Pinhoe, Exeter EX4 9HH (please include 51.40)

R.A. Local Groups

EAST DEVON
Secretary: Mrs Hilda Smith
Seaton (0297) 22438
6 Riverdale, Colyford Rd, Seaton

EXETER
Secretary: Mr C Dodd
Topsham (039 287) 4628
30 Winslade Park Ave, Clyst St Mary, Exeter

Water Skiing

MOORLAND
Secretary: Miss P Waldron
Lustleigh (064 77) 452
Leacroft, Lustleigh, Newton Abbot

NEWTON ABBOT
Secretary: Mr R W B Sanders
Newton Abbot (0626) 2813
14 Rowantree Rd, Newton Abbot

NORTH DEVON
Secretary: Mr W G Elliott
Croyde (0271) 890530
Greenleafe, Millers Brook, Croyde,
Braunton

NORTH WEST DEVON
Secretary: Mrs E C B Clissold
Milton Damerel (040 926) 220

PLYMOUTH
Secretary: Mr D Allen
Plymouth (0752) 779184
20 Elphinstone Rd, Peverell, Plymouth

SOUTH DEVON
Secretary: Mr Ian Norden
Torquay (0803) 6776
16 Courtland Rd, Torquay

SOUTH HAMS
Secretary: Mrs Peggy Eagle
Loddiswell (054 855)
The Bungalow, Stile Orchard, Loddis-
well, nr Kingsbridge

TAVISTOCK
Secretary: Mr S Eslick
198 Whitchurch Rd, Tavistock

TIVERTON
Secretary: Mr E A Harris
Tiverton (088 42) 2785
5 Middlemead Rd, Tiverton

Water skiing is best undertaken as a member of a recognised club. The British Waterski Federation (BWF) is the governing body for sport in Britain and most clubs are affiliated to it, including all those listed below.

If you wish to learn how to water ski contact a club near you. Clubs with vacancies may be able to provide equipment and instruction. The BWF run many courses and should be contacted for details.

Most clubs will hire equipment such as wet suits and usually provide boats. In many cases members are not allowed to use their own boats since the number of boats operating in any one area of water must be carefully controlled.

For any information on the sport contact:

BRITISH WATER SKI FEDERATION
Secretary: Gillian Hill
01-387 9371 Upper Woburn Place,
London WC1H OQL

Water Ski Clubs

AUNE VALLEY WATER SKI CLUB
Secretary: Mr Iain Garland
Salcombe (054 855) 227
Courtlands Centre, Nr Kingsbridge
River Avon

EXE POWERBOAT & WATER SKI CLUB
Secretary: Mr D Frost
22 Marions Way, Exmouth
River Exe, Exmouth

SOUTH DEVON WATER SPORTS CLUB

Secretary: Mr R Wilson
Newton Abbot (0626) 66644
Pine Villa, Wolborough Close, Newton Abbot
Combe Cellars, Coombe in Teignhead, near Newton Abbot
Facilities for jump & slalom

Windsurfing

If you are a capable windsurfer and have your own sailboard you can use it in safe harbour waters or the inland waters of Devon, though these are mostly controlled and only private clubs have access to them for sports such as windsurfing. If you undertake this sport it is advisable to seek tuition from your local club. This section gives details of clubs and of courses for learning windsurfing. Some clubs are purely for windsurfing. Some clubs, particularly sailing clubs, offer a wide range of facilities from bars and restaurants to dressing rooms and showers. It is usually necessary to wear a wetsuit when windsurfing in this country and they can often be hired, as can the sailboards.

BLUE WATER SAILING (SALCOMBE) LTD

Kingsbridge (0548) 3605
PO Box 6, 11 Saffron Park, Kingsbridge
School run from a ship, the 'Blue Arcadia', moored on Salcombe Estuary

Courses: mainly residential for all proficiencies, price depends on time of year (telephone for details)
Changing and shower facilities
✕ ♀

EXE SAILING CLUB

Tornado, Estuary Rd, Exmouth
Membership: apply to secretary
Club sails on the sea via a tidal bowl approx. 5ft deep; active racing programme for all levels
Changing and shower facilities, social activities
P � ♀

FREE POWER WINDSURFING SCHOOL

Windsurfing Centre, 22 North St, Exeter
Courses: March-Nov (depending on weather); £30 full day (including equipment)
Board hire: £4 hour, £10 half day, £18 all day

HARBOUR SPORTS WINDSURFING SCHOOL

Paignton (0803) 550180
The Harbour, Paignton
Courses: April-Oct, half day £14 (equipment); group reductions 5«
Board Hire: for qualified windsurfers only
Changing and shower facilities
P ⊠ ⊟ ♀

MAYFLOWER SAILING CLUB

Plymouth (0752) 662526
Phoenix Wharf, The Barbican, Plymouth
Membership: details on application
Courses: for members only, all levels, all year
Board storage, changing and shower facilities
⊟

MELDON SAILING CLUB

Okehampton (0837) 84258
c/o Cawsand House, South Zeal, Okehampton (based at Meldon Reservoir, Dartmoor)
Membership: details on application

PAIGNTON SAILING CLUB
Paignton (0803) 525817
The Harbour, Paignton
Membership: details on application
Full racing programme on Sunday
afternoons and Thursday evenings,
social gatherings, beach parties
Changing & shower facilities, board
storage

**TORBAY BOARDSAILING CENTRE
& SCHOOL**
Torquay (0803) 212411
55 Victoria Rd, Ellecombe, Torquay
Courses: all year (weather permit-
ting), £6 hour
Board Hire: on application
All ages and proficiencies; boardsail-
ing on special windsurfing lane

WINDSURFING MID-DEVON
Okehampton (0837) 84258
Cawsand House, South Zeal,
Okehampton
Courses: April-Oct (telephone for
details)
This school is in association with
Windsurfing Plymouth and sails on
Meldon Lake Reservoir

Women's Institute

The Women's Institute is a completely
independent voluntary organisation,
with a total membership of about
400,000 women in England, Wales,
the Channel Islands and the Isle of
Man.

The broad purpose of the WI is to
give country women the opportunity
of working together to improve the
quality of life in rural areas; and to
provide a wide variety of educational
and leisure activities. New members
are always welcome. WIs usually
meet once a month in a hall, parish
room or perhaps a school
   If you want to find out more about
the WI in your area contact the NFWI
the local secretary in Devon given
below.

**THE NATIONAL FEDERATION OF
WOMEN'S INSTITUTE**
Membership Secretary
01 730 7212
39 Eccleston Street
London SW1W 9NT

**DEVON FEDERATION OF
WOMEN'S INSTITUTE**
Secretary: Mrs Manning
Exeter (0392) 55386
56 Heavitree Road, Exeter EX1 2LH

Woodland

This section includes forests, woods,
arboretums. Many of them are owned
and managed by the Forestry Commissions (FC). Woodlands mentioned
are open at all times and access is
free unless otherwise stated.

ABBEYFORD WOODS
Map 1 Bc
½m N of Okehampton town centre
on B3217
Interesting mixed conifer woodland;
variety of woodland birds, good views,
woodland walks.
🅿 🛏

ASHCLYST FOREST
Map 4 Aa
Exeter (0392) 832262
2m NE Exeter off B3181
Extensive oak woods mixed with
sweet chestnut, ash, beech & conifer
provides superb habitat for rich variety
of plants & animal life, marked
woodland walks (self guiding) conducted walks: Telephone FC office,
Bullers Hill, Exeter (0392) 832262
FC & NT
🅿 ⛱

BELLEVER FOREST FC
Map 3 Bb
5m SW Moretonhampstead on
B3212 Plantation of Norway and sitka
spruce and contorta pine; good views
of river Dart & moorland forest walks
Lavatories
🅿 ⛱

BOVEY VALLEY WOODLANDS
See Nature Reserves Bovey Valley
Woodlands Nature Reserve.

EXETER FOREST
Map 4 Aa
Haldon, 9m SW Exeter off A38
Mixed woodlands, interesting area for
flowers, insects & bird life; superb
views, conducted walks available early
April-late Sep by arrangement with FC
office, Bullers Hill Exeter (0392)
832262
Lavatories, information office
🅿 ⛱

DENDLES WOOD
See Nature Reserves: Dendles
Wood

DUNSFORD & MEADHAYDOWN
WOOD
See Nature Reserves: Dunsford &
Meadhaydown Wood

EGGESFORD FOREST
Map 1 Bc
On A377, 7mls NW Crediton
Mixed woodland of conifers contain-
ing some of the oldest trees planted
by the FC Commission, forest walk
approx 1 mile
Leaflet available
🅿 ⛱

FERNWORTHY FOREST
Map 3 Ba/p27
5m SW Chagford off B3212
Part of Dartmoor National Park, coniferous woodlands surrounding a
reservoir with fine moorland views &
varied plant, animal & bird life.Forest
trail 1½m, booklet available
🅿 ⛱

HALDON FOREST
See Exeter Forest

HEMBURY WOODS
Map 3 Bb
1m N Buckfastleigh off A38 2m NW
Totnes
Coppice Oakwoods in valley of river
Dart, demonstrates how trust is bringing these woods into production
whilst preserving their beauty and
value as habitat for wildlife, woodland
walk 1½m

HEYWOOD WOOD
Map 1 Bb
1¾m N Eggesford Station, 7m NW
Crediton on A377
Predominantly Douglas fir plantation
of mixed ages; landscaped clear felled
areas create good vistas; forest walks
2½m & shorter versions of 1m and
1½m, guide available

HOLSWORTHY WOODS
Map 1 Ac
1½m S Holsworthy on A388
Spruce & pine wood, difficulties of
forestry on heavy soil, well illustrated;
forest walk
🅿

KILLERTON FOREST
Map 2 Ac
4m N Exeter off B3185, access from several car parks. Predominantly oak woodlands with some conifers, forest walks ½m-2ms
🅿

MELBURY WOOD
Map 1 Ab
2½m SW Bideford on unclassified Clovelly to Stibbs Cross road
Conifer plantation where development of woodland condition on moorland can be seen, woodland walk
🅿 🛋

PLYM BRIDGE WOODS
Map 3 Ab
1½m N Plymouth off A386
Woods extending up steep sided valley of river Plym; wildlife & remains of 19th century slate quarries; woodland walk 1½m, leaflet available (40p)

STOKE WOOD
Map 4 Aa
1m NE Exeter town centre on A396
Mixed woodland, varying from 150 year old oaks to young conifers; also areas of coppice, ash & sycamore; good views, woodland walks 1½m, leaflet available (10p)
🛋

WARLEIGH POINT WOOD
See Nature Reserves: Warleigh Point Wood

WELLSFORD WOOD
Map 1 Ac
Wellsford, 1½m SE Hartland on A39
200 hectares of largely coniferous wood; information centre, open Easter-end Sept; small display illustrating where one can go in Devon & Cornwall to FC woodlands; nature trail 1½m & 2½m self guided trail, leaflet available

WISTMANS WOOD
See Nature Reserves: Wistman's Wood Forest Nature Reserve

YARNER WOOD
See Nature Reserve: Yarner Wood National Nature Reserve

Zoos

DARTMOOR WILDLIFE PARK
Map 3 Bb
Cornwood (075 537) 209
3m NE Plympton on the Sparkwell to Cornwood Rd
Open: all year, daily 10.00-dusk
Charge: £1.80 (ch 90p), group reductions by arrangement (prices subject to alteration)
Guided tours by arrangement
25 acres with over 100 species of animals and birds, including deer, timber wolf pack and Siberian tiger; donkey rides for children
🅿 🛋 ♿

EXMOOR BIRD GARDEN
Map 1 Bb
Parracombe (059 83) 352
Bratton Fleming, 3m S Parracombe off B3226
Open: all year, daily 10.00-18.00 (dusk if earlier)
Charge: £1.20 (ch 60p); groups (20«) 80p per person (ch 45p, OAPs 70p) by arrangement
Tropical birds including penguins, waterfowl and rare breeds of poultry, also wallabies, ponies and goats
Children's corner and play area
🅿 🛍 🛋 ♿

Zoos

HIGHER LEIGH MANOR
See Monkey Sanctuary

MONKEY SANCTUARY
Map 1 Ba/p30
Combe Martin (027 188) 2486
Open: Easter-end Sep, daily 10.00-
17.00
Charge: £1.50 (ch 75p), group
reductions 20«
15 acres garden with fine views of
the sea, animal sanctuary including
variety of monkeys, sea lions,
wallabies; model railway, children's
fun fair, pets' corner
🅿 ⚓ �🍴 ⚲

WILDLIFE COLLECTION
Map 4 Ab
Shaldon (062 687) 2234
Ness Drive, Shaldon 1 m S
Teignmouth on A379
Open: Easter-end Sep, daily 10.00-
dusk; Oct-Easter by arrangement
Charge: 85p (ch 50p), group reduc-
tions by arrangement
Collection of small mammals, exotic
birds, reptiles, monkeys, chipmunks
and birds
Guided tours by arrangement
🅿

WILDLIFE GARDENS
Map 1 Aa
Bicclescombe Park, Ilfracombe
Open: Easter-end May, daily 11.00-
16.30; end May-end Sep, daily
10.00-dusk (weather permitting)
Charge: 60p (ch 40p), group reduc-
tions by arrangement
Children's play area
Variety of animals and exotic birds,
including monkeys, rare ocelots, hand
reared puma
🅿 🚾 ♿

ZOOLOGICAL & BOTANIC
GARDENS
Map 4 Ab/p88
Paignton (0803) 557479
Totnes Rd, Paignton
Open: all year, daily 10.00-dusk
(closed 25 Dec)
Charge: £2 (ch £1, OAPs £1.50),
group reductions 30« by arrangement
100 acres of grounds, tropical plants,
extensive collection of animals from all
over the world; breeding colony of lar
gibbons, monkey house, tropical
house, aquarium, reptile house, pea
fowl; children's playground, miniature
railway
No dogs but kennels available in car
park
🅿 ⚓ 🚾🍴 ⚲ 曱♿

Notes

Acknowledgements

The author and publishers would like to thank the following individuals and organisations for their help and co-operation in providing information for this book:

Mr F.S. Candy, Ramblers' Association; Cosira; Dartmoor National Park; Devon County Council; Forestry Commission; Mrs Macleod, South West Way Association; National Gardens Scheme; National Trust; Nature Conservancy Council; Royal National Lifeboat Institute; Royal Society for Nature Conservation; Caroline Steele, Devon Trust for Nature Conservation; South West Water Authority; Mr W. Stutchbury, Devon Cricket Association.

Thanks also go to the many individuals who provided information through tourist information offices and through other societies and organisations too numerous to mention.